DATABASE MANAGEMENT SYSTEMS

Useful for students of both undergraduate and post graduate programme related to computer science and information technology including engineering discipline (Degree and Diploma engineering)

By

Ivan Bayross

BPB PUBLICATIONS
B-14, CONNAUGHT PLACE, NEW DELHI-110001

FIRST EDITION 2010

ISBN : 978-81-8333-363-4

LIMITS OF LIABILITY AND DISCLAIMER OF WARRANTY

The information contained in this book is to the best of the Author/Publishers knowledge true and correct. The Author/Publishers has made every effort to ensure accuracy of this publications, but cannot be held responsible for any loss or damage arising from any information in this book.

All trademarks referred to in the book are acknowledged as properties of their respective owners.

GTU is in no way connected with this book. This is written solely for the benefit and guidance of the students.

Distributors:

COMPUTER BOOK CENTRE
12, Shrungar Shopping Centre, M.G. Road,
BANGALORE-560001 Ph: 25587923, 25584641

MICRO BOOKS
Shanti Niketan Building, 8, Camac Street
KOLKATA-700017 Ph: 22826518/9

BUSINESS PROMOTION BUREAU
8/1, Ritchie Street, Mount Road,
CHENNAI-600002 Ph: 28410796, 28550491

MICRO MEDIA
Shop No.5, Mahendra Chambers, 150 D.N. Rd,
Next to Capital Cinema V.T. (C.S.T.) Station,
MUMBAI-400001 Ph: 22078296, 22078297

DECCAN AGENCIES
4-3-329, Bank Street,
HYDERABAD-500195 Ph: 24756400, 24756967

BPB PUBLICATIONS
B-14, Connaught Place, NEW DELHI-110001
Ph: 23329760, 23723393, 23737742

BPB BOOK CENTRE
376, Old Lajpat Rai Market, DELHI-110006
Ph: 23861747

INFOTECH
G-2, Sidhartha Building, 96, Nehru Place,
NEW DELHI-110019
Ph: 26438245, 26415092, 26234208

INFOTECH
Shop No.2, F-38, South Extention Part-1
NEW DELHI-110049
Ph: 24691288

Published by Manish Jain for BPB Publications, B-14, Connaught Place, New Delhi-110001 and Printed by him at Akash Press, New Delhi.

have a ready reference book, with real world examples, which covers DBMS codespec and real world examples and which is closely mapped to their DBMS syllabus.

I've tried to write this book with a view that the students will one day evolve into programmers who will work in India's dynamic software development industry.

As far as is practical, each chapter has concepts and how these concepts are applied using code to real world situations. All this is bound to ANSI SQL, which is the natural language of all RDBMS.

I've tried to use my extensive application development experience to create material that should cover most of the areas that seem to puzzle students as they work through their syllabus and grow from strength to strength in the use of DBMSystems.

Concepts are built using simple language, examples have easily understood logic. I really hope that this book makes students as excited about RDBMS as I am. I'm proud to say that for the last 30 years the only environment that I've done any serious programming in is RDBMS.

This foreword will not be complete without my thanking the many people who encouraged me and put up with the many revisions and updations of the manuscript with patience and tolerance.

My sincere **THANKS** go to:

- My publisher Mr. Manish Jain I believe that he is a really great human being.
- The students who read this material, without you, I would not be an author. I welcome both your brickbats and bouquets. Do visit my website www.ivanbayross.com there's quite a bit of great tech reference material there available free.
- Kavita, Meher and Prerna, without whom I would be totally handicapped. Your diligent attention to detail, meticulous testing of the codespec examples, adds quality to this book that I would find impossible to do on my very own.
- Finally, my wife Cynthia who has always believed in me and encouraged me. You have always helped to keep my feet firmly on the ground; in you I am truly blessed.

Ivan N. Bayross

Table Of Contents

1. Introductory Concepts Of DBMS

What Is Database

A database can be defined as a collection of coherent, meaningful data. The phrase collection of coherent data needs to have a point of reference to be understood. A simple point of reference would be the example of a postal address, this would generally contain:

- A building name
- A flat number in the building (if it is co-op housing society rather than a bungalow)
- A road name
- An area name
- A state name
- A pincode
- A country name (This is optional, but necessary if the letter is destined to a foreign country)

To project on this further, multiple addresses kept together in one place, such as an address book, could be termed as a coherent collection of data. Thus the **address book** is a **database** and the **postal addresses** in the book, is the **data** that fills the database.

What Is Database Management Systems (DBMS)

To be able to successfully design and maintain databases we have to do the following:

1. Identify which part of the world's data is of interest to us
2. Identify what specific objects in that part of the world's data are of interest
3. Identify a relationship between the objects

Hence, the objects, their attributes and the relationship between them (that are of interest to us) are stored in the database that is designed, built and populated with data for a specific purpose.

Software houses took up the challenge of designing a system that would help in **managing** data in such a database. These systems were called Database Management Systems (DBMS). DBMS is a system that allows inserting, updating, deleting and processing of data. Some of the DBMS developed by software houses were Oracle, Ingress, Sybase, Dbase 3+, Foxbase, Foxpro, MS Access, Dataease, Dataflex, Advanced Revelation, and so on.

Benefits of DBMS

1. The amount of data redundancy in stored data can be reduced
2. No more data inconsistencies
3. Stored data can be shared by a single or multiple users
4. Standards can be set and followed
5. Data integrity can be maintained. Data integrity refers to the problem of ensuring that database contains only accurate data

6. Security of data can be simply implemented
7. Data independence can be achieved, **i.e.** data and programs that manipulate the data are two different entities

The Purpose Of Database Systems

Changing A Database's Contours

Adding a telephone number to the address held in the address book changes the contours of the database. It should no longer be considered an Address database but a Contact Information database.

This is because a telephone number brings a dimension to the address book that is, strictly speaking, unnecessary for a letter to be delivered to its destination. Hence, the addition of the telephone number changes the contours (shape) of the database.

From this simple analogy there are a few interesting things that come into focus. For a database to exist apparently the following must exist:

A coherent collection of data	The Addresses
An **object** that holds this coherent collection of data.	The Address Book

This concept belongs to the real world, i.e. the world that human beings live in. With a little imagination multiple databases can be identified in the real world.

Real world database
Recipes in a cook book

A coherent collection of data	A recipe and its ingredients
An **object** that holds this coherent collection of data	The cook book

Database
Telephone numbers added to the memory of a mobile phone

A coherent collection of data	Each telephone number and name combination
An **object** that holds this coherent collection of data	The mobile phone's internal memory

When this is modeled using computers it gives rise to a few problem areas that must be addressed. Take the address database, in the real world there maybe areas, which have not yet been assigned a pincode. In other areas of the real world there could be post offices that will not accept a letter for delivery unless it has a legitimate pincode. Hence an **address database's** contour can change from one real world domain space to another.

This is the first problem area that needs to be addressed when trying to model a real world database in a computer. A fixed, pre-created, database cannot be used because the very same database may have different contours in different real world domain spaces.

To solve this problem **D**ata**B**ase **M**anagement **S**ystem (DBMS) software has been created that will allow a programmer to structure a database that will model exactly to the collection of coherent (meaningful) data that belongs to a specific real world domain space.

Some of the names of such database management systems are:

M. S. Access (i.e. a Microsoft DBMS product), FoxPro, MySQL, M.S. SQL Server, Oracle, Sybase and a host of such products.

Each database management system facilitates the very same thing. They empower a programmer to structure (create) a specific database that will model correctly to the information belonging to a specific slice of the real world. This is shown as a picture (diagram 1.1) because often a picture is easier to understand.

From diagram 1.1 it is apparent that a programmer must learn to communicate with a DBMS and tell it to build a structure of specific dimensions to hold information that belongs to a specific slice of the real world.

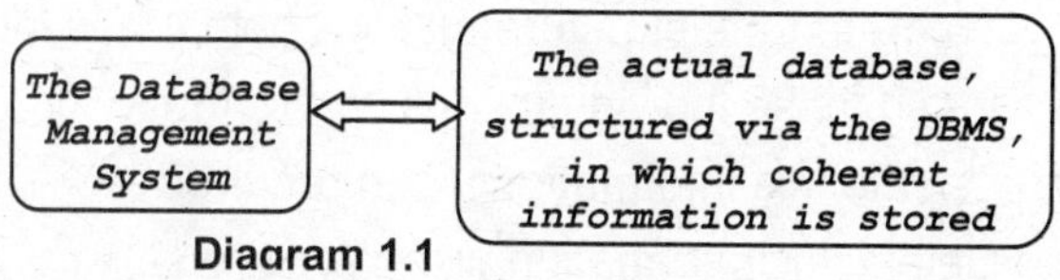

Diagram 1.1

Obviously, to communicate effectively with a DBMS a programmer must learn the natural language of the DBMS.

Once a structure exists that maps to the structure of the information in the real world, this real world information can be inserted into the structure for permanent storage and re-use later on.

The DBMS mentioned earlier on M. S. Access (i.e. a Microsoft DBMS product) FoxBase, FoxPro, Quick Silver, Oracle, Sybase and so on each, have a proprietary language and a programmer has to learn (and be proficient in) multiple DBMS languages.

Since each of these DBMS use proprietary languages information held by one DBMS could not be shared with the other. This could lead to a lot of duplication of the very same information if it is held in different DBMS in the same office. Such duplicate data is termed as **redundant** data.

To help overcome the prospect of redundant data standards were defined for a common DBMS language simply called **S**tructured **Q**uery **L**anguage (SQL). An apex body called the **A**merican **N**ational **S**tandards **I**nstitute (ANSI) defined these standards. The combination came to be known as ANSI-SQL.

For a product to be qualified as a DBMS system by ANSI, it had to conform to the standards laid out in ANSI–SQL. DBMS could have their own proprietary languages but were **also** required to conform to ANSI-SQL standards. Most DBMS conformed to this rule because by then users of DBMS had matured to a point that a product would not be bought if it were unable to share its data with other ANSI-SQL compliant products.

Because all major DBMS began to conform to ANSI-SQL standards (or perish by losing market share to those who did) programmers today need to learn only ANSI-SQL to be able to work efficiently across a multiple DBMS. Additionally, (and this is really useful) because of ANSI-SQL, information can be shared seamlessly across multiple DBMS.

This is how diagram 1.1 changes to reflect the above concepts.

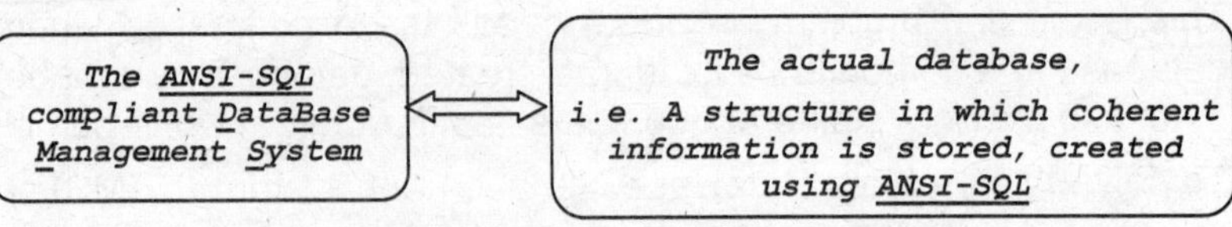

Diagram 1.2

The steps used to create and maintain a database using a DBMS is as follows:

- Identify which slice of real world information is of prime interest and must be converted to a database
- Decompose the slice of real world information into individual units that make up the whole slice
- Design a structure that is capable of storing these individual units of information

Use any DBMS and ANSI-SQL:

- To **create** the structure that will hold these individual units
- Insert these individual units of information into the structure created to hold them
- Update this information when required
- Delete this information when required
- View this data from any conceivable angle.

This is how and why DataBase Management Systems are used.

The Structure Of A Database

Obviously it is the structure used to store individual units of data that is important. The storage structure itself is very simple. It really is a two dimensional matrix, consisting of Rows and Columns.

The **intersection** of Rows and Columns gives rise to a **cell**. Each cell in the storage structure will have to have a **unique name** to reference it by. A cell is a single unit of storage in which a single unit of information, obtained from the real world, is stored.

The Data Storage Structure

Address Book

House	**Flat No.**	**Road**	**Area**	**Place**	**Pin Code**	**Country**
Diamond Queen	F/12	West Avenue	Santacruz (West)	Mumbai	400054	India
Jay Chambers	A/5	Nanda Patkar Road	Vile Parle (East)	Mumbai	400057	India

Table 1.1

With reference to table 1.1, **Address book** is the name of the data storage structure created using ANSI-SQL. This is really a two dimensional matrix consisting of a number of rows and columns as can be seen from table 1.1. Each junction of a row and column creates a cell.

Each cell has a unique name. A single unit of information that must be stored is placed within a cell.

A group of **cells** in the same horizontal plane make a **record**. Multiple records of **equal length** stored one below the other make a **table**.

> ***Note:*** *Hence a DBMS and ANSI-SQL can be used to create any number of carefully designed tables to store information in.*

Once the tables are created using ANSI-SQL, information can be Inserted, Viewed, Updated or Deleted from the table.

This is how diagram 1.2 changes to accommodate the above concepts.

Diagram 1.3 indicates that any number of addresses can be stored in the Address book table one below the other.

The ANSI-SQL compliant DataBase Management System ← A data storage structure created and communicated with using ANSI-SQL

Address Book

House	**Flat No.**	**Road**	**Area**	**Place**	**Pin Code**	**Country**
Diamond Queen	F/12	West Avenue	Santacruz (West)	Mumbai	400054	India
Jay Chambers	A/5	Nanda Patkar Road	Vile Parle (East)	Mumbai	400057	India

Diagram 1.3

The actual number of addresses storable being limited only by the physical size of the permanent storage media used in the computer, (i.e. its hard disk drive size).

Once information required is stored in the table it can be manipulated at incredible speed using ANSI-SQL or the native (proprietary) language of the DBMS being used.

Manipulating Information Stored In A Table

A table can be conceptualized as an **empty storage structure** in which information can be stored. Hence, there must be some way to Insert, View, Update or Delete information stored in the table. These are the table **operations** that manipulate table information.

The DBMS has (ANSI-SQL) syntax that allows a programmer to pass it explicit instructions on how to structure the table. A programmer needs to learn this syntax after which the programmer can communicate with the DBMS (in a language it understands) and pass appropriate instructions to it.

> **Note:** *Since all DBMS are required to understand ANSI-SQL it stands to reason that if a programmer learns ANSI-SQL syntax, the programmer can communicate effectively with all DBMS that are ANSI-SQL compliant.*

Similarly, there is ANSI-SQL syntax that permits the manipulation of information (i.e. data) held in a table. Such as:

Insertion of table data

- Updation of table data
- Deletion of table data
- Viewing of table data

Inserting, Updating and Deleting table data are termed as table **write** operations and the Viewing of table data is termed as a table **read** operation. Table write operations cause **permanent changes** to table data, whereas a table read operation does **not make any change** to table data at all.

Once a table is fully populated with data (i.e. collection of coherent (meaningful) information) this data can be viewed in any number of ways. Please refer to table 1.2.

Address Book

House	Flat No.	Road	Area	Place	Pin Code	Country
Diamond Queen	F/12	West Avenue	Santacruz (West)	Mumbai	400054	India
Jay Chambers	A/5	Nanda Patkar Road	Vile Parle (East)	Mumbai	400057	India
The Emblem	F/1	North Avenue	Santacruz (West)	Mumbai	400054	India
Odina	10	Central Avenue	Santacruz (East)	Mumbai	400055	India
ShirDhar Co-op	F/33	Delile Road	Matunga	Mumbai	400067	India
Panchratna	109 1st Floor	Sardar Patel Road	New Marine Lines	Mumbai	400012	India
Hi Fives	701 7th Floor	Bhavani Shankar Road	Dadar	Mumbai	400034	India
Sharda	201 1st Floor	H.F.Society Road	Jogeshwari	Mumbai	400060	India
Dixit Niwas	2	Behind Ruia College	Matunga	Mumbai	400016	India
Neel Gagan	2637/20	Ansari Road	Daryaganj	New Delhi	110002	India
Modern House	7/18	Capt. Chhabra Road	Carol Bagh	New Delhi	110005	India
Rachana Apts.	C/2	Hospet Road		Chennai	700020	India
Ganesh Bhuvan	Ground floor	Raasta Peth	Near KEM Hospital	Pune	411004	India
Kasturi Apts.	A/103	Panchal Road	Nallasopara	Thane	401211	India
Rameshwar	B/24	Annasaheb Road	Pashan	Pune	411102	India
Soni Bhavan	30	Telang Road	Matunga (East)	Mumbai	400016	India
Yojana	2456	Saibaba Road	Saibaba Nagar	Chennai	700006	India
Satnam Apts.	4/10	Safdarjung Road	Sher-e-Punjab	New Delhi	110013	India
Sudha-Shrusthi	B/45	Pestom Sagar	Chembur	Mumbai	400096	India
Everest Bldg	A/10	Venkatraman Road	Borla Village	Chennai	710102	India
Shanta Sadan	Grd. Floor	Ganesh Galli	Ghatkopar	Mumbai	400110	India
Vijay Apts.	315 3rd Floor	Cmdr. Rai Road	Defense Colony	Delhi	112008	India
Parvathi	1165/5	Laxminarayan Road	Laminarayan Temple	Chennai	700109	India

Sujan Bldg.	A/14	Babhai Road	Ghatkopar	Mumbai	400089	India
Munish Plaza	4637/20	Ajmal Road	Fidai Bagh	New Delhi	110001	India
VijayaShanti	B/33	S.V.Road	5 Gardens	Chennai	700068	India
Durga Bhavan	A/05	Chatopadhyay Road	Near Bus Depot	Calcutta	600011	India
Apna Bazar Bldg.	2nd Floor	Plot No.3	Sector 17	Chennai	700056	India
Shanta Sadan	Ground Floor	Saraswat Colony	Mahim (West)	Mumbai	400014	India
Amar Mahal	C/11	Saki Road	Gulshan Bagh	New Delhi	110002	India
Shyam Niwas	12	Market Road	Bogarves	Chennai	700001	India
Maya	G/42	Biswas Road	Horniman Circle	Calcutta	600023	India
Shamiana	F/7	Jaini Road	Faridabad	New Delhi	11000	India

Table 1.2

The data stored in the table address book (table 1.2) can be viewed in any number of different ways.

- What are the addresses that are located at Mumbai?
- What are the addresses that are located at Delhi?
- What are the addresses that are located at Chennai?
- What are the addresses that are located at Pune?
- How many people live on the first floor?
- How many people live on the seventh floor?
- How many people live in Santacruz?
- How many people live in Santacruz West?
- How many people live in Santacruz East?

These (and much more) are the different **Views** of table data that are available. In fact viewing table data is limited only to the imagination. The technique of being able to view table data any desired way is really an extremely powerful business tool.

Imagine a place like Shopper's Stop or Globus or any such type of mega store. If they can capture shopper's data along with the goods purchased, over a period of time, by viewing this data shrewdly their management will be able to recognize a shopper's **buying patterns** and thus stock the mega store appropriately.

Everyone knows that if a shopper is provided with the right goods, at the right price in a place that is clean, helpful and convenient this delightful shopping experience will make the shopper return for more. This simply translates into profits for the mega store.

Tip: *Maximizing profits from simply capturing shopper's data, storing it and having managers look at the data shrewdly.*

Other than capturing, storing and viewing shopper's data there is little or no processing done to the data. Yet by its **visual analysis** by experienced managers there could be a real impact o the mega store's profits.

Hence the simple process of viewing and analyzing table data is an extremely powerful business tool.

Data Models

The above material should have sown the seeds of understanding and appreciating the value that a DBMS brings to business.

A look at how business is run in the modern dynamic business world and how the use of a DBMS can help enhance business and make it both competitive and profitable. This creates a strong belief that a DBMS and business must go hand in hand.

All businesses have a business model at their core. What this really means is that a business is not a haphazard collection of processes but a set of processes that are clearly defined and have a definite hierarchy in the way they run.

Each of these processes will both generate and manipulate business data. Each of these processes will have a specific cost attached. These type of processes bring a **cost** to the company.

The cost to company processes always give rise to another set of processes that bring **returns** to the company.

Making profit, is simply ensuring that the processes that bring returns to the company bring in **more money** than the processes that are a cost to the company.

Database Languages

Since a DBMS is used to create the data model, bound to a business model, a programmer has to be able to communicate with the DBMS in a language it understands. This is because to be able to build a data model using a DBMS a programmer must be in a position to communicate with the DBMS and describe the structure of the data model.

Most DBMS have proprietary languages but today almost all conform to (i.e. understand) ANSI SQL as mentioned earlier. Most data modeling can be done using ANSI SQL. However, there are times when knowing and using the proprietary language of the DBMS will provide a specific advantage such as an increase in the speed of data manipulation, under a special set of circumstances.

Storage Management

All DBMS store business data in tables. This means that the DBMS needs to have syntax to create tables. Subsequently, the DBMS needs syntax that will permit the management of data stored in the tables. The management of table data basically being Inserting, Viewing, Updating and Deleting table data.

Additionally, table data can be extracted and manipulated in any number of different ways.

Any type of arithmetic data manipulation imaginable can be applied to table data such as exponentiation, addition, subtraction, multiplication, division and more. Logical operations such as decision making using AND, OR, NOT operators and so on.

All this is based on appropriate DBMS syntax and comes under the head of **storage management**.

Overall Systems Structure

Most DBMS are built around rigid (and robust) system architecture. This allows simple to use, user interfaces, to be built via which a user can harness the raw power of a DBMS to do useful work. Refer to diagram 1.4.

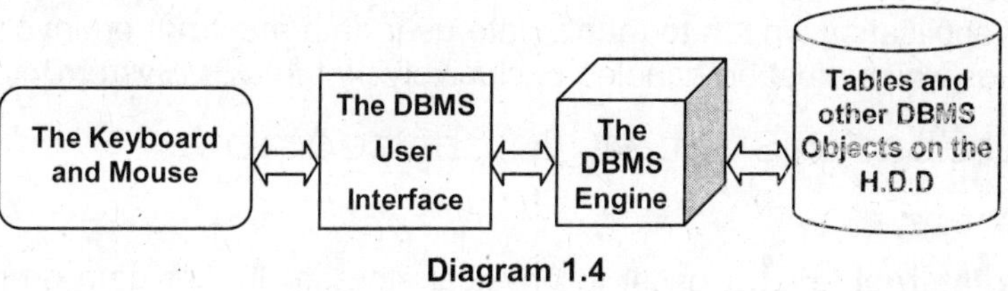

Diagram 1.4

Data Independence

Data independence is a technique employed by all database management systems that keeps user data isolated from all programs that use such data. The technique of data independence in a DBMS, ensures that the data cannot be redefined or reorganized by any of the programs that use this data. In this manner, the data remains accessible, but is also stable and cannot be corrupted by the programs / applications that access it.

All DBMSystems use centralized database management techniques within their environment that ensures data independence. While data transparency still exists as far as the ability of different applications to access and use user data to completing their tasks, no program or application belonging to the DBMS environment can begin to make changes to user data itself. This ensures the consistency of user data and in turn makes the overall process of maintaining and managing user date within a single database or multiple databases fairly simple and convenient.

One of the functions of data independence is that user applications are restricted in their access to the storage structure of user data. By effectively hiding the specifics of the storage structure of user data from applications, the potential for any application to alter the nature of the user data becomes impossible. Thus, the essential data retains its integrity and remains consistent no matter how many databases or database applications access user core data.

There are normally two levels or types of Data independence. Logical data independence makes it possible to change the storage structure of user data independent of modifying the applications or programs that make use of such data. There is no need to rewrite current applications as part of the process of adding to or removing data from the DBMS data storage system.

The second type or level of data independence is known as physical data independence. This approach is associated with altering the codespec of data storage procedures, rather than modifying user data itself.

Accomplishing this for user data does not require any modification to the external structure of applications, meaning that users of the applications are not likely to notice any difference at all in the function of their programs.

Data independence is the type of data transparency that matters for a centralized DBMS. It refers to the immunity of user applications to make changes to the definition and organization of data.

Physical data independence deals with hiding the details of the user data storage structure, from all user applications that manipulate user data held within the storage structure. Hence, any application written to manipulate user data must not be involved with data storage structure issues which must be handled exclusively by the DBMSystem.

Database System Architecture

Levels

The internal level: closest to physical storage of user data on permanent storage (i.e. the hard disk drive). The internal level of DBMS system architecture is concerned with the way user data is stored inside the DBMSystem.

The external level: closest to users, concerned with the way user data is seen by individual users

The conceptual level: a level of interaction between the external and internal levels.

External level

The external level is an individual user level.

Each user has a programming language at their disposal:

For the application programmer, the language could be a conventional programming language (Java, C++, etc.) that can communicate natively with a DBMS or using appropriate middleware or a language specific to the DBMSystem i.e. the natural language of the DBMS.

For an end user, the language is either a query language (probably SQL) or some special-purpose language, perhaps menu- or forms-driven.

All these languages include **D**ata **S**ub **L**anguage (DSL) which is concerned with various database objects and their operations.

One particular DSL supported by almost all current DBMSystems is SQL (to be used both a stand-alone query language and embedded within other languages).

Any DSL is really a combination of two child languages:

1) A **D**ata **D**efinition **L**anguage (DDL).

2) A **D**ata **M**anipulation **L**anguage (DML).

Programmers use DDL to define (or declare) DBMS objects like table, views and so on.

Users of DBMS make extensive use of its DML.

DML supports the processing or "manipulation" of database objects.

Conceptual level

The conceptual level is a representation of the entire information content of the database.

The form of the representation is abstract in comparison with the way in which the data is physically stored.

The form is also, in general, different from the way the data is viewed by any particular user.

The conceptual views are intended to be a view of the data "as it really is" rather than as users (are forced to) see it.

The conceptual view consists of many occurrences of many types of conceptual records.

Example: It might consist of:

- A collection of department record occurrences
- A collection of employee record occurrences
- A collection of supplier record occurrences,

And so on.

The conceptual view is defined by means of conceptual schema, which includes definitions of each of the various conceptual record types.

In most existing systems the conceptual schema is little more than simple union of all the individual external schemas, plus certain security and integrity constraints.

Internal level

The internal level is a low-level representation of the entire database.

It consists of many occurrences of many types of internal records (i.e. data rows in tables).

The internal view is described by means of the internal schema.

The internal schema defines various stored record types, plus specifies what indexes exist, how stored fields are represented, what physical sequence of stored records are in, and so on.

The internal schema is written using the internal DDL of the DBMSystem.

*User Interface
User A1
Host language + DSL
User A2
Host language + DSL
User B1
Host language + DSL
User B2
Host language + DSL
User B3
Host language + DSL
*External Schema A
External View A
*External Schema B
External View B
Schemas and mappings built end maintained by the database administrator (DBA)
External/conceptual mapping A
External/conceptual mapping B
Conceptual schema
Conceptual View
Database Management System DBMS
Conceptual/internal mapping
Storage structure defination (internal schema)
Stored Database (internal view)

Diagram 1.5

Summary

Database system architecture consists of three levels.

The internal level is the one closest to physical storage.

The external level is the one closest to the users.

The conceptual level is a level of interaction between these two.

The data as perceived at these levels is defined by a schema or schemas.

Mappings define correspondence between a given external schema and the conceptual schema, and the conceptual schema and internal schema.

Users interact with the data by means of DSL.

DSL consists of at least two subcomponents: DDL and DML.

Database Users

All others who have access to and use DBMS resources such as its user interfaces, tables, table data, form creation interface, reports generation interface and so on are termed as database users.

Database user names are global across a database. Database users interact with database objects. Every database object has its owner - the user that created it. Every user and role has a creator.

There are following kinds of database objects:

- Standalone tables
- Collection of tables belonging to a single logical schema

- Table indexes
- Database modules

There are two types of database users:

- The **D**ata**B**ase **A**dministrator (DBA user)
- Ordinary users

The Database Administrator

All DBMS have the concept of a **D**ata**B**ase **A**dministrator (DBA). This is the individual who has complete and total charge of the DBMS.

DBMS are pretty complex systems but their user interface has been designed so that even a fairly inexperienced individual can carry out day-to-day database management tasks. ANSI SQL is a language that is pretty close to ordinary English.

> **Note:** *The simplicity of most DBMS, user interfaces, is really a testimony of the skills of the systems programmers that created (i.e. coded) the DBMS.*

A user interface is what programmers (or any other user of the DBMS) use to structure their commands in ANSI SQL and then have these commands passed to the DBMS for execution as shown in diagram 1.6.

Even though using a DBMS is fairly simple ensuring that all the tables on the hard disk drive work together in perfect harmony especially when holding huge volumes of business data is a specialized task and requires an individual with specialized skills.

The individual entrusted with this responsibility usually has an intimate knowledge of the architecture of the DBMS, knows all its idiosyncrasies, and can ensure smooth functioning of the DBMS.

his is an individual, (usually an experienced programmer), who has subsequently undergone specialized training and certification, bound to the DBMS in use. This is the individual who is called the **D**ata**B**ase **A**dministrator (DBA).

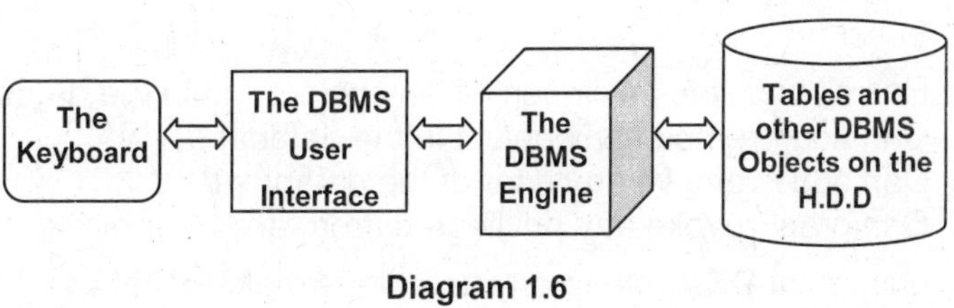

Diagram 1.6

It is the DBA's responsibility to ensure that the DBMS functions smoothly all the time, irrespective of how many users are simultaneously requesting the DBMS for data.

Another area of responsibility for the DBA is to backup user data regularly on CDROM or magnetic tape. These backups will be used to restore the DBMS to normalcy in case the DBMS crashes for any reason.

Finally, DBA's restore the DBMS in case of a system crash. After the DBMS is successfully restored, (reinstalled from scratch if necessary) the data backups are used to return the DBMS to its fully operational state.

In very large software development houses (or very large users of DBMS based software) the DBA is a **unique** individual whose sole mandate is to keep the DBMS working smoothly all the time. In smaller software houses (or users of DBMS based software) a senior programmer may play a dual role of programmer and DBA.

Before anyone can make use of DBMS resources such as its user interfaces, tables, table data, form creation interface, reports generation interface and so on they have to have their **user account** created with the DBMS. Creating user accounts is also the prerogative of the DBA. Unless a user account is created and registered with the DBMS, generally the DBMS will prevent a user from accessing any of its resources.

Most DBMS have separate DBA syntax, this is generally a super set of ANSI SQL, (i.e. contain verbs (syntax) **not specified** in the ANSI SQL specification but required for managing user accounts and a host of other DBA related duties).

When a DBA creates a user account, the DBA can exercise a great deal of control over exactly what DBMS resources a user can access.

The DBA accesses a special graphical user interface (GUI), via which all DBA activity is carried out. Access to the DBA GUI is via a **special user name** and **password** (i.e. a **special** user account) created when the DBMS was **being installed** on the system. Anyone who knows the user name and password associated with the DBA user account can log into the DBMS as the DBA and would be recognized by the DBMS as the DBA.

When the DBA is creating user accounts and registering them with the DBMS **each** user account is created having a **unique** user name and password, which is then given to the user for use. Only the DBA can change user names or passwords. Users themselves generally cannot change this.

Formally, a DBA user is a user that has **D**ata **B**ase **A**dministrator role.

DBA user type

1. Has all possible privileges on any object within the database schema
2. Can add / remove any object in the database
3. Can add / remove any user of the database
4. Can grant/revoke any privilege to/from any user of the database
5. Can grant **DBA** role to any user, thus making that user also a DBA user (not recommended, as the database with multiple DBA users is hard to administrate). Any DBA user can also revoke the DBA privileges from another DBA user

A user

- Can act upon the user data held within the DBMS only according to the privileges assigned by the DBA to that user
- Can grant and revoke any privileges on a database object that is owned, to another user
- Can remove database objects that are owned and drop users that they have created

Every user has a name and password assigned to them by the DBA on being added as user to the DBMS

To create a user use the CREATE USER statement:

CREATE USER "user-name" WITH PASSWORD "user-password"

This statement creates a user with name user-name with password user-password.

To remove an existing user, use DROP USER statement:

DROP USER "user-name"

To change user password use the ALTER USER statement. A user can change a password for themselves or for a user they has created.

A DBA user can change a password for any user of the database.

ALTER USER "user-name" WITH PASSWORD "new-password"

This statement changes the password of the user user-name to new-password.

In order to startup the database instance, a freshly installed and configured DBMS always contains one predefined DBA user with name ROOT and an associated password defined at DBMS install and configure time.

To start work with the DBMS, you first have to connect to the DBMS instance running in memory as ROOT with the appropriate password, only then can you:

Create other users

Grant then privileges on DBMS resources

Change default password for ROOT if any

Privileges and Roles

Whenever any database object is created, it is immediately bound to an owner. This is normally the user who created the database object. Only a database object owner and the DBA user can do anything with the database object.

In order to allow other users to use a database object, they have to be granted access privileges.

There are several possible privileges, here are some of them:

- CREATE-USER
- CREATE-DOCUMENT
- CREATE-COLLECTION
- CREATE-INDEX
- LOAD-MODULE
- LOAD
- DROP
- QUERY
- INSERT
- DELETE
- RENAME
- RETRIEVE-METADATA

Users can be grated privileges to specific objects within a database or to the whole database. Using the key word **ALL** when assigning user privileges to a database object grants all access permissions on the specified object.

When the LOAD privilege on a database is granted to a user this allows that user to load documents into the DBMS collection.

When the DROP privilege on collection is granted to a user, this means that the user can drop any document in the DBMS collection.

A simple technique used by Database administrators to assign privileges to users quickly is to create a database object called a ROLE.

Then the DBA binds specific privileges to the ROLE. Once this is done whenever a DBA creates a new user the ROLE can be bound to a user. The user then automatically acquires all privileges assigned to the ROLE.

Hence, a ROLE is a **named** group of related privileges. ROLE's provide easy and controlled way to manage user privileges.

To create a ROLE a CREATE ROLE statement is used:

CREATE ROLE "dataentyronly"

This statement creates role with name **dataentyronly**. When created a role does not contain any privileges.

> **Note:** *It is not recommended to create any role whose name is that of an existing user. This is because all the privileges assigned to that role will be immediately granted both to the* ***user*** *and to the ROLE.*

It is not allowed to use "DBA" and "PUBLIC" as ROLE names as they are reserved by the system.

Granting privileges

Privileges are granted to users so that they can access and operate database objects **or** to process some tasks with a database engine **or** a combination of both.

User privileges can be granted in two different ways:

1. Privileges can be granted to a user explicitly
2. Privileges can be granted to role, and the role can be bound to one or more users at their creation time.

Roles allow easier and simpler management of privileges, thus privileges are normally granted to roles and not to specific users. Roles can be granted both to users and to roles.

A user who has been granted a privilege (or a role) can in turn be the grantor of this privilege (or role).

To grant a privilege on a database object you must be an owner of this object or the DBA. To grant one or more privileges on a database object to one or more users or roles use:

GRANT "privilege" | ALL
ON [DOCUMENT|COLLECTION] "database-object-name"
TO "user-name|role-name" | PUBLIC

The key word PUBLIC is used when the privileges are to be granted to all users, including those that may be created later. PUBLIC may be thought of as an implicitly defined role that every user has.

If the kind of the database object (DOCUMENT or COLLECTION) is not specified, the database object is considered to be a document.

To grant a privilege on a database you must be a DBA. To grant one or more privileges on a database to one or more users or roles use:

GRANT "privilege" | ALL
ON DATABASE
TO "user-name|role-name" | PUBLIC

To grant a role to any user you must be:

Allowed to grant every privilege set within the role

Be the owner of every database object of bound to the privileges of the role

To grant a role to one or more users or roles use:

GRANT "role-name" TO "user-name|role_name" | PUBLIC

<u>Revoking privileges</u>

Privileges or roles can be revoked from the user or role. Only grantor of the privilege (role) or DBA user can revoke privilege (role).

REVOKE statements are similar to GRANT statements.

To revoke one or more privileges on a database object from one or more users or roles use:

REVOKE "privilege" | ALL
ON [DOCUMENT|COLLECTION] "database-object-name"
FROM "user-name|role-name" | PUBLIC

If the kind of the database object (DOCUMENT or COLLECTION) is not specified, the database object is considered to be a document.

To revoke one or more privileges on a database from one or more users or roles use:

REVOKE "privilege" | ALL
ON DATABASE
FROM "user-name|role-name" | PUBLIC

To revoke a role from one or more users or roles use:

REVOKE "role-name"
FROM "user-name|role-name" | PUBLIC

DBA is a reserved name for a role. A role with the name **DBA** cannot be created, privileges or roles cannot be granted to DBA role.

A DBA can grant DBA privileges to another user, thus making that user a DBA as well. This is not recommended, as multiple powerful users of a database can lead to hard database administration, and can cause unsecure usage of the database and database objects.

Client Authentication

All database engines require that a user logs in to the db engine prior being able to access/use any database object. Most database engines use a character based client for login, some database engines use a GUI based client for login.

When a user or any client application wishes to connect to the database engine / server, either must specifies which user name they want to connect as. It is the User name that determines access privileges to database objects therefore, client access authentication is mandatory for any DBMS.

Authentication is the process by which the database server (or engine) establishes the identity of the client wishing to gain access to its resources and determines whether the client application (or the user who runs the client application) is permitted to connect to database resources with the user name that was provided at login time.

When any user is created with the -db-security authorization 'ON', the database engine will check the user password on session open.

Currently, most database servers use password authentication. The client application that connects to the database must specify both a user name and user password.

A newly created database always contains one predefined DBA user with name "SYSTEM" and password "MANAGER". To start your work with the database, you first have to connect as this initial user.

> **Note:** *A DBA named SYSTEM with the associated password MANAGER is normally associated with the Oracle RDBMS.*
> *To know the default DBA and its associated Password created at install time read the technical reference manual for that DBMS.*

Self Review Questions

Fill In The Blanks

1. A __________ can be defined as a collection of coherent (meaningful) data.
2. ________________ software allows a programmer to structure a database that belongs to a specific real world domain space.
3. For a product to be qualified as a DBMS system by ANSI it had to conform to the standards laid out in _________.
4. ANSI stands for _________________________.
5. Each junction of a row and column creates a _________.
6. A group of cells in the same horizontal plane make a __________.

7. The Viewing of table data is termed as a table __________ operation.
8. A table __________ operation does not make any change to table data at all.
9. All businesses have a business __________ at their core.
10. ROI stands for ____________________.
11. The data captured by a program when submitted to the management for reaction is called __________ __________.
12. A single unit of work is termed as a __________.
13. Multiple addresses kept together in one place, such as an address book, could be termed as a _________ collection of data.
14. The structure of a database is _________ dimensional.
15. A DBMS and ANSI-SQL can be used to create _________ number of carefully designed tables to store information in.
16. A _________ can be conceptualized as an empty storage structure in which information can be stored.
17. The cost to company processes always give rise to another set of processes that bring _________ to the company.
18. All the replies received from brokers need to be _________ and an appropriate short list created.
19. If a transaction fails then in addition to automatic roll back of table data a programmer can instruct the DBMS to write to an __________ table.
20. The ____________________ is the individual who has complete and total charge of the DBMS.

True Or False

1. Addresses kept at different locations could be termed as coherent collection of data.
2. A fixed, pre-created, database cannot be used because the very same database may have different contours in different real world domain spaces.
3. ANSI-SQL, information cannot be shared seamlessly across multiple DBMS.
4. The cell is a single unit of storage in which a single unit of information, obtained from the real world, is stored.
5. These table operations are what facilitate table information manipulation.
6. Multiple records of equal length stored one below the other make a column.
7. Table write operations cause permanent changes to table data.
8. Inserting, Updating and Deleting table data are termed as table read operations.

9. Making profit ensures that the business process brings in more money rather than acting as a cost.
10. The trick in building a successful business model is simply to ensure that the ROI is greater than the cost to company.
11. All DBMS store business data in rows.
12. A DBMS and ANSI-SQL can be used to create any number of carefully designed tables to store information in.
13. DBMS could not have their own proprietary languages as they were confined to ANSI-SQL standards.
14. Table read operation does not make any change to table data at all.
15. A document (content) need not be structured.
16. Broadly speaking a business model always has only one set of process.
17. Data modeling cannot be done using ANSI SQL.
18. If a single sub process fails for any reason the master process must be flagged as failed.
19. On a current account the amount withdrawn and the number of withdrawals is limited.
20. Table data can be extracted and manipulated in any number of different ways.
21. The individual who ensures that all the DBMS tables on the hard disk drive work together in perfect harmony is called the database user.
22. It's the DBA's responsibility to ensure that the DBMS functions smoothly at all times.

Objective Questions

1. What is a Database?
2. What is a Database Management System?
3. What is ANSI-SQL?
4. What are the different ways that data can be manipulated in a table?
5. How do the contours of a database change, explain with a small example?
6. What is data independence?
7. Why is data independence important?
8. What are privileges and roles?
9. How does a DBA grant user privileges on database objects?
10. How does a DBA revoke user privileges on database objects?

2. Relational Model

A DBMS has always been a preferred tool for managing business data. This is because using a DBMS to store and manage business data is simplicity itself. Another great advantage is the fact that DBMS provide complete data independence at logical schema level and physical data storage levels as well.

Once a DBMS has been used to craft storage structures for a business application complete data independence is assured by the DBMS engine. This means that business applications can be modified without any effect on the DBMS data storage structures, and/or DBMS storage structures can be modified without causing business application code spec to fail immediately.

Tip: *Traditionally, there are three techniques that DBMS use to manage user data held in their storage structure called tables:*

Hierarchical

Network

Relational

Fortunately today DBMS do not use the Hierarchical technique for managing table data at all DBMS have almost ended using the Network technique for managing user data.Almost all (except very specialzed DBMSystems) have adopted the Relational technique of managing user data. The Relational technique is the one that is constantly growing and being made easier to use and is the most commonly found technique in DBMSs for managing user data today.

The DataBase Management System (DBMS)

Since early days, managing business data using a computer was done via an **application** where the data manipulation code and the structure in which user data was stored were tightly linked. Applications could be **generic**, where the application offers extensive, in-built, facilities to customize it to fit any business model **or** the application could be tailormade to fit a specific business model and cannot be used anywhere else.

A financial accounting system for instance is a perfect example of a generic application used in the business world. A hospital management system is an example of an application that can be used only with the hospital business model.

A **D**ata**B**ase **M**anagement **S**ystem (DBMS) is an application with simple to use, built-in tools, which allow it to be extensively customized to fit **any** business model under the sun.

Creators Of DBMS

The computer application development domain can be quickly segregated into two. The **Systems** domain and the **Commercial Application development** domain. This gives rise to two unique type of programmers, System programmers and Commercial Application development programmers.

System programmers are those who create DBMS.

Systems programmers are proficient with machine language, assembly language, **and** other low level languages especially ANSI **C**.

Additionally, these programmers usually have quite an intimate knowledge of electronic circuitry such as computer motherboard architecture, GUI interfacing, Hard disk drive controllers, networking and so on.

These skills give them the unique ability to code generic applications, with simple to use user interfaces. These programmers create **D**ata**B**ase **M**anagement **S**ystems and belong to the Systems domain space, which can be visualized as a super set of the software development domain.

> **Tip:** *To map these concepts to what was learned earlier:*
> *Software development* **is often considered as a** *Parent process*
> *System* **software development is one of its** *sub-process*
> *Commercial Application* **software development is another one of its** *sub-process*

System programmers write the source code for **DBMS engines**.

The DBMS is the application first loaded into a computer's memory which acts as an interface that sits between the Programmer and user data stored in its structures.

Commercial application programmers communicate all their instructions to the DBMS which in-turn will communicate with the CPU beneath it.

Commercial application programmers communicate with the DBMS engine, via simple to use, **Character based** or **Graphical User Interface** provided for them by the Systems programmers who wrote the DBMS. Refer to diagram 2.1.

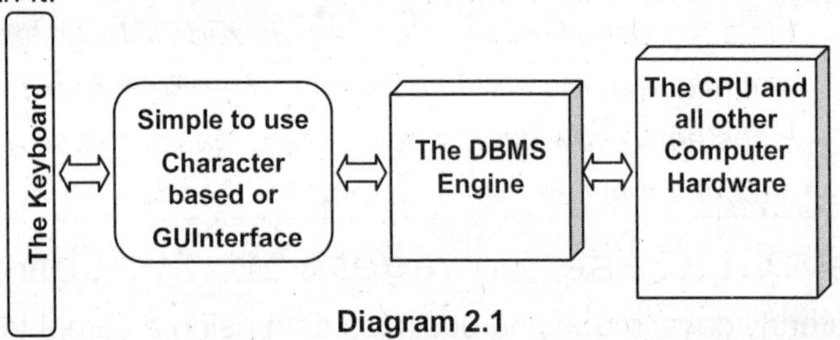

Diagram 2.1

Application programmers normally communicate with the user interface provided using a **keyboard** via which they pass their instructions (**i.e.** what they want done).

The user interface accepts their instructions, checks for its correctness, (**i.e.** syntax and semantics) and if all is acceptable passes these instructions to the DBMS engine for execution.

> **Caution:** *If the instructions contain syntax and/or semantic errors the interface, will display an appropriate error message to the programmer, on the VDU. These instructions are not passed to the DBMS.*

The DBMS engine executes these instructions (**i.e.** does what it's been instructed to do by the programmer) and displays appropriate output to the user via the VDU. This completes the work cycle.

The DBMS engine communicate with all that is necessary to execute the users commands such as computer hardware, memory, user tables populated business data and so on.

To communicate with all its resources DBMS use, **S**tructured **Q**uery **L**anguage (SQL).

For any application to qualify as a DBMS, SQL must be its native language. The **A**merican **N**ational **S**tandards **I**nstitute (ANSI) has defined the standards to be followed by SQL.

To be able to set the standards for SQL table structures must in turn be standardized as well as the way that table data is manipulated. Since the structure of DBMS tables and their access is standardized all DBMS can use SQL as their natural language.

Tables use a **mathematical** technique called a **R**elational **D**ata **M**odel (RDM) to store, access and manipulate table data. Hence all DBMS that are built around engines that use this model to store, access, and manipulate table data are called **R**elational **D**ata**B**ase **M**anagement **S**ystems (RDBMS).

In essence the power of the Relational Data Model is that it completely frees an **application** programmer from being concerned about how to create data storage structures (**i.e.** tables), store data in them, then access such data and so on.

The programmer is completely free to focus on designing the software application model to fit the actual business model exactly.

The Relational Data Model - Basics.

The **R**elational **D**ata **M**odel (RDM) came into existence many years ago. It has moved through several stages after first coming into existence as is now a tried and tested commercial product. Today several commercial RDBMS products exist, some of their names are:

- Oracle
- Sybase
- Ingres
- DB2
- MSSQL Server
- MySQL

There are a host of other RDBMS products.

Note:	*All of these products attempt to implement the **RDM 100%**, regretfully **none** of them actually **achieve this**, thus theoretically **none** no product currently calling itself an RDBMS is a true RDBMS.*

The principles of **R**elational **D**ata **M**anagement are very simple:

1. Users can express their queries using the powerful **S**tructured **Q**uery **L**anguage of the RDM.
2. In the RDM the **Relation** (**i.e.** a table) is the **only structure** required to represent the attributes of various business entities (**i.e.** a business's Master and child processes) as well as any specific relationship between these attributes.

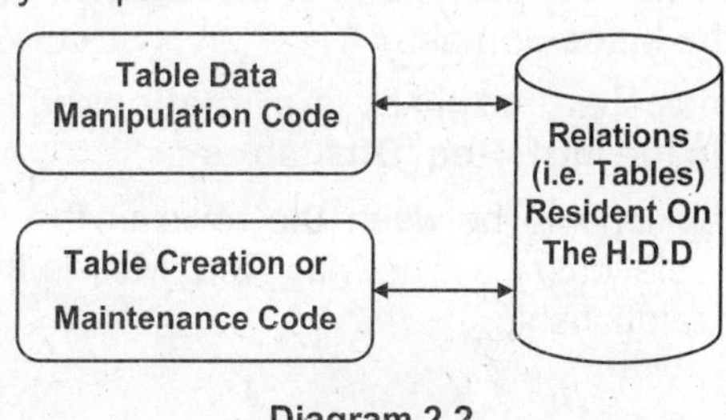

Diagram 2.2

The RDM approach immediately **separates** the **code** used to **define** and **create** a Relation from the **code** used to **manipulate** its data (**i.e.** table data). By using a RDBMS programmers are immediately freed of the responsibility of making changes in their program code when they need to make any change to the structure of a Relation (**i.e.** a table). Refer to diagram 2.2.

Note: *For the purpose of simplicity and to maintain a link with commercial application development the words Relation and Table can and will be used completely interchangeably in this material.*

3. Another huge advantage of using an RDBMS is that the programmer **does not** have to code for how table data must be accessed.

Accessing and manipulation table data is **completely transparent** to the programmer and handled by the **RDBMS** independently.

4. A **Relation** can be simply conceptualized as a **Named Table**.

MaterialRequisition Master :
Mtrl_Req_Mast

Rq_Number	Date	Dept_Name

Table 2.1

Material Requisition Details:
Mtrl_Req_Dtls

Rq_Number	Material Name	Qty_Reqd.

Table 2.2

Tables 2.1 and 2.2 show two Relations (i.e. tables) M[illegible]_Req_Mast and Mtrl_Req_Dtls using a tabular structure. Each relation is uniquely name[illegible] [illegible]ach column of the relation, representing attributes of the Relation and is also named.

Note: *Rows* ***in a Relation*** *(i.e.* ***table) are called*** *Tuples* ***of the Relation. The*** *Columns* ***of the Relation are its*** *Attributes.*

In the RDM:

5. No **two** rows (**i.e.** tuples) of a table (**i.e.** Relation) are **identical**
6. The **ordering** of a Relation's rows is **completely insignificant**

<u>These are the simple principles of the **R**elational **D**ata **M**odel.</u>

Here the columns **Rq_Number** in both tables (**i.e.** Relations) contain identical values. The column names have been deliberately kept the same to indicate that they hold **values** drawn from the **same** domain.

This indicates that there is a **relationship** between the **rows** in the **Mtrl_Req_Mast** and the **rows** in the **Mtrl_Req_Dtls** tables.

The relationship between the rows in the Mtrl_Req_Mstr and the Mtrl_Req_Dtls is a **one**-to-**many** relationship. The Mtrl_Req_Mstr is the controller and the Mtrl_Req_Dtls is the controlled in this relationship.

Note:	*The Mtrl_Req_Mstr.Rq_Number is the Primary Key of the Relation. The Mtrl_Req_Detls.Rq_Number is the Foreign Key between the Relations.A* ***period*** *is used to separate the attribute from the Relation name because in* ***both*** *cases the* ***attribute name*** *is the* ***same.***

To tie up this information with what was learned earlier. Systems programmers must understand RDM principles thoroughly. Then code these principles **into** the **RDBMS engine** they are creating.

This will give rise to a sophisticated block of code that will be completely generic in nature. This will allow programmers to:

- Define and create table structures to store business data
- These structures will be completely independent of the code used to manipulate the business data held within the tables
- The order in which the rows of data are stored in a table will be completely inconsequential to the programmer and controlled by the RDBMS
- The programmer need not indicate how the table data will be accessed. The RDBMS must do this based on the Relational Data Model automatically

This is what a **R**elational **D**ata**B**ase **M**anagement **S**ystem is all about.

Diagram 2.3 shows **where** the **R**elational **D**ata **M**odel (RDM) is introduced in a DBMS to evolve the DBMS to an **R**DBMS.

This in brief is how a **R**elational **D**ata**B**ase **M**anagement **S**ystem (RDBMS) is structured.

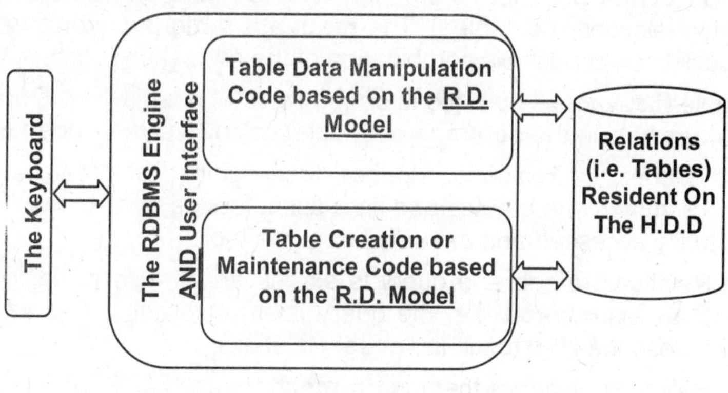

Diagram 2.3

Relational Algebra

Conceptually, Relational Algebra is a **collection** of **operations** that manipulate Relations. Hence, Relational Algebra is a collection of operations that manipulate data in a table (or tables).

Relational Algebra is associated with table **Read operations** or **Write operations**. Table Read operations do **not change table data** in any way but permit table data to be accessed and displayed in **any conceivable way** with reference to a business model.

Table **Write operations** are where table data is **physically** and **permanently** changed in the table.

Note:	*Relational Algebra is a* ***procedural language****, used with tables. (****i.e.*** *Relational Algebra is* ***fully modeled*** *in* ***ANSI SQL*** *that is the natural language of all RDBMS).*

Relational Algebra is used to specify table data operations that must be carried out on tables to derive result values. Relational Algebraic operations can be quickly divided into set-oriented table operations and relational-oriented operations.

Basic Operations

The basic set-operations are in Relational Algebra are:

- Union
- Difference
- Intersection
- Cartesian Product

Difference and **Intersection** are childsets of **Union**, hence if these operations are to be carried out on any tables they must be **Union compatible**.

Tip:	*Being Union compatible means that the columns of the table on which these operations are carried out have the same column name* ***and*** *the resultant table created (which displays the table data required) inherits the same column name as well.* *Additionally, the* ***values*** *held in these columns must belong to a* ***common*** *domain*

A **Cartesian product** of two Relations is simply the **concatenation** of the tuples (**i.e.** rows) of both Relations (**i.e.** tables). The **resultant table** (**i.e.** Relation) created by the Cartesian product consists of all possible combination of the rows (**i.e.** Tuples) of the tables.

Tuple (**i.e.** various operations on the **rows** of a table) and Domain (**i.e.** various operations on the **values** held in the **columns** of a table) calculi are referred to **Relational Algebra**.

All queries, in Relational Algebra, fired against table/data are **nonprocedural** in nature. The programmer who creates and fires such queries **is not** involved in the details of **how** this data is actually accessed and extracted from the table.

In Relational Algebra, a query is expressed as a **formula**, consisting of a number of variables and **an expression** (**i.e.** the query itself) involving these variables. The formula, in essence, fully describes the result table (**i.e.** Relation).

In Relational Algebra there is **no mechanism** (**i.e.** RDBMS syntax) provided to specify how the formula should be evaluated by the RDBMS.

This is completely up to the **RDBMS engine** to transform all such (*nonprocedural*) queries into efficient, procedural queries and execute them against the table or tables specified in the query formula.

All that the commercial application programmers really must know is how to use **S**tructured **Q**uery **L**anguage (**i.e.** ANSI SQL). It is this language that allows programmers to define variables and formulas with which to effectively manipulate business data held within tables.

Inserting Data Into A Table From Another Table

In addition to inserting data one row at a time into a table, it is quite possible to populate a table with data that already exists in another table. The syntax for doing so is described under

Syntax:

```
INSERT INTO tablename
SELECT columnname, columnname,
FROM tablename;
```

Example:

1. Insert records into table supplier_master from the table client_master;

```
INSERT INTO SUPPLIER_MASTER
SELECT CLIENT_NO, NAME, ADDRESS1, ADDRESS2,
CITY, STATE, PINCODE, REMARKS
FROM CLIENT_MASTER;
```

Insertion Of A Data Set Into A Table From Another Table:

Syntax:

```
Insert into tablename
SELECT columnname, columnname
from tablename
where column = expression;
```

Example:

1. Insert records into the table supplier_master from the table client_master where the field client_no contains the value 'C01001';

```
INSERT INTO supplier_master
SELECT client_no, name, address1, address2,
city, pincode, state, remarks
FROM client_master
WHERE client_no = 'C01001';
```

Delete Operations

The verb DELETE in SQL is used to remove either

- All the rows from a table **OR**
- A set of rows from a table

Removal Of All Rows

Syntax:

DELETE FROM ***tablename;***

Example:

1. Delete all rows from the table client_master;

   DELETE FROM **client_master**;

Removal Of A Specified Row/S

Syntax:

DELETE from ***tablename*** **WHERE** ***search condition;***

Example:

2. Delete rows from the table client_master where the value in the bal_due field is less than 500;

   DELETE FROM **client_master** WHERE **bal_due < 500**;

Updating The Contents Of A Table

The **UPDATE** command is used to change or modify data values in a table. To **update**

- All the rows from a table **OR**
- A select set of rows from a table

Updating Of All Rows

Syntax:

UPDATE ***tablename***

SET ***columnname = expression, columnname = expression;***

Example:

1. Give every employee a bonus of 15%. Calculate the 15% amount based on the value held in the column basic_sal of the table emp_master and update the values held in the column net_sal.

   UPDATE **emp_master**

   SET **netsal = net_sal+ basic_sal* 0.15**;

Updating Records Conditionally

Syntax:

UPDATE ***tablename***

SET ***columnname = expression, columnname = expression...***

WHERE ***columnname = expression;***

Example:

2. Update the table client_master change the contents of the field *name* to 'Vijay Kadam' and the contents of the field *address* to 'SCT Jay Apartments' for the record identified by the field *client_no* containing the value 'C02000';

   UPDATE **client_master**

   SET **name = 'Vijay Kadam' , address1 = 'SCT Jay Apartments'**

   WHERE **client_no = 'C02000'**;

Viewing Data In The Tables

Once data has been inserted into a table, the next most logical operation would be to view what has been entered. The '**SELECT**' SQL verb is used to achieve this.

All Rows And All Column

In order to view global table data the syntax is:

Global data extract

Syntax:

SELECT (*columnname1*...... *columnname* n) FROM tablename;

Note: *Here* *columnname1.......columnname n* ***represents table columns.***

Syntax:

SELECT * FROM tablename;

Example:

1. Retrieve the names of the employees and their salaries from the table emp_master;
   SELECT name, salary **FROM** emp_master;
2. Retrieve all records from table client_master;
   SELECT * FROM client_master;

> **Tip:** *When data from all rows and columns from the table are to be viewed the syntax of the SELECT statement will be:*
>
> ***SELECT * from tablename;***
>
> *Oracle allows the user to use the meta character asterisk (*), which is expanded by Oracle to mean all columns in the table. The Oracle Server compiles the sentence, executes it, and retrieves data for all columns/rows from the table.*

Filtering Table Data

While viewing data from a table it is rare that all the data from the table will be required **each time**. Hence, SQL must give us a method of filtering out data that is not required.

The ways of filtering table data will be

- Selected columns and all rows
- Selected rows and all columns
- Selected columns and selected rows

Selected Columns And All Rows:

The retrieval of specific columns from a table:

Syntax:

```
SELECT columnname, columnname
FROM tablename;
```

Examples:

1. Retrieve the contents of the columns *client_no* and *name* from the table client_master

```
SELECT client_no, name
FROM client_master;
```

Selected Rows And All Columns

If information of a particular client must be retrieved from the table, its retrieval must be based on a specific condition.

The SELECT statement used until now displayed all rows. This is because there was no condition set that informed Oracle about the need to view a specific data set from the table.

Oracle provides the option of using a 'where clause' in an SQL sentence to apply a filter on the rows the select statement will retrieve.

When a 'Where Clause' is added to the SQL sentence, the Oracle Server compares each record from the table with the condition specified in the where clause. Oracle displays only those records that satisfy the specified condition.

Syntax:

```
SELECT *
FROM tablename
WHERE search condition;
```

Example:

1. Retrieve all client_information from the table client_master where the value in the bal_due field is greater than 0;

```
SELECT *
FROM client_master
WHERE bal_due > 0;
```

> **Note:** *In the search condition all standard operators such as logical, arithmetic, predicates etc. can be used. Their usage in SQL sentences is extensive in later chapters.*

Selected Columns And Selected Rows

To view a specific data set from the table and also a select number of columns the syntax will be as follows

Syntax:

```
SELECT columnname, columnname
FROM tablename
WHERE search condition;
```

Example:

2. Retrieve the *client_no*, *name* from the table client_master where the value in the bal_due field is greater than *5000*;

```
SELECT client_no, name
FROM client_master
WHERE bal_due > 5000;
```

Elimination Of Duplicates From The Select Statement

A table could hold duplicate rows. In such a case, to see only unique rows the syntax is

Syntax:

```
SELECT DISTINCT columnname,columnname
FROM  tablename;
```

The **SELECT DISTINCT** SQL syntax scans through the values of the column/s specified and displays unique values from amongst them.

Syntax:

```
SELECT DISTINCT *
FROM  tablename;
```

The **SELECT DISTINCT** SQL syntax scans through entire rows, and eliminates rows that have exactly the same contents in each column.

Example:

1. Eliminate the duplicate job descriptions when retrieving data from the job column of the table employee.

```
SELECT DISTINCT job
FROM employee;
```

2. Select only unique rows from the table client_master;

```
SELECT DISTINCT *
FROM client_master;
```

Sorting data in a table

Oracle allows data from a table to be viewed in a sorted order. The rows retrieved from the table will be sorted in either ascending or descending order depending on the condition specified in the select sentence.

The syntax for viewing data in a sorted order is as follows

Syntax:

```
SELECT *
FROM tablename
ORDER BY columnname, columnname[sort order];
```

Example:

1. Retrieve all rows from the table client_master and display this data sorted on the value contained in the field client_no in ascending order;

```
SELECT *
FROM client_master
ORDER BY client_no;
```

Note:	*For viewing the data in descending sorted order the word 'desc' must be mentioned after the column name and before the semi colon in the order by clause. In case there is no mention of the sort order, the Oracle engine sorts in ascending order by default.*

Example:

```
SELECT client_no, name, address1, address2, city, pincode
   FROM client_master
   ORDER BY client_no desc;
```

Computations Done On Table Data

None of the techniques used till now allows display of data from a table after some arithmetic has been done with it.

Computations may include displaying an employee's name and the employee's salary from the Employee_Master table along with the **annual salary** of the employee (**i.e.** Salary*12). The arithmetic (Salary * 12) is an example of table data arithmetic.

Arithmetic and logical operators give a new dimension to SQL sentences.

Arithmetic Operators

Oracle allows arithmetic operators to be used while viewing records from a table or while performing Data Manipulation operations such as Insert, Update and Delete. These are:

+	Addition	*	Multiplication
-	Subtraction	**	Exponentiation
/	Division	( )	Enclosed operation

Example:

List the fixed deposits held by the customers and also show what will be the amount payable by the bank if the fixed deposits are cancelled by the **end of the day**.

Synopsis:

Tables:	FD_DTLS
Columns:	FD_NO, TYPE, PERIOD, OPNDT, DUEDT, AMT, INTRATE, DUEAMT
Technique:	**Functions:** ROUND(), **Operators:** *, -, /, **Clauses:** WHERE, **Others:** SYSDATE

Solution:

SELECT FD_NO, TYPE, PERIOD, OPNDT, DUEDT, AMT, INTRATE, DUEAMT,
ROUND(AMT **+** (AMT * ROUND(SYSDATE – OPNDT)/365 * (INTRATE/100)), **2)**
FROM FD_DTLS **WHERE** DUEDT > **SYSDATE;**

Output:

```
FD_NO  TYPE  PERIOD OPNDT      DUEDT         AMT  INTRATE  DUEAMT
---------------------------------------------------------------
                   ROUND(AMT+(AMT*ROUND(SYSDATE-
                   OPNDT)/365*(INTRATE/100)),2)
---------------------------------------------------------------
F6     S        732 19-JUL-03  20-JUL-05    5000        9  5902.47
                                                  5429.04
F7     S        366 27-JUL-03  27-JUL-04    5000        8   5401.1
                                                   5372.6
```

Explanation:

Here, **ROUND(AMT + (AMT * ROUND(SYSDATE – OPNDT)/365 * (INTRATE/100)),2)** is **not** a column in the table **FD_DTLS**. However, the arithmetic specified is done on the contents of the columns **AMT, OPNDT and INTRATE** of the table **FD_DTLS** and displayed in the output of the query.

By default, the Oracle engine will use the column names of the table **FD_DTLS** as column headers when displaying column output on the VDU screen.

Since there are no columns with the arithmetic expression applied on the table **FD_DTLS**, the Oracle engine performs the required arithmetic and uses the **formula** as the **default** column header when displaying output as seen above.

Logical Operators

Logical operators that can be used in SQL sentences are:

The AND Operator:

The AND operator allows creating an SQL statement based on two or more conditions being met. It can be used in any valid SQL statement such as select, insert, update, or delete. The AND operator requires that each condition must be met for the record to be included in the result set.

The Oracle engine will process all rows in a table and display the result only when **all** of the conditions specified using the **AND** operator are satisfied.

Example:

Display all those transactions performed today for amount ranging between 500 and 5000 **both inclusive**.

Synopsis:

Tables:	TRANS_MSTR
Columns:	All Columns
Technique:	**Functions:** TO_CHAR(), **Operators:** AND, **Clauses:** WHERE, **Others:** SYSDATE

Solution:

```
SELECT * FROM TRANS_MSTR WHERE AMT >= 500 AND AMT <= 5000
    AND TO_CHAR(DT, 'DD/MM/YYYY') = TO_CHAR(SYSDATE, 'DD/MM/YYYY');
```

Output:

TRANS_NO	ACCT_NO	DT	TYPE	PARTICULAR	DR_CR	AMT	BALANCE
T7	CA7	14-MAR-2004	B	Initial Payment	D	2000	2000

Explanation:

Here, the AND operator is used to compare the value held in the amount field with a constant. Only those transactions carried out today, that satisfy this comparison, are shown. This is done by comparing transaction dates with the current date after converting them to characters.

The OR Operator:

The OR condition allows creating an SQL statement where records are returned when any one of the conditions are met. It can be used in any valid SQL statement such as select, insert, update, or delete. The OR condition requires that any of the conditions must be met for the record to be included in the result set.

The Oracle engine will process all rows in a table and display the result only when **any of** the conditions specified using the **OR** operator is satisfied.

Example:

Display the customers whose belong to Information Technology or are self-employed.

Synopsis:

Tables:	CUST_MSTR, ADDR_DTLS
Columns:	CUST_NO, FNAME, MNAME, LNAME
Technique:	**Operators:** LIKE, AND, OR, **Clauses:** WHERE, **Others:** CONCAT

Solution:

```
SELECT CUST_NO, FNAME || ' ' || MNAME || ' ' || LNAME "Customers"
  FROM CUST_MSTR, ADDR_DTLS
    WHERE CUST_MSTR.CUST_NO = ADDR_DTLS.CODE_NO
      AND (OCCUP = 'Information Technology' OR OCCUP = 'Self Employed')
      AND CUST_NO LIKE 'C%';
```

Output:

```
CUST_NO  Customers
---------------------------------------
C1       Ivan Nelson Bayross
C10      Namita S. Kanade
C7       Anil Arun Dhone
```

Explanation:

Here, the **OR** operator is used to compare the value held in the **OCCUP** field. If the comparison condition is satisfied then only those customers who belong to Information Technology or are self-employed are shown. The **LIKE** operator is used to avoid display of those rows held in the **CUST_MSTR** table, which identify corporates.

Combining the AND and OR Operator:

The **AND** and **OR** conditions can be combined in a single SQL statement. It can be used in any valid SQL statement such as select, insert, update, or delete.

When combining these conditions, it is important to use brackets so that the database knows what order to evaluate each condition.

The Oracle engine will process all rows in a table and display the result only when **all** of the conditions specified using the **AND** operator are satisfied and when **any of** the conditions specified using the **OR** operator are satisfied.

Example:

Display all the customers whose **last name** is **Bayross** and are **less than 25** yrs old <u>**or**</u> all those customers who are **more than 25** but **less than 50** yrs old.

Synopsis:

Tables:	CUST_MSTR, ADDR_DTLS
Columns:	CUST_NO, FNAME, MNAME, LNAME
Technique:	**Operators:** LIKE, AND, OR, **Clauses:** WHERE, **Others:** CONCATENATE

Solution:

SELECT CUST_NO, FNAME || ' ' || MNAME || ' ' || LNAME "Customers",
ROUND((SYSDATE - DOB_INC)/365) "Age" **FROM** CUST_MSTR
WHERE (ROUND((SYSDATE - DOB_INC)/365) < 25 **AND** LNAME='Bayross')
OR (ROUND((SYSDATE - DCB_INC)/365) > 25
AND ROUND((SYSDATE - DOB_INC)/365) < 50) **AND** CUST_NO **LIKE** 'C%';

Output:

```
CUST_NO Customers                  Age
--------------------------------------
C2      Chriselle           Ivan 22
        Bayross
C3      Mamta Arvind Muzumdar    29
C4      Chhaya          Sudhakar 28
        Bankar
C5      Ashwini Dilip Joshi      26
C8      Alex Austin Fernandes    42
C10     Namita S. Kanade         26
6 rows selected.
```

Explanation:

This would return all the records where the value calculated by the arithmetic expression **i.e.** age is less than 25 and the value held in the field **LNAME** is **Bayross**. This will also return those records where the value calculated by the arithmetic expression **i.e.** age is more than 25 but less than 50. The brackets determine what order the **AND** / **OR** conditions are evaluated in.

The NOT Operator:

The Oracle engine will process all rows in a table and display only those records that **do not** satisfy the condition specified.

Example:

List the accounts details of those accounts which are **neither** Singly and **nor** Joint Accounts.

Synopsis:

Tables:	ACCT_MSTR
Columns:	ACCT_NO, TYPE, OPR_MODE, OPNDT, CURBAL, STATUS
Technique:	**Operators:** NOT, OR, **Clauses:** WHERE

Solution:

SELECT ACCT_NO, TYPE, OPR_MODE, OPNDT, CURBAL, STATUS
FROM ACCT_MSTR **WHERE NOT (**OPR_MODE = 'SI' **OR** OPR_MODE = 'JO');

Output:

ACCT_NO	TYPE	OPR_MODE	OPNDT	CURBAL	STATUS
CA4	CA	AS	05-FEB-03	2000	A
SB6	SB	ES	27-FEB-03	500	A
CA7	CA	AS	14-MAR-03	2000	A
CA10	CA	AS	19-APR-03	2000	A

Explanation:

The Oracle engine **will not** display rows from the ACCT_MSTR table where the value of the field **OPR_MODE** is either **SI** (Single) or **JO** (Joint). This means that all those records, which satisfy the condition specified using the NOT operator, will not be shown.

Self Review Questions

Fill In The Blanks

1. The ____________ technique of managing table data is totally obselete.
2. The ___________ technique of managing table data is the one that is constantly growing and is the most commonly found technique in DBMS form.
3. ________________________ is an application that falls into the category of applications that have excellent built-in tools
4. The computer software domain space can be quickly segregated into two, the __________ domain and the __________ domain.
5. System software development is a _________ entity of Software development.
6. Application programmers normally communicate with the Graphical User Interface (G.U.I.) using the ___________.
7. The DBMS engine has to communicate with two distinct domains, the first is all the computer hardware the second the __________ which contain business data in them.
8. To communicate with its tables all DBMS use, ____________________.
9. The ___________________________ has set the standards of SQL.
10. A Relation can be simply conceptualized as a __________ Table.
11. Rows in a Relation (i.e. table) are called _________ of the Relation.
12. The Columns of the Relation are its ___________.
13. The Mtrl_Req_Mstr is the _________ and the Mtrl_Req_Dtls is the controlled in this relationship.
14. A ___________ is used to separate the attribute from the Relation name.
15. Relational Algebra is really a collection of ____________ that manipulate Relations.
16. Relational Algebra is a ___________ ___________, used with tables.

17. Difference and ___________ are childsets of Union.
18. A Cartesian product of two Relations is simply the ___________ of the tuples (i.e. rows) of both Relations (i.e. tables).
19. Views are ___________ (ANSI SQL) bound to physical tables.
20. Table creation is done using the ___________ syntax.
21. The ___________ command is used to change or modify data values in a table.

True Or False

22. There are three techniques that DBMS uses to manage data held in their tables.
23. Managing business data through a computer is usually done via a programmer.
24. System programmers are those who create DBMS applications.
25. Software development is a sub-process.
26. System programmers create (write code for) what is called the DBMS engine.
27. Application programmers can communicate directly with the CPU.
28. Tables use a mathematical technique called a Relational Data Model (RDM) to store, access and manipulate table data.
29. Another huge advantage of using the RDBMS model is that the programmer does not have to code for how a Relation (i.e. table) data is to be accessed from the Relation.
30. Table Read operations are where table data is physically and permanently changed in the table.
31. Relational Algebraic operations can be quickly divided into basic set-oriented table operations and relational-oriented operations.
32. In Relational Algebra there is a mechanism provided to specify how the formula should be evaluated by the RDBMS.
33. Predicates are a formal language used to symbolize logical arguments in mathematics.
34. The Oracle engine will process all rows in a table and display the result only when none of the conditions specified using the NOT operator are satisfied.

Objectives Questions

1. Define DBMS and RDBMS. State the difference between DBMS and RDBMS.
2. What are the principles of Relational Data Management?
3. Define the Structure of RDBMS.
4. What are the basic sets of operations in Relational Algebra?
5. What is Cartesian Product?
6. What are the different ways for filtering Data from a table?
7. State the use of DISTINCT keyword in a SELECT statement.
8. Which keyword is used to sort the data in a table? Explain the syntax.
9. What are the different Arithmetic operators?
10. What are Logical Operators? State the use of it.

3. Entity Relationship Model

All business models such as Banks, HRD, Manufacturing, Marketing and so on generate a whole lot of business data on a day to day basis. To manage the large quantities of business data generated accurately and at very high speed a computer it is always used.

A computer will run an application, specifically designed to handle business data, which will be used to manage and manipulate the vast quantities of data generated by any business. A common application used to manage business data is a **D**ata**B**ase **M**anagement **S**ystem (DBMS).

All business models consist of multiple **Master business processes**, which in turn can (and often do) have multiple **child processes** that must run and work together in perfect harmony for the master process to execute successfully. Each **Master Process** in a business model can be referred to as an **Entity**.

> **Note:** *It's the business owner who knows all the Entities which constitute the business model as well as how these Entities **relate** to one another.*

A Business Model For Retail Banking

Banking Business Model Specifications

Banking, like any other business model has a master business process (**i.e.** Retail Banking), which is supported by a number of sub processes. This concept is described in diagram 3.1.

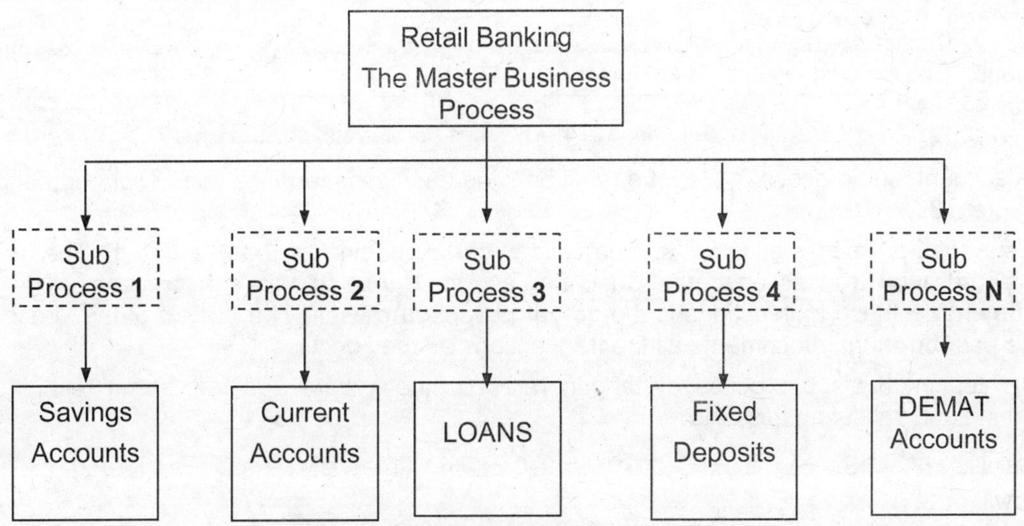

Diagram 3.1: The Retail Banking Business Model

To create a full-fledged, retail banking, commercial product, all the sub processes of the retail banking business model have to be fully computerized.

Each sub process described above, in turn has multiple child processes that work together in harmony for the sub process to be successful. This concept is described below.

Savings Account (It's child processes described)

- Collecting the account opening forms from the bank
- Getting support documents together to be submitted to the bank for opening the Savings account
- Submitting the documents to an account opening officer at the bank
- The documents submitted are verified and validated by the account opening officer at the bank
- Once acceptable, an unique account number is assigned to the Customers Savings account
- A cheque book, as well as cash and cheque deposit books, are given to the Customer by the bank
- The Savings account is opened. Banking transactions can now begin

Savings Bank Transactions

Saving bank transactions, both **deposits** and **withdrawals**, are at the heart of any Savings account. These transactions continue until the account is closed.

Each deposit or withdrawal, whether by **cheque**, **bank draft** or **cash** is documented by the bank. This documentation is available to the account holder in the form of a hand written **or** especially printed out **passbook or** a **computerized print out** that is universally accepted as the passbook.

This document (**i.e.** either the passbook or the computer printout) is accepted by all government authorities such as Income tax, Professional tax, Sales tax and so on, as **valid proof** of all transactions carried out by the account holder.

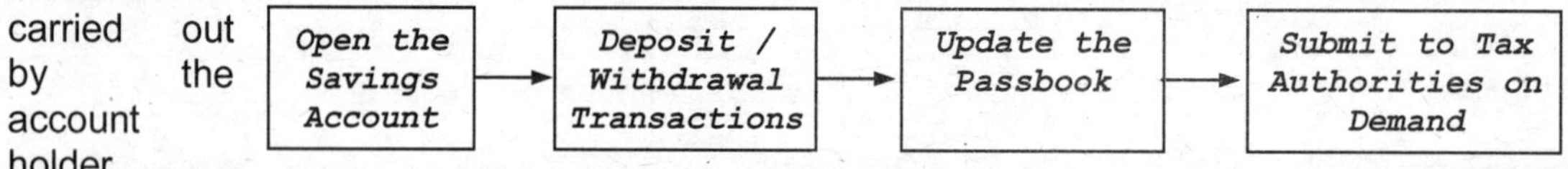

Diagram 3.2: The Savings Account sub process cycle.

The Savings bank account, sub process **cycle**, of a retail banking business model can be described as shown in diagram 3.2.

The start of the Savings account, sub process **cycle** is opening the bank account. The **deposit** and **withdrawal** transactions of a Customer are the **input** to this sub process. The bank **documenting** these transactions is the **actual processing** itself. The **output** of this processing is **the passbook** that documents all the transactions as they occur.

Each step in this sub process cycle generates business data and has some technique of capturing and validating this data.

Opening A Savings Bank Account (Details of the process flow)

This requires that a **Savings** account opening form is collected from the bank, then filled in with all the information that a bank demands prior opening the Savings account on behalf of the Customer.

Some of the information required by the bank prior account opening is:

- Customers Name
- Address
- Contact Information **i.e.** Residence, Office & Mobile telephone numbers
- Introducer's Name and Account number

And so on.

Additionally, a Customer must submit specific support documents along with the appropriately filled in Savings bank account opening form, to the bank. The documents are:

- A Xerox copy of the Customers Income Tax, **P**ermanent **A**ccount **N**umber

Or

- Form **60** providing supplemental taxation details
- A Xerox copy of the Customer's Ration card, or passport, or latest Electricity or Telephone bill needs to be submitted as address proof
- Two, colored passport sized photographs, of the Customer

Once these documents and support material is submitted to a bank they are checked by a bank employee. The bank employee **signs** and **dates** the application form, if everything submitted conforms exactly to the banks requirements.

The bank employee then passes these documents and their support material to the bank manager for perusal. The bank manager does a second validation check of all the material submitted. The bank manager then signs and dates the application form and issues the Savings account number, which from that day onwards is bound to the Customer until the account is closed.

A cheque book as well as withdrawal and deposit slip book is issued to the Customer.

The Savings bank account is opened ready for all transactions. The process of opening a Savings bank account is complete. Deposit and withdrawal transaction can commence.

Opening A Current Account (Details of the process flow)

This requires that a **Current** account opening form is collected from the bank, then filled in with all the information that a bank demands prior opening the Current account on behalf of the Customer.

Some of the information required by the bank prior account opening is:

- Company Name
- Full Postal Address
- Directors Contact Information **i.e.** Full postal Address, Residence, Office & Mobile telephone numbers
- Introducer's Name and Account number

And so on.

Additionally, a Customer must submit specific support documents, along with the appropriately filled in Current bank account opening form, to the bank. The documents are:

If the company is a Private or Public Limited company then:

- A copy of its Memorandum Of Understanding
- A letter with an **extract of a board meeting** where it is resolved to open a Current account with the bank

If the company is a proprietorship:

- A letter signed by the proprietor indicating a desire to open a Current account with the bank
- A Xerox copy of the company's Income Tax, **P**ermanent **A**ccount **N**umber

Or

- A form **60** providing supplemental taxation details
- Two, colored passport sized photographs, of each individual who will operate the account

Once these documents and support material is submitted to a bank they are checked by a bank employee. The bank employee **signs** and **dates** the application form, if everything submitted conforms exactly to the banks requirements.

The bank employee then passes these documents and their support material to the bank manager for perusal. The bank manager does a second validation check of all the material submitted. The bank manager then signs and dates the application form and issues the Current account number, which from that day onwards is bound to the company or proprietor until the account is closed.

A Cheque book as well as withdrawal and deposit books are issued.

The Current account is opened ready for all transactions. The process of opening a Current bank account is complete. Deposit and withdrawal transactions can commence.

It may appear that a Current account is exactly the same as a Savings account. While the account opening process may appear to be the same there are differences in the running of each account.

Some of the differences are:

- The monies deposited (and held) in a Savings account attract an annual interest of 4.5%
- The monies deposited into a Current account attract nothing. In fact, banks normally charge a customer to setup and run a Current account
- A bank normally has **R**eserve **B**ank Of **I**ndia (RBI) guidelines to follow which restricts the amount of money that can be withdrawn from a Saving bank account
- There are no such limitations on the withdrawal of money from a Current account
- There is always a minimum balance that has to be maintained in a savings and/or current account. However, the minimum balance to be maintained in a current account is **substantially larger** than the minimum balance that has to be maintained in a savings account

Having said all this, the way both the accounts **are operated** by their respective account holders is identical.

Money is **deposited** and money is **withdrawn**. There is simply a running check kept of all deposit and withdrawal transactions in each type of account. Money can be deposited by cash, cheque or bank draft (**i.e.** a bankers cheque). Money can be withdrawn by cash, cheque or bank draft (**i.e.** a bankers cheque).

The monthly statement of an account holder's transactions (i.e. deposits and withdrawals) is accepted by all government agencies such as Income Tax, Sales Tax and so on as proof that the transaction actually took place. This (as mentioned earlier) is the significance of running a Savings or Current account with a bank.

Fixed Deposits (It's child processes described)

Another banking product is **fixed deposits**. This product offers an attractive rate of return, on funds that are parked as fixed deposits with a bank.

There is a higher degree of safety of the principal amount and the interest thereon, when fixed deposits are used to generate additional funds when compared to placing the same funds in company stock. Retired people, (or anyone who wishes to hedge risk) normally opt for a fixed deposit with a bank to generate additional funds.

A fixed deposit, as the name suggests, is when funds are parked with a bank for a fixed, predetermined period. Most banks define the period during which the funds are locked in **time slabs**.

The rate of interest applicable to a fixed deposit is proportional to the period of lock in (**i.e.** longer the period of lock in the greater the interest rate applicable). Refer to table 3.1 as an example.

Period of Fixed Deposit	Interest Rate Applicable
15 days and above to 30 days	5.00%
31 days and above upto 45 days	5.25%
45 days and above but less than 3 months	5.50%
3 months and above but less than 6 months	5.75%
6 months and above but less than 12 months	6.00%
12 months and above but less than 36 months	6.25%
36 months and above upto 120 months	6.50%

Table 3.1

Bank Customers make a choice of the time slab and then instruct the bank the amount of funds that will be parked in the fixed deposit. Once the time slab and amount is finalized the bank will create a fixed deposit receipt and hand this over to the customer.

The fixed deposit receipt mentions, the period of lock in, the principal amount and the rate of interest applicable. When the period of lock in completes the customer surrenders the fixed deposit receipt and the bank pays back the principal amount together with the interest, which has accrued on the principal amount to the customer.

Opening A Fixed Deposit (Details of the process flow)

This requires a **F**ixed **D**eposit (FD) opening form be collected from the bank, then filled in with all the information that a bank demands prior issuing the fixed deposit receipt to the customer.

Some of the information required by bank prior issuing the FD receipt is:

- Customer Name
- Full Postal Address
- Contact Information (**i.e.** Residence, Office & Mobile telephone numbers)
- Introducer's Name and Account number (if available)

And so on.

Additionally, a Customer must submit specific support documents, along with the appropriately filled in fixed deposit opening form, to the bank. The documents are:

- A Xerox copy of the most recent Electricity bill, Telephone bill, Ration card or Passport to verify the postal address provided above
- A Xerox copy of the Customer's Income Tax, **P**ermanent **A**ccount **N**umber

Or

- A form **60** providing supplemental taxation details
- Three, colored passport sized photographs, of the customer

Once these documents and support material is submitted to a bank they are checked by a bank employee. The bank employee **signs** and **dates** the Fixed deposit opening form, if everything submitted conforms exactly to the banks requirements.

The bank employee then passes these documents and their support material to the bank manager for perusal. The bank manager does a second validation check of all the material submitted. The bank manager then signs and dates the fixed deposit opening form. This finalizes the fixed deposit opening form, data validation.

Once this is complete the bank manager issues instructions to a bank employee for the preparation of the fixed deposit receipt. This depends on whether the FD is being opened with cash, bank draft or cheque. If the FD is being opened by Cash or Bank Draft the FD receipt is issued immediately.

If the FD is being opened by a cheque **and** the bank account on which the cheque is drawn is external to the bank that is issuing the FD receipt, then the bank will wait until the cheque clears and only then issue the FD receipt.

Note:	*Since funds for the FD are being parked with the bank, the bank draft or cheque used to pay for the FD must be made in the (FD receipt issuing) banks name.*

As soon as the funds are available with the bank the FD receipt is issued to the customer.

Once the FD receipt is issued to the customer, the customer has to wait until the lock in period mentioned on the FD receipt is over before encashing the FD.

To encash a FD the customer has to discharge the FD to the bank that issued it. This is done by the customer pasting a revenue stamp on the reverse of the FD receipt (at an appropriate place) signing on partly on the revenue stamp and partly on the reverse of the FD receipt.

The receipt is then handed over to the bank. The bank then immediately repays the principal amount mentioned on the receipt **and** the interest accrued based on the interest percentage mentioned on the FD receipt. Once this is done the current FD process is complete.

Premature Discharge Of A Fixed Deposit

Fixed deposits can be discharged prematurely. Irrespective of the completion date mentioned on the FD it can be discharged at any time. The penalty for premature discharge is bound to the rate of interest of the FD.

Generally, if a FD is prematurely terminated, the bank only pays **simple interest** on the funds parked in the FD.

> **Note:** *This banking project covers only the opening and running of Savings and Current accounts together with Fixed Deposits. Loans, DEMAT accounts and so on are not covered in this project.*

Since only the Savings account, Current account and Fixed deposit business processes, of the banking business model, are being dealt with in this project the first order of the day is to go to the bank and collect all the **application forms** necessary used to initiate each of these business processes.

When collecting the application forms for each of these business processes, establish exactly what **additional support documents** have to be submitted by a customer (to the bank) to complete each business process.

> **Note:** *Given below are scanned images of bank documents, which are required by each banking business process being dealt with (i.e. Savings accounts, Current accounts and Fixed deposits). Refer to diagrams 3.3.1 to 3.8.*
>
> *Table structures used to capture form data are designed based on the application forms for each banking business process.*

Table Structuring Principles

Fundamentally, a **mother table** for each form is created by simply ensuring that there is a **column** in the table for **each data capture field** visible on the form.

Once the mother table has been structured, it is **normalized**. The mother table can then decompose into several master / detail tables (*if necessary*) to ensure that the **minimum** of redundant data is stored.

Once a mother table is decomposed into appropriate master / detail tables (appropriately normalized), these become **production tables** in which data captured by the applications forms is stored. Application forms **always** work against production tables.

Actual Table Structures

The structure of the **production tables** for the Savings account, Current account and Fixed deposit, business processes of a banking business model, are given immediately after the scanned images of bank documents.

Scanned Banking Model Forms

Savings Accounts Opening Form:

THE SOUTH INDIAN CO-OPERATIVE BANK LTD.

SICB

.... BRANCH

SAVING ACCOUNT OPENING FORM DATE : ________

S.F. No. ____________ A/c. No. [ ]

Dear Sir,

Please open a Savings Account in my/our name/s in your Bank. I/We agree to comply with and be bound by the Bank rules and regulations prevailing now and as may be changed from time to time.

The account shall be operated by me/us.

☐ Singly ☐ Either or Survivor ☐ Jointly ☐ Anyone or Survivor

Please issue pass book.

Yours faithfully

FULL NAME/S OF ACCOUNT HOLDER/S	SPECIMEN SIGNATURES
1.	1.
2.	2.

Manager / Accountant Date :

Diagram 3.3.1: The Front Of The Savings Account Opening Form

FULL NAME/S, ADDRESSES OF ACCOUNT HOLDER/S

1. Name ________

Off. Address ________

Tel. : ________

Resi. Address ________

Tel. : ________

2. Name ________

Off. Address ________

Tel. : ________

Resi. Address ________

Tel. : ________

FULL NAME & ADDRESS OF INTRODUCER :

I know the applicant/s desirous of opening the A/c with you for ________ Years and recommend the same.

Introducer's Signature ________ Name of the Introducer ________

S.F.S.B./C. A/c. No. ________

Address ________

Tel. No. ________

Diagram 3.3.2: The Rear Of The Savings Account Opening Form

Fixed Deposit Opening Form:

THE SOUTH INDIAN CO-OP. BANK LTD., MUMBAI

FIXED DEPOSIT / REINVESTMENT CERTIFICATE	S. B. A/c. No.	C. A/c. No.	S. F. No.

I/We desire to invest a sum of Rs. ________ (Rupees ________) in your Bank as Fixed Deposit / Re-Investment Certificate for a period ________ at @ ________ p.a. We have read and understood the rules in respect of the said account and agree to be bound by them as now in force or any change that may be made therein from time to time.

Signature

INTRODUCED BY :

Name : ________

Address : ________

A/c. No. ________ S. F. No. ________

INSTRUCTIONS

FULL NAME (IN BLOCK LETTERS)	SPECIMEN SIGNATURE
1.	
2.	
3.	
	Signature of the Officer

Diagram 3.4.1: The Front Of The Fixed Deposit Form

THE SOUTH INDIAN CO-OP. BANK LTD.,
MUMBAI.

SICB

Name : ________

Address : ________

Occupation : ________ Tel. No. : ________

F. D. / R. I. C. No.	AMOUNT	DATE OF DEPOSIT	DATE OF EXPIRY	INTEREST RATE	PERIOD

Diagram 3.4.2: The Rear Of The Fixed Deposit Form

Current Account Opening Form:

CURRENT ACCOUNT OPENING FORM
For Partnerships/Limited Company/Trusts/Society, etc.

To,

The South Indian Co-operetive Bank Ltd.
MUMBAI.

S I C B

Account No. ____________
Ledger/Folio ____________
Date ____________
Branch ____________

Dear Sir,

I/We request you to open/continue a Current Deposit Account with your Bank, as per particulars given below. I/We have read and understood the rules in respect of Current Deposit A/c. and agree to be bound by them as now in force or to any change that may be made therein from time to time.

Name / Title of Account ____________
(In Block Letters)
Address ____________
Constitution ____________
Occupation/Line of Business ____________
Instructions for operation ____________
Necessary documents are attached herewith (as per details given below)

____

____

I/We further declare that we have got no Account/Account with ____________ Bank(s) and do not enjoy / enjoy credit facilities with them, as per sheet attached.

Please supply a cheque book for my/our use and issue a Pass Book/note to send a statement of account every ____________

Yours faithfully

____________ ____________

____________ ____________

SPECIMEN SIGNATURES-CUM-INDEMNITY FOR COLLECTION OF BILL ETC.

I/we may have occation from time to time to handle your collection or negotiation of Cheques, Drafts or Bills of Exchange (with or without documents attached) and I/we hereby agree to your forwarding the same to your agents for the time being for collection or negotiation. In the event of your having no independent Collecting Agents at any centre. I/We hereby authorise you to send cheqes by mail directly to the drawee bank itself. I/We shall keep/hold you harmless, free from responsibility and indemnified by you in handling this business due to any cause whatsover including delay in transit presentation, payment or default by your agents.

In addition to your ordinary rights as holders of such cheques, Drafts or Bills of Exchange, you are authorised to accept in payment thereof a banker's cheque or banker's cheque payable in your station or at other places and in the event of such cheque or cheques not being paid on presentation to debit the amount to our account with all charges incurred thereon. I/We confirm that you can present Bills and receive the amount in respect thereof in accordance with the usage of the place where the Bills are made payable. It is understood that these transactions are in all respects at our entire risk and responsibility.

Full Name		Specimen Signature
Mr. ____________	will sign as	____________
Mr. ____________	will sign as	____________
Mr. ____________	will sign as	____________

Introduced by

Name ____________
Address ____________
Signature ____________

Signatures

Open the Account

Manager

Diagram 3.5.1: Page One Of The Current Account Opening Form

(A) FOR SOCIETIES CLUBS OR SIMILAR BODIES

In terms of the certified copy of the resolution of the Executive/Governing body of ______________________.
dated__________ handed over to you separately, kindly authorise the operation on the accounts by Mr.______________ ______________(designation) or by Mr. ______________________(designation) and counter signed by its Secretary or Mr.______________________(designation) and debit the amount hereof to the account.

Chairman/President Secretary

It is hereby confirmed and declared by me/us that I/We have no beneficial interest in the account referred to on the reverse hereof and it is understood that all money's herein or hereafter standing to the credit of this account will in the event of my/our death during the currency of account form no part or my/our estate and that account thereafter will be operated upon by my/our successor(s) in office for the time being.

(B) FOR PARTNERSHIP ACCOUNTS

We the undersigned beg to inform you that we are the only partners in the firm of ______________________ ______________________ and are jointly and severally responsible for the liabilities thereof. We shall advise you in writing of any change that may take place in the partnership and all the ;present partners will be liable to you jointly and severally on any obligation which may be standing in the firm's name in your books on the date of the receipt of such notice and until all such obligations shall have been liquidated.

We confirm that our partnership is registered not registered with the Registrar or Firms and is written/verbal.

I/We hereby jointly and severally free you from any liability for the funds and the securities if any, charged to or deposited in the account that may be withdrawn by the remaining partners after the death bankruptly or retirement of any partner(s) of our firm. We further hereby agree to indemnify you against all claims, actions and demands arising from such withdrawal of the funds and the securities by the remaining partners. We also agree and declare that this agreement shall be binding upon ourselves and our respective legal representatives and you will not be liable in any way for the operations on the account in the name of the firm by any one or more of us or for withdrawal of the funds and securities by any one or more of us or any survivors of us.

______________ ______________ ______________ ______________

______________ ______________ ______________ ______________

Signature

(D) FOR LIMITED COMPANY A/CS

Extracts or minutes of the meeting of the Board of Directors of ______________________
____
held at its registered office at ______________________
______________ on ______________________
RESOLVED

(a) That an account in the name of the Company be opened with **The South Indian Co-operative Bank Ltd.** at............
and that Mr.______________________
(give name & designation)

★ and Mr.______________________
(give name & designation)

is/are authorised to do so and sign the necessary forms and documents thereafter.

(b) And that the bank be instructed to honour all cheques, promissory notes, and other orders drawn by and all bills accepted on behalf of the company whether such account be in credit or overdrawn, and to accept and credit to the account of the company all moneys deposited with or owing by bank on any account or accounts at any time or times kept or to be kept in the name of the company and the amount of all cheques, notes, bills other negotiable instruments, orders or receipt provided they are endorsed/signed by Mr.______________ ★ and Mr.______________ for the time being of the company on behalf of the company and such signatures(s) shall be sufficient authority to bind the company in all transactions between the bank and the company including those specifically referred to herein.

Diagram 3.5.2: Page Two Of The Current Account Opening Form

(c) And that Mr. ______________________★and Mr. ______________________ be authorised to withdraw and deal with any of the company's securities or properties or documents of title thereto which may be deposited with the bank from time to time whether by way or security otherwise.

(d) And that Mr. ______________________★and Mr. ______________________ is/are authorised to acknowledge all types of debts and liabilities on behalf of the company.

(e) And that the bank be furnished with a copy of its memorandum and Articles of Association and a list of names and specimen signatures of the Directors and other officer (s) of the company authorised to sign on behalf of the company and be informed from time to time by a notice in writing under the hand of the Chairman of any changes which may take place therein and be entitled to act upon such notice until, the receipt of further notice under the hand of the Chairman.

(f) And that a copy of any resolution of the Board if purporting to be certified as correct by the Chairman of the meeting or by the Secretary of the company shall as between the bank and the company, be conclusive evidence of the resolution so certified

(g) And that this resolution be communicated to the bank and shall remain in force until notice in writiog of its withdrawal or cancellation is given to the bank by the Chairman of the company.

Certified that the above is a corract copy of the resolution passed on ______________________ by the Board of Directors of ______________________ and that it has been entered in the usual course of business in the minitues book of the company and signed therein by the Chairman of the meeting/company and is in accordance with the memorandum of Articles of Association of the Company.

____

____
Chairman of the meeting

★ Delete one name if authority is to be vested in a single person.

Indicative Guidelines for filling up Current A/c. Opening Form

(1) List of Documents to be submitted according to the consititution in original (for inspection & return wherever applicable)

(a) For partnership Firm

(i) Partnership deed and/or copy of registration certificate.

(b) For Joint Stock Companies

(i) Copy of Memorandum and the Articles of Association.
(ii) Certificate of Incorporation.
(iii) Certificate of commencement of business/Registration Certificate.
(iv) Certified copy of a Resolution of Board of Directors regulating Conduct of such account (as per proforma given in this form)

(c) For Trust Accounts

(i) Trust Deed
(ii) Resolution of Trustees
(iii) List of Trustees

(d) For Clubs, Societies, Association & other similar bodies

(i) Constitution & bye-laws
(ii) Certificate of Registration
(iii) Resolution

(e) For HUF—Letter to be filled up

(2) The Account is to be introduced by a persons well-known to the bank such as an account-holder or share-holder

(3) **Instructions for Operation**

Please write the mode of operation of the account-viz, joint operation by all account-holders, Former or Survivor Either or Survivor, and the names of officials along with their designations [in case of incorporate body].

Diagram 3.5.3: Page Three Of The Current Account Opening Form

The Bank Account Deposit Slip:

THE SOUTH INDIAN CO-OP. BANK LTD.

SICB

Date 200

Wanted a FD / CC Share No. ....

In Favour of ....

the sum of Rupees ....
(in words)

Cash / Cheque Rs. ....

Recd. by ....

PARTICULARS OF PAYMENT

By Cash (Notes)	Rs.	P.
x 1000		
x 500		
x 100		
x 50		
x 20		
x 10		
x 5		
Coins		
(By Cheque Details overleaf)		
TOTAL		

Recd. by ....

THE SOUTH INDIAN CO-OP. BANK LTD.

SICB

Voucher No. : Date :

Wanted a FD / CC Share No

For Rs.

In Favour of : Rs.

Office Use

Officer

APPLICANT'S SIGNATURE

Diagram 3.6.1: The Front Of The Pay In Slip

Particulars of Cheque

Drawee Bank / Branch	Cheque No.	Place	Amount Rs.	P

Drawee Bank / Branch	Cheque No	Amount Rs.	P

Diagram 3.6.2: The Rear Of The Pay In Slip

Whether a Savings account, Current account or a Fixed deposit is being opened, each process begins with a customer depositing money with the bank. This is done via a **Pay In slip** as shown in diagrams 3.6.1 and 3.6.2. A Pay In slip is instrument that is used to document all customer **deposit transactions** with the bank.

For customer **withdrawals transactions** the bank provides a **Withdrawal slip** and a **Chequebook** to their customers. Refer to diagrams 3.7.1, 3.7.2 and 3.8.

Occasionally, account withdrawals (Savings or Current) can be done using a **Bank draft**.

The Banks Withdrawal Slip:

The South Indian Co-Operative Bank Ltd.
PASS BOOK MUST ACCOMPANY THIS WITHDRAWAL SLIP

____________________ Branch

S.B A/c. No. [ ]

Date ____________________

Pay self the sum of Rupees ____________________________________
(in words)

____ Rs. [ ]

L.F. ____________________

Entered by ____________________

Vr.No. [ ]

Signature ____________________

Diagram 3.7.1: The Front Of The Withdrawal Slip

I authorise Shri/Smt. ____________________________________

Whose signature is attested below to receive the payment of the amount mentioned overleaf

____________________ ____________________
Signature of authorised Agent Depositor

Diagram 3.7.2: The Rear Of The Withdrawal Slip

The Banks Cheque:

In most cases the bank does not encourage its customers to withdraw money from an account using a withdrawal slip. Most banks prefer that a customer use a cheque for the withdrawal of money from any account. A sample of the bank's cheque is shown in diagram 3.8.

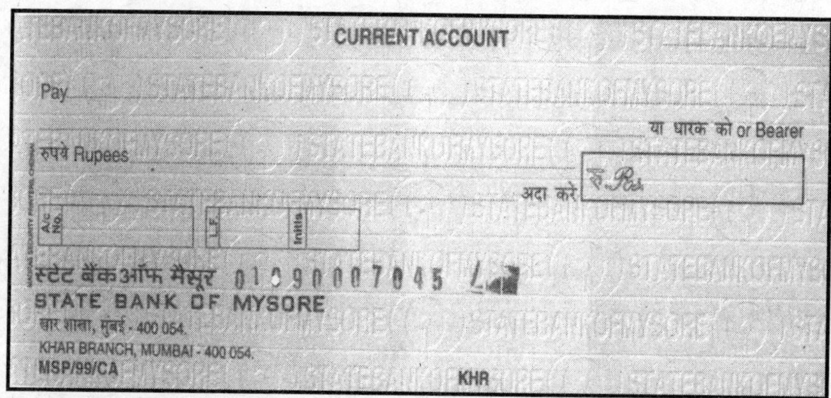

CURRENT ACCOUNT

Pay ____________________________________ या धारक को or Bearer

रुपये Rupees ____________________________________ रु. Rs.

____________________________________ अदा करें

A/c No. [ ] L.F. [ ] Initls. [ ]

स्टेट बैंक ऑफ मैसूर 01090007045
STATE BANK OF MYSORE
खार शाखा, मुंबई - 400 054.
KHAR BRANCH, MUMBAI - 400 054.
MSP/99/CA

KHR

Diagram 3.8: A Cheque Sample Issued By The Bank.

This completes all the paper forms used by the bank to carry out the business processes that this project has undertaken to computerize. Based on a study of the business data being captured by these forms table structures will be designed.

Table structure definitions now follow.

Project Planning For The Retail Banking model

Based on the business model for Retail Banking presented above, the following table structures are identified.

Table Definitions For Retail Banking

Branches Of The Bank

Table Definition:

Table Name : **BRANCH_MSTR**

Primary Key : BRANCH_MSTR.BRANCH_NO

Foreign Key : - -

Column Definition:

Column Name	Data Type	Width	Allow Null	Default
BRANCH_NO	VarChar2	10		
NAME	VarChar2	25		

Table Description:

Column Name	Description
BRANCH_NO	A system generated number auto posted to this table column
NAME	Branch location

Explanation:

The BRANCH_MSTR table stores the Unique ID Number and location of different branches of the bank.

Employees Of The Bank

Table Definition:

Table Name : **EMP_MSTR**

Primary Key : EMP_MSTR.EMP_NO

Foreign Key : EMP_MSTR.BRANCH_NO → BRANCH_MSTR.BRANCH_NO

Column Definition:

Column Name	Data Type	Width	Allow Null	Default
EMP_NO	VarChar2	10		
BRANCH_NO	VarChar2	10		
FNAME	VarChar2	25		

MNAME	VarChar2	25		
LNAME	VarChar2	25		
DEPT	VarChar2	30		
DESIG	VarChar2	30		
MNGR_NO	VarChar2	10		

Table Description:

Column Name	Description
EMP_NO	A system generated number auto posted to this table column
BRANCH_NO	A unique branch Id number This value must be present in the BRANCH_MSTR table
FNAME	First name of a bank employee
MNAME	Middle name of a bank employee
LNAME	Last name of a bank employee
DEPT	Bank employee's department
DESIG	Bank employee's official designation
MNGR_NO	Employer Id number of the manager to whom the employee reports This value must be present in the EMP_MSTR table

Explanation:

The EMP_MSTR table stores bank employee information (*across all branches*).

Each branch of the bank will access this repository as though it was local to the branch. This requires that each branch be connected to the central repository via a WAN, which has excellent bandwidth.

The WAN is expected to have a consistent 512 kpbs bandwidth to start with using dedicated ISDN lines. Once more than 10 branches go live, this bandwidth will be quickly ramped up to GB size with failsafe and Server redundancy built-in to ensure 24/7 operations for the bank.

This means that, a Savings account or Current account opened at one branch can be accessed at any other branch as though it were local to the branch. Thus cash, bank draft or cheque transactions can be carried out for a customer at any branch of the bank.

Additionally, fixed deposits can be opened at any branch. Any branch employee can verify the fixed deposit opening transaction. Finally the fixed deposit receipt can be issued from any branch convenient to the customer. If required the fixed deposit itself can be transferred to any branch on instructions from the customer. A truly open, multi user, multi location, retail banking.

Customers Of The Bank

Table Definition:

Table Name : **CUST_MSTR**
Primary Key : CUST_MSTR.CUST_NO
Foreign Key : - -

Column Definition:

Column Name	Data Type	Width	Allow Null	Default
CUST_NO	VarChar2	10		
FNAME	VarChar2	25		
MNAME	VarChar2	25		
LNAME	VarChar2	25		
DOB_INC	Date/Time			
OCCUP	VarChar2	25		
PHOTOGRAPH	VarChar2	25		
SIGNATURE	VarChar2	25		
PANCOPY	VarChar2	1		
FORM60	VarChar2	1		

The **CUST_MSTR** table structure details continued:

Table Description:

Column Name	Description
CUST_NO	A system generated number auto posted to this table column
FNAME	Customer's first name
MNAME	Customer's middle name
LNAME	Customer's last name
DOB_INC	Customer's date of birth (for individuals) or data of incorporation (for organizations)
OCCUP	Customer's occupation or line of business
PHOTOGRAPH	Location to customer's scanned photograph (for individuals only)
SIGNATURE	Location to customer's scanned signature (for individuals only)
PANCOPY	Holds **Y** if a copy of PAN card has been submitted
FORM60	Holds **Y** if the Form 60 has been submitted

Explanation:

The CUST_MSTR stores customer information collected once, when a customer opens a new account or creates a fixed deposit with the bank.

Accounts Opened With The Bank

Table Definition:

Table Name : **ACCT_MSTR**
Primary Key : ACCT_MSTR.ACCT_NO
Foreign Key : ACCT_MSTR.BRANCH_NO →BRANCH_MSTR.BRANCH_NO
: ACCT_MSTR.INTRO_CUST_NO → CUST_MSTR.CUST_NO
: ACCT_MSTR.INTRO_ACCT_NO → ACCT_MSTR.ACCT_NO
: ACCT_MSTR.CORP_CUST_NO → CUST_MSTR.CUST_NO
: ACCT_MSTR.VERI_EMP_NO → EMP_MSTR.EMP_NO

Column Definition:

Column Name	Data Type	Width	Allow Null	Default
ACCT_NO	VarChar2	10		
SF_NO	VarChar2	10		
LF_NO	VarChar2	10		
BRANCH_NO	VarChar2	10		
INTRO_CUST_NO	VarChar2	10		
INTRO_ACCT_NO	VarChar2	10		
INTRO_SIGN	VarChar2	1		
TYPE	VarChar2	2		
OPR_MODE	VarChar2	2		
CUR_ACCT_TYPE	VarChar2	4		
TITLE	VarChar2	30		
CORP_CUST_NO	VarChar2	10		
APLNDT	Date			
OPNDT	Date			
VERI_EMP_NO	VarChar2	10		
VERI_SIGN	VarChar2	1		
MANAGER_SIGN	VarChar2	1		
CURBAL	Number	8, 2		0
STATUS	VarChar2	1		A

Table Description:

Column Name	Description
ACCT_NO	A system generated number auto posted to this table column
SF_NO	Holds the account's S. F. number
LF_NO	Holds the account's Ledger / Folio number
BRANCH_NO	This value must be present in BRANCH_MSTR table
INTRO_CUST_NO	Introducers, customer identity number This value must be present in the CUST_MSTR table
INTRO_ACCT_NO	Introducers, bank account number This value must be present in the ACCT_MSTR table
INTRO_SIGN	Holds **Y** if the introducer's has signed the account opening, application form
TYPE	Can hold the values: **CA** - Current Account, **SB** - Savings Bank Account
OPR_MODE	Can hold the values: **SI** for singly operated account **ES** for account operated by either or survivor **JO** for jointly operated account **AS** account operated by anyone or survivor
CUR_ACCT_TYPE	Can hold the values: **ØS** for Individuals/Savings Bank Account **1C** for Propriety/Sole Trading Concerns **2C** for Partnership Concerns **3C** for Hindu Undivided Family Businesses **4C** for Limited Companies **5C** for Trust Accounts **6C** for Clubs/Societies **7C** for Legislative Bodies
TITLE	Holds an account name in those cases where an organization has opened the account
CORP_CUST_NO	Customer number of the Corporate account holder This value must be present in the CUST_MSTR table
APLNDT	The date of submission of the account opening application form
OPNDT	The date on which the account was actually opened
VERI_EMP_NO	The employee ID number of the bank officer who physically verified the customers application form This value must be present in the EMP_MSTR table

The **ACCT_MSTR** table structure details continued:

Table Description:

VERI_SIGN	Holds **Y** if the bank official who verified the application form has signed and dated the form
MANAGER_SIGN	Holds **Y** if the bank branch manager has signed and dated the form
CURBAL	Holds the current balance of an account
STATUS	Can hold the following values: **A** for active accounts **S** for suspended accounts **T** for terminated accounts

Explanation:

The ACCT_MSTR table stores all the details of opening any type of account, whether Savings or Current, with the bank. This information is largely one time information gathered and registered with the bank when an account is opened for the first time. Additionally, this table holds the current, real time, balance held in a specific account.

Account Opening Support Documents

Table Definition:

Table Name : **SPRT_DOC**
Primary Key : SPRT_DOC.ACCT_CODE
Foreign Key : - -

Column Definition:

Column Name	Data Type	Width	Allow Null	Default
ACCT_CODE	VarChar2	4		
TYPE	VarChar2	30		
DOCS	VarChar2	75		

Table Description:

Column Name	Description
ACCT_CODE	Can hold the values: **ØS** for Individuals/Savings Bank Account **1C** for Propriety/Sole Trading Concerns **2C** for Partnership Concerns **3C** for Hindu Undivided Family Businesses
ACCT_CODE	Also, can hold the values: **4C** for Limited Companies **5C** for Trust Accounts **6C** for Clubs/Societies **7C** for Legislative Bodies

The **SPRT_DOC** table structure details continued:

Table Description:

TYPE	Describes the organization type
DOCS	Stores document(s) required by the bank for verification prior account opening

Explanation:

The SPRT_DOC table stores information related to the documents submitted to the bank via which a customer's details, written in the application form, are verified and supported.

Different support documents must be submitted to the bank depending upon whether an **individual** or an **organization** is opening the account, **or** fixed deposit.

Fixed Deposits With The Bank

Table Definition:

Table Name : FD_MSTR
Primary Key : FD_MSTR.FD_SER_NO
Foreign Key : FD_MSTR.BRANCH_NO → BRANCH_MSTR.BRANCH_NO
: FD_MSTR.INTRO_CUST_NO → CUST_MSTR.CUST_NO
: FD_MSTR.INTRO_ACCT_NO → ACCT_MSTR.ACCT_NO
: FD_MSTR.ACCT_NO → ACCT_MSTR.ACCT_NO
: FD_MSTR.CORP_CUST_NO → CUST_MSTR.CUST_NO
: FD_MSTR.VERI_EMP_NO → EMP_MSTR.EMP_NO

The **FD_MSTR** table structure details continued:

Column Definition:

Column Name	Data Type	Width	Allow Null	Default
FD_SER_NO	VarChar2	10		
SF_NO	VarChar2	10		
BRANCH_NO	VarChar2	10		
INTRO_CUST_NO	VarChar2	10		
INTRO_ACCT_NO	VarChar2	10		
INTRO_SIGN	VarChar2	1		
ACCT_NO	VarChar2	10		
TITLE	VarChar3	30		
CORP_CUST_NO	VarChar2	10		
CORP_CNST_TYPE	VarChar2	4		
VERI_EMP_NO	VarChar2	10		
VERI_SIGN	VarChar2	1		
MANAGER_SIGN	VarChar2	1		

Table Description:

Column Name	Description
FD_SER_NO	A system generated number auto posted to this table column
SF_NO	Holds the account's S. F. number
BRANCH_NO	This value must be present in the BRANCH_MSTR table
INTRO_CUST_NO	Customer number of the Introducer (*Optional*) This value must be present in the CUST_MSTR table
INTRO_ACCT_NO	Introducer's bank account number. (*Optional*) This value must be present in the ACCT_MSTR table
INTRO_SIGN	Holds **Y** if the introducer has signed the fixed deposit opening application form (*Optional*)
ACCT_NO	Bank Account number (if any) held by the F. D. holder(s) This value must be present in the ACCT_MSTR table
TITLE	Holds an account name in those cases where an organization has opened the account
CORP_CUST_NO	Customer number of the Corporate account holder. (**Foreign Key:** Should be present in CUST_MSTR table)
CORP_CNST_TYPE	Can hold the values: **ØS** for Individuals/Savings Bank Account **1C** for Propriety/Sole Trading Concerns **2C** for Partnership Concerns **3C** for Hindu Undivided Family Businesses **4C** for Limited Companies **5C** for Trust Accounts **6C** for Clubs/Societies **7C** for Legislative Bodies
VERI_EMP_NO	Employee ID number of the bank officer who physically verified the account application form. This value must be present in the EMP_MSTR table
VERI_SIGN	Holds **Y** if the above verifier has signed the form
MANAGER_SIGN	Holds **Y** if the bank manager has signed the form

The **FD_MSTR** table structure details continued:

Explanation:

The FD_MSTR table stores all the details of **opening** a fixed deposit with the bank. This information is one time information gathered and stored when a customer opens a fixed deposit with the bank.

Table Definition:

Table Name : **FDSLAB_MSTR**
Primary Key : FDSLAB_MSTR.FDSLAB_NO
Foreign Key : - -

Column Definition:

Column Name	Data Type	Width	Allow Null	Default
FDSLAB_NO	Number	2		
MINPERIOD	Number	5		
MAXPERIOD	Number	5		
INTRATE	Number	5, 2		

Table Description:

Column Name	Description
FDSLAB_NO	A system generated number auto posted to this table column
MINPERIOD	Minimum period in months
MAXPERIOD	Maximum period in months
INTRATE	Rate of Interest charged on the Deposit

Explanation:

The FDSLAB_MSTR is a **lookup** table that stores details of the interest payable on a fixed deposit bound to specific time slabs.

Fixed Deposit Details

Table Definition:

Table Name : **FD_DTLS**
Primary Key : FD_DTLS.FD_NO
Foreign Key : FD_DTLS.FD_SER_NO → FD_MSTR.FD_SER_NO
: FD_DTLS.PAYTO_ACCTNO → ACCT_MSTR.ACCT_NO

Column Definition:

Column Name	Data Type	Width	Allow Null	Default
FD_SER_NO	VarChar2	10		
FD_NO	VarChar2	10		
TYPE	VarChar2	1		
PAYTO_ACCTNO	VarChar2	10		
PERIOD	Number	5		
OPNDT	Date			
DUEDT	Date			

AMT	Number	8, 2		
DUEAMT	Number	8, 2		
INTRATE	Number	8, 2		
STATUS	VarChar2	1		A
AUTO_RENEWAL	VarChar2	1		

The **FD_DTLS** table structure details continued:

Table Description:

Column Name	**Description**
FD_SER_NO	This value must be present in the FD_MSTR table
FD_NO	Unique Identity Number for each fixed deposit A system generated number auto posted to this table column
TYPE	Can hold the values: **S** of standard fixed deposits **R** for recursive fixed deposits
PAYTO_ACCTNO	Account number to which the F.D. amount should be transferred on maturity (*Optional*) This value must be present in the ACCT_MSTR table
PERIOD	Period of the fixed deposit in days
OPNDT	The date on which the fixed deposit is opened
DUEDT	The maturity date of the fixed deposit
AMT	Principle amount for the fixed deposit
DUEAMT	Amount due when the fixed deposit matures
INTRATE	The rate of interest applicable to the fixed deposit
STATUS	Can hold the values: **A** for active **C** for Cancelled **M** for Matured
AUTO_RENEWAL	Holds **Y** if the F. D. should be automatically renewed on maturity

Explanation:

The FD_DTLS table stores specific and complete details of every fixed deposit **receipt** issued to a bank customer.

The fixed deposit, banking business model, sub process, involves three tables. FD_MSTR, FD_SLAB and FD_DTLS.

- The table FD_MSTR stores all the information bound to the documentation of a fixed deposit being opened with the bank.
- The table FD_SLAB is a lookup table. This table stores information about the rate of interest payable on a fixed deposit based on the period of time that the money is locked with the bank.
- The table FD_DTLS stores information about every fixed deposit receipt issued by the bank to a customer.

When the fixed deposit receipt is being printed out from the FD_DTLS tables, the FD_SLAB table is referenced and the appropriate rate of interest is printed on the FD receipt. Additionally, the FD_DTLS table also stores a flag indicating the status of all fixed deposits created with the bank. An FD status could be A, C or M. A = Active, C = Cancelled, M = Matured.

Bank Account Nominee Information

Table Definition:

Table Name : **NOMINEE_MSTR**
Primary Key : NOMINEE_MSTR.NOMINEE_NO
Foreign Key : NOMINEE_MSTR.ACCT_FD_NO → ACCT_MSTR.ACCT_NO **OR**
NOMINEE_MSTR.ACCT_FD_NO → FD_MSTR.FD_SER_NO

The **NOMINEE_MSTR** table structure details continued:

Column Definition:

Column Name	Data Type	Width	Allow Null	Default
NOMINEE_NO	VarChar2	10		
ACCT_FD_NO	VarChar2	10		
NAME	VarChar2	75		
DOB	Date			
RELATIONSHIP	VarChar2	25		

Table Description:

Column Name	Description
NOMINEE_NO	Unique Identity Number for each nominee A system generated number auto posted to this table column
ACCT_FD_NO	Identifies the account or F.D. to which the individual is a nominee This should be present in either ACCT_MSTR table **or** FD_MSTR table
NAME	The name of the nominee
DOB	The date of birth of the nominee
RELATIONSHIP	The nominee's relationship with the account or F.D. holder(s)

Explanation:

The NOMINEE_MSTR table stores account or fixed deposit, nominee information. Nominees can be set for Savings accounts, Current accounts and Fixed deposits.

Bank Account Or Fixed Deposit Identity Details

Table Definition:

Table Name : **ACCT_FD_CUST_DTLS**

Primary Key : - -

Foreign Key : ACCT_FD_CUST_DTLS.ACCT_FD_NO → ACCT_MSTR.ACCT_NO
OR
ACCT_FD_CUST_DTLS.ACCT_FD_NO → FD_MSTR.FD_SER_NO
: ACCT_FD_CUST_DTLS.CUST_NO → CUST_MSTR.CUST_NO

Column Definition:

Column Name	Data Type	Width	Allow Null	Default
ACCT_FD_NO	VarChar2	10		
CUST_NO	VarChar2	10		

Table Description:

Column Name	Description
ACCT_FD_NO	Identifies the account / F.D. to which the customer is bound. This value must be present in either ACCT_MSTR table or FD_MSTR table
CUST_NO	Customer number associated with an account / F.D. This value must be present in the CUST_MSTR table

Explanation:

The ACCT_FD_CUST_DTLS table stores a list of bank accounts or fixed deposit identity numbers. Each Savings or Current account and fixed deposit identity number will have a customer number bound to it.

The contents of this table allow the linking of a Savings account, Current account or Fixed deposit with a specific **customer** and **contact** information.

The **ACCT_FD_CUST_DTLS** table structure details continued:

Without this table, a **one to many** relationship, cannot be maintained between Current accounts, Savings accounts and Fixed deposits with multiple customers.

All contact information such as a **multiple** postal addresses together with **multiple** telephone, mobile and pager numbers and/or Email addresses and Web Site URLs can be bound to specific Savings accounts, Current accounts and Fixed deposits due to the contents of the ACCT_FD_CUST_DTLS table.

Bank Customers Address And Contact Information

Table Definition:

Table Name : **ADDR_DTLS**
Primary Key : ADDR_DTLS.ADDR_NO
Foreign Key : ADDR_DTLS.CODE_NO → CUST_MSTR.CUST_NO **OR**
ADDR_DTLS.CODE_NO → NOMINEE_MSTR.NOMINEE_NO **OR**
ADDR_DTLS.CODE_NO → BRANCH_MSTR.BRANCH_NO **OR**
ADDR_DTLS.CODE_NO → EMP_MSTR.EMP_NO

Column Definition:

Column Name	Data Type	Width	Allow Null	Default
ADDR_NO	Number	6		
CODE_NO	VarChar2	10		
ADDR_TYPE	VarChar2	1		
ADDR1	VarChar2	50		
ADDR2	VarChar2	50		
CITY	VarChar2	25		
STATE	VarChar2	25		
PINCODE	VarChar2	6		

Table Description:

Column Name	Description
ADDR_NO	A system generated number auto posted to this table column
CODE_NO	Identifies a person or organization to whom the address belongs Should be present in either BRANCH_MSTR table, CUST_MSTR table, EMP_MSTR table or NOMINEE_MSTR table
ADDR_TYPE	Can hold the values: **C** for Current Residential address **N** for Native place **i.e.** Permanent Residential address, **H** for Head Office or **B** for Branch
Addr1	Postal Address (House number & Name, Road name)
Addr2	Postal address (Locality & area)
City	Postal address (City name)
State	Postal address (State name)
Pincode	Postal address (Pin code)

Explanation:

The ADDR_DTLS table stores multiple postal addresses of customers who have either Savings accounts, Current accounts or Fixed deposits with the bank.

Table Definition:

Table Name : CNTC_DTLS

Primary Key : - -

Foreign Key : CNTC_DTLS.ADDR_NO → ADDR_DTLS.ADDR_NO

: CNTC_DTLS.CODE_NO → CUST_MSTR.CUST_NO **OR**

CNTC_DTLS.CODE_NO → NOMINEE_MSTR.NOMINEE_NO **OR**

CNTC_DTLS.CODE_NO → BRANCH_MSTR.BRANCH_NO **OR**

CNTC_DTLS.CODE_NO → EMP_MSTR.EMP_NO

Column Definition:

Column Name	**Data Type**	**Width**	**Allow Null**	**Default**
ADDR_NO	Number	6		
CODE_NO	VarChar2	10		
CNCT_TYPE	VarChar2	1		
CNCT_DATA	VarChar2	75		

Table Description:

Column Name	**Description**
ADDR_NO	This value must be present in the ADDR_DTLS table
CODE_NO	Identifies the person or organization to whom the address belongs Should be present in either BRANCH_MSTR table, CUST_MSTR table, EMP_MSTR table or NOMINEE_MSTR table
CNCT_TYPE	Can hold the values: **R** for Residence telephone number **O** for Office telephone number **M** for Mobile telephone number **P** for Pager number **E** for Email address **F** for Fax number **W** for Website's URL
CNCT_DATA	Actual contact details of a client, **i.e.** A telephone, mobile, Fax, pager number, Email address or Web site URL

Explanation:

The CNTC_DTLS table stores complete contact information for a bank's branch employees, customers, or nominees to any account or fixed deposit. There can be multiple contact details for each.

The tables ADDR_DTLS and CNTC_DTLS are common to the system. They hold the complete Postal address and Residence, Office, Mobile, Pager, Fax, Email and Web site URLs (if any) of all the banks branch employees, customers and their nominees.

Banking Transactions

Table Definition:

Table Name : **TRANS_MSTR**

Primary Key : TRANS_MSTR.TRANS_NO

Foreign Key : TRANS_MSTR.ACCT_NO → ACCT_MSTR.ACCT_NO

The **TRANS_MSTR** table structure continued:

Column Definition:

Column Name	Data Type	Width	Allow Null	Default
TRANS_NO	VarChar2	10		
ACCT_NO	VarChar2	6		
DT	Date			
TYPE	VarChar2	1		
PARTICULAR	VarChar2	30		
DR_CR	VarChar2	1		
AMT	Number	8,2		
BALANCE	Number	8,2		

Table Description:

Column Name	Description
TRANS_NO	A system generated number auto posted to this table column
ACCT_NO	This value must be present in the ACCT_MSTR table
DT	Transaction date
TYPE	Can hold the values: **B** for Cheque transaction **C** for Cash transaction or **D** for Demand Draft transaction

PARTICULAR	Short summary for the transaction
DR_CR	Transaction type (**D** - Deposit or **W** - Withdrawal)
AMT	The amount of the transaction
BALANCE	A calculated, real time, balance held in the account

Explanation:

The TRANS_MSTR table stores the daily transactions of deposits or withdrawals carried out by all customers of the bank.

Banking Transaction Details

Table Definition:

Table Name : TRANS_DTLS

Primary Key : - -

Foreign Key : TRANS_DTLS.TRANS_NO → TRANS_MSTR.TRANS_NO

Column Definition:

Column Name	Data Type	Width	Allow Null	Default
TRANS_NO	VarChar2	10	No	
INST_NO	Number	6	No	
INST_DT	Date		No	
PAYTO	VarChar2	30	No	
INST_CLR_DT	Date		No	
BANK_NAME	VarChar2	35	No	
BRANCH_NAME	VarChar2	25	No	
PAIDFROM	VarChar2	10	No	

The **TRANS_DTLS** table structure continued:

Table Description:

Column Name	Description
TRANS_NO	This value must be present in the TRANS_MSTR table
INST_NO	Instrument number (**i.e.** Cheque number)
INST_DT	Instrument date (**i.e.** Cheque date)
PAYTO	The name to whom the cheque is made out to
INST_CLR_DT	Date on which an instrument (**i.e.** Cheque) deposited with the bank is cleared by the bank on which it was drawn
BANK_NAME	Name of the drawee bank
BRANCH_NAME	Branch of the drawee bank
PAIDFROM	The Account number at the bank on which the cheque is drawn

Explanation:

The TRANS_DTLS table stores the daily cheque transactions carried out by the bank's customers. The information in the TRANS_MSTR and TRANS_DTLS tables are combined to obtain the entries to be written / printed in a customer's passbook **or** computerized passbook.

Entity Relationship Diagram For Retail Banking

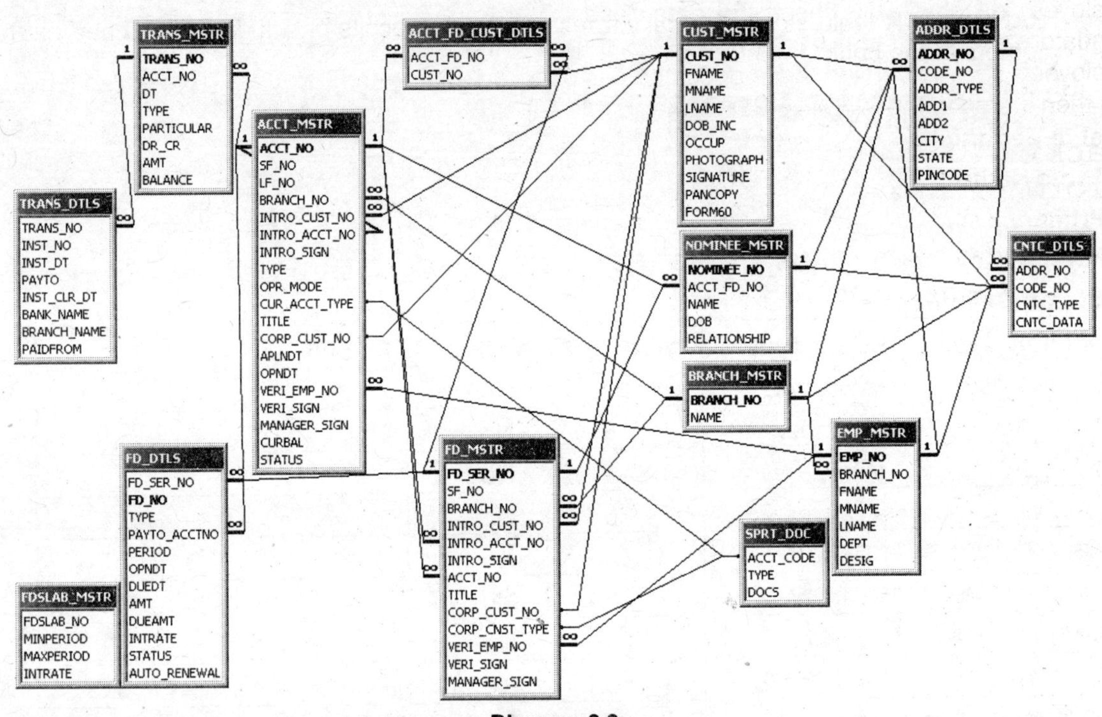

Diagram 3.9

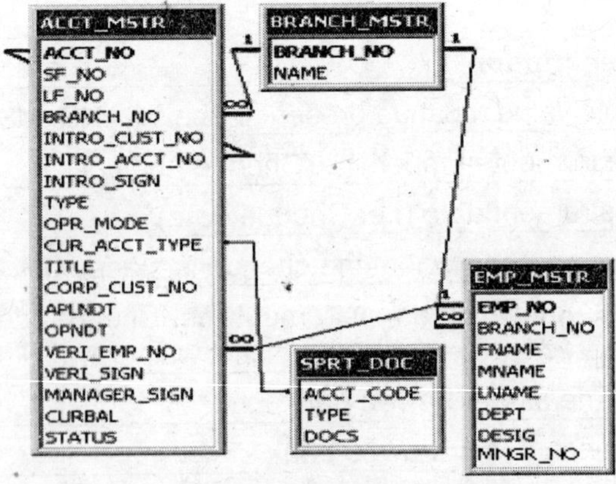

Diagram 3.10

The above diagram, attempts to give a visual representation of the entity relationship between various tables required under the project. The symbols '**1**' and '**oo**' indicate a **one-to-many** relationship.

The **ACCT_MSTR** table references the **BRANCH_MSTR** and **EMP_MSTR** tables. Refer to diagram 3.10.

When any Savings or Current **account opening form** is submitted to the bank, a bank employee will physically check the data filled in the form for its correctness as well as the mandatory **account support documents** that have to be submitted by the customer. The bank employee's ID who verified these documents is checked against the **EMP_MSTR look up** table, and then stored in the **ACCT_MSTR** table.

Tracking A Customer's Or Nominee's Address And Contact Information

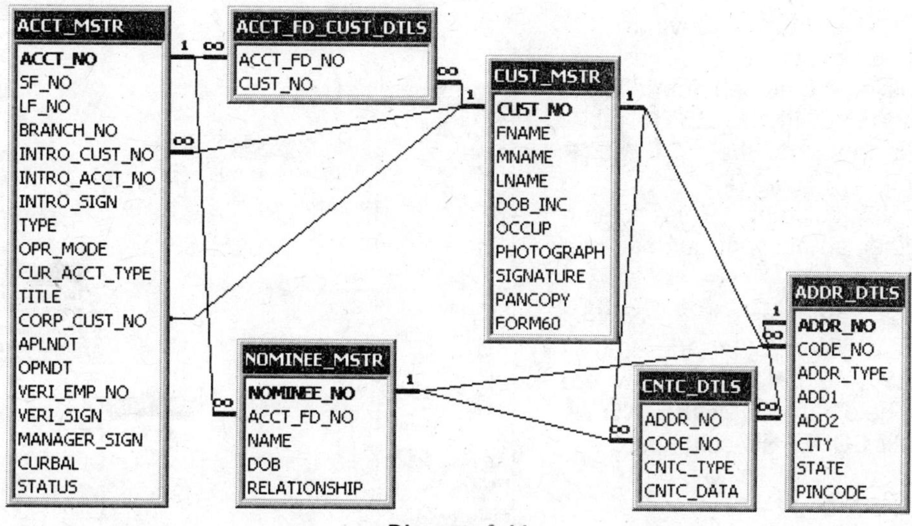

Diagram 3.11

When a customer opens an account with the bank **or** creates a fixed deposit, the customers and their nominee's full postal address and contact information needs to be stored in the retail banking system. The tables that store such information are **CUST_MSTR**, **NOMINEE_MSTR**, **ADDR_DTLS** and **CNTC_DTLS**.

The CUST_MSTR table is bound to the ACCT_MSTR table via the column **ACCT_FD_NO** in the **ACCT_FD_CUST_DTLS** table, which stores the value held in ACCT_MSTR.ACCT_NO. The NOMINEE_MSTR table is bound to the ACCT_MSTR table via the column **ACCT_FD_NO**, which stores the value held in ACCT_MSTR.ACCT_NO. The ADDR_DTLS and the CNTC_DTLS tables are bound to the ACCT_MSTR and the NOMINEE_MSTR / CUST_MSTR tables via the column **CODE_NO**.

This column will hold either the value held in CUST_MSTR.CUST_NO **or** the value held in NOMINEE_MSTR.NOMINEE.NO.

Employee Details

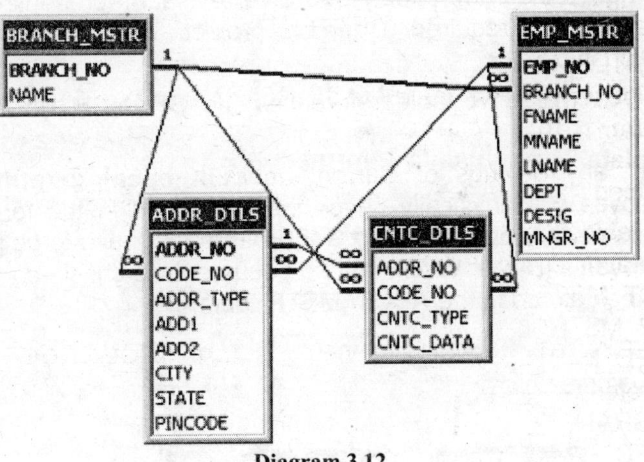

Diagram 3.12

ADDR_DTLS and **CNTC_DTLS** are common lookup tables used across the system for storing the contact information of Branches, Employees, Customers, and Nominees. The column **CODE_NO** in these tables will hold BRANCH_NO, EMP_NO, CUST_NO or NOMINEE_NO thus binding address and contact information to any of the four.

Nominee Details

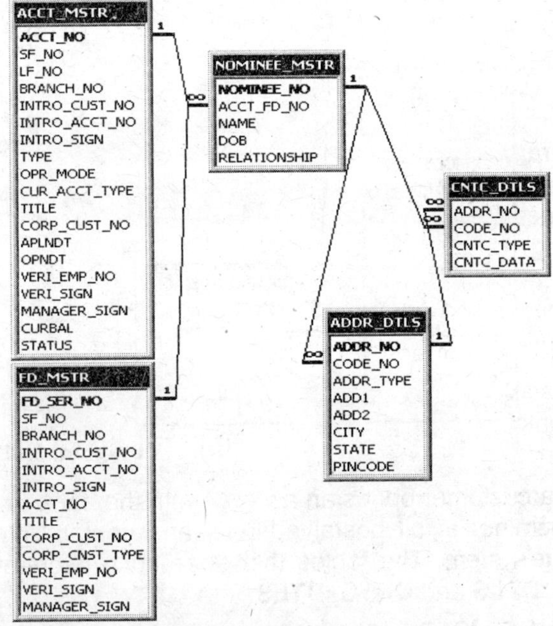

Diagram 3.13

Nominees can be setup for Savings or Current accounts as well as Fixed Deposits. Nominee information is stored in the **NOMINEE_MSTR** table. This table is bound to the **ACT_MSTR** and/or the **FD_MSTR** via the **ACCT_FD_NO** column. This column can hold either an account number or a fixed deposit number.

A nominee's address and contact information is stored in the tables **ADDR_DTLS** and **CNTC_DTLS** where the value held in **NOMINEE_NO** is stored in their **CODE_NO** columns.

Fixed Deposits

When creating fixed deposits with the bank there are two sets of information to be captured and stored. The table **FD_MSTR** stores information about the bank application documentation that leads to the issue of a fixed deposit receipt. The table **FD_DTLS** stores the details of the fixed deposit.

Fixed deposits are created for a specific time duration called a slab. Depending upon this time slab an interest rate will be applied to the fixed deposit. Whenever a fixed deposit is being created, the interest rate applicable to the deposit is obtained from the **FDSLAB_MSTR** lookup table.

Information printed on the fixed deposit receipt is taken from the FD_DTLS table. The fixed deposit receipt, which is the output of this sub system, is a combination of a **fixed template** and **dynamic information** obtained from the FD_DTLS table.

The table FD_MSTR also references several other **look up** tables they are, ACCT_MSTR, CUST_MSTR, EMP_MSTR:

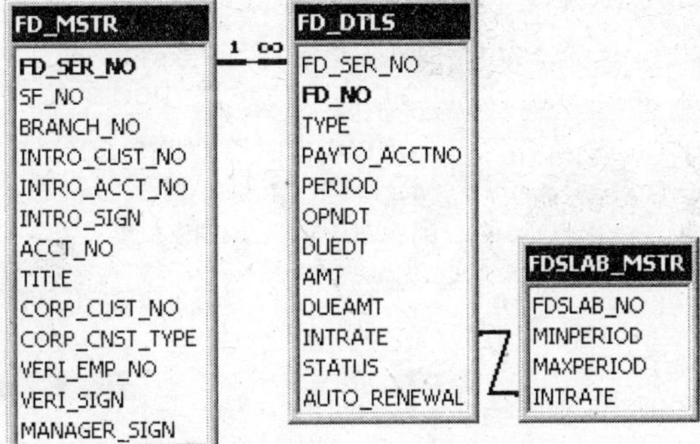

Diagram 3.14

- FD_MSTR.BRANCH_NO references BRANCH_MSTR.BRANCH_NO
- FD_MSTR.INTRO_CUST_NO references CUST_MSTR.CUST_NO
- FD_MSTR.INTRO_ACCT_NO references ACCT_MSTR.ACCT_NO
- FD_MSTR.ACCT_NO references ACCT_MSTR.ACCT_NO
- FD_MSTR.CORP_CUST_NO references CUST_MSTR.CUST_NO
- FD_MSTR.VERI_EMP_NO references EMP_MSTR.EMPNO

Banking Transactions

The transactions of both Savings and Current accounts are identical. Transactions documented in this retail banking are either deposits or withdrawals. Transactions can be done via Cash, Bank draft or Cheque.

TRANSACTIONS

Transactions must occur for a specific Account. Hence, the table TRANS_MSTR references ACCT_MSTR.ACCT_NO.

Transactions (**i.e.** Deposits or Withdrawals) can be Cash, Bank draft or Cheque. This information is stored in TRANS_MSTR.TYPE.

If the transaction is via Bank draft or Cheque their details are stored in:

TRANS_DTLS.INST_NO

TRANS_DTLS.INST_DT

TRANS_DTLS.BANK_NAME

Diagram 3.15

The type of transaction (i.e. whether a Deposit or Withdrawal) is stored in TRANS_MSRT.DR_CR.

The transaction amount and the running balance of the account are stored in TRANS_MSTR.AMT and TRANS_MSTR.BALANCE respectively.

Once calculated, the running balance is immediately posted to ACCT_MSTR.CURBAL.

The passbook or computer printout of a customer's banking transactions (generally month wise) is taken from the TRANS_MSTR and TRANS_DTLS tables. This documentation of a customer's day-to-day transactions is the output of this sub system.

The Complete Entity Relationships For Account Opening

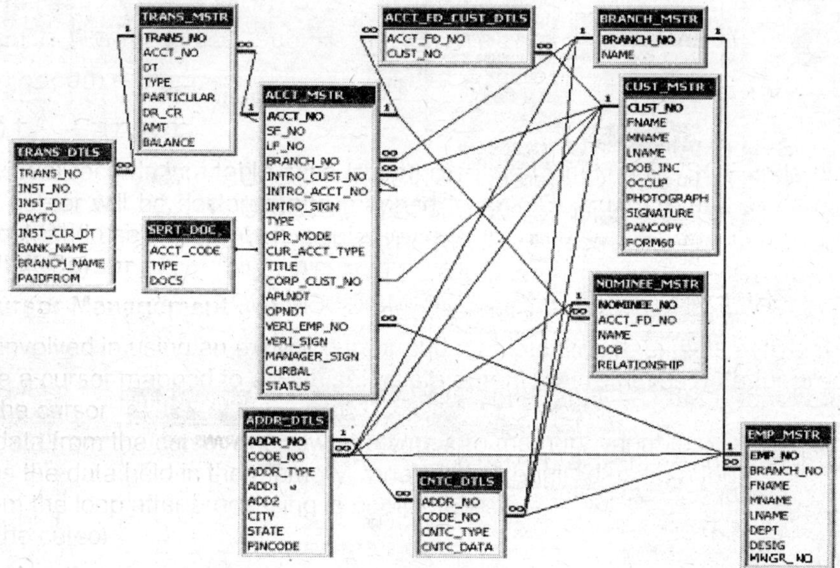

Diagram 3.16

The Complete Entity Relationships For Fixed Deposit Creation

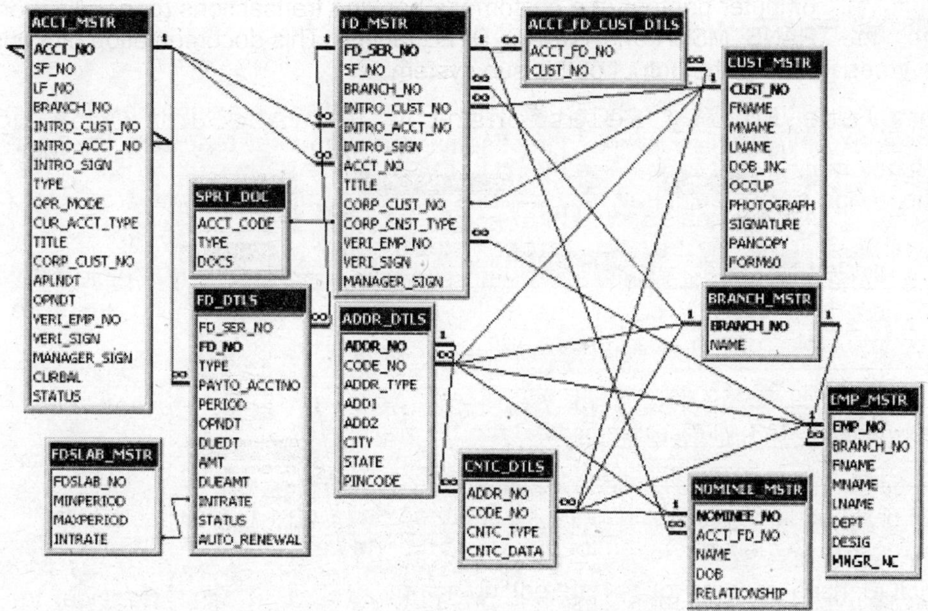

Diagram 3.17

4. Relational Database Design

Pitfalls In Relational Database Design

When designing any database schema, a careful study of the master / detail relationships in business model will go a really long way in offsetting the amount of redundant data captured and stored in the db tables.

The DB schema designer goals should be:

- Avoid redundant data by the normalization of table data
- Ensure that all relationships between business data is expressed fully in table data columns
- Appropriate data integrity constraints that check business data being stored in tables is applied to a table column as a constraint.

Note:	*The application of appropriate data constraints ensures that erroneous business data is captured in any table column.*

Faulty relational database design often leads to:

- A load of redundant business data being captured and stored in table columns
- An increase in the length of time for extracting reports from tables

Example: Shows how faulty table design can lead to **redundant** data. Consider the following relational schema. A bank decides to capture and store all its business data associated with loan applications. The loan schema designed, is as follows:

Lending-schema = (branch-name, branch-city, branch-assets, customer-name, loan-number, loan amount)

Schema 1

Data Redundancy

Here the branch-name, branch-city and branch-assets are being captured and stored, when capturing and storing information about every loan made by that branch to any customer. This information will also be captured in some Master table in the business schema and need not be captured a second time if there is simply a reference stored in this record to an appropriate master table in the schema.

NOT NULL Data Type

Often **all** the table columns are flagged as NOT NULL. Generally this is done in the belief that the RDBMS engine will prevent the data entry operator from leaving out any business data at data entry time.

If the customer-name, loan-number, amount, table columns are flagged as **NOT NULL**, then Branch information **cannot be** stored in the table **if loan information does not exist**. Additionally, the RDBMS engine has to work to check the NOT NULL constraint when data is being inserted into each column.

As far as practical, no table column should be flagged as NOT NULL unless the data being entered is considered as absolutely mandatory for the system.

Decomposition

A technique to resolve these types of issues is to decompose Schema 1 shown in Schema 2, (i.e. more granular levels) then create a relationship between the two schemas because of this decomposition.

Decompose the relation schema **Lending-schema** into:

Branch-customer-schema = (branch-name, branch-city, assets, customer-name)

Customer-loan-schema = (customer-name, loan-number, loan-amount)

Schema 2

All the **attributes** (table columns) of the original Schema 1 (i.e. Relation **R**) must appear in the decomposition (R_1, R_2), **i.e. R = R1 Union R2**. This is shown in schema 2.

Note: *Customer-name* ***is the attribute that links the data held in the two schemas.***

When decomposing a relational schema decide whether a particular relation R is in **good** form (**i.e.** fully decomposed).

If a relation **R** is not in **good** form, decompose it into a set of relations {R_1, R_2, **...**, R_n} such that:

- Each relation is in good form

  i.e. minimum redundant data is stored in the tables
- The decomposition is a lossless-join decomposition

  i.e. when extracting data from the table by using a **simple join** all relevant data can be extracted from the tables.

The rules that help decide whether a relation is in good form is based on the relation's functional dependencies and its multi valued dependencies

Normalization Using Functional Dependencies

When the Relation schema **R** is decomposed into a set of functional dependencies **F** (**i.e.** R_1 and R_2) a lossless join should result.

The relations R_1 and R_2 preferably should be in either Boyce-Codd Normal Form **or** Third Normal Form.

Normalization and De-Normlization

Normalization is a process that helps analyst or database designers to design table structures for an application. The focus of normalization is to attempt to reduce **redundant** table data to the very minimum.

Through the normalization process, the collection of data in a single table is replaced, by the same data being distributed over multiple tables with a specific relationship being setup between the tables. By this process table designers try their best to reduce redundant table data to the very minimum.

Note: *It is essential to remember that **redundant data cannot be reduced to zero** in any database management system.*

Having said this, when the process of normalization is applied to table data, and this data is spread across several **associated** tables, it takes a query much longer to run and retrieve user data from the set of tables.

Hence, often in a commercial application after **100%** normalization is carried out across the master tables often the table structures are **de-normalized** deliberately to make SQL queries run faster. This means that in commercial applications there is often a **trade off** between **redundant** table data and the **speed** of query execution.

Normalization is carried out for the following reasons:

- To structure the data between tables so that data maintenance is simplified
- To allow data retrieval at optimal speed
- Simplify data maintenance through updates, inserts and deletes
- To reduce the need to restructure tables as new application requirements arise
- Normalization can improve the quality of design for an application by rationalization of table data

Normalization is a **technique** that:

- Decomposes data held in a single table into multiple tables with a defined relationship
- Eliminate all table data relationships which does not fully depend upon a primary key
- Eliminate all table data relationships that contains transitive dependencies

First, Second and Third Normal Form(at)

First Normal Form

When table data is decomposed into two-dimensional tables with all **repeating groups** of data eliminated, the table data is said to be in **First Normal Form(at)**.

The portion of data record that is repeated is termed as **Repeating Group.**

For Example, a client gives a set of printed challans to an systems analyst or database designer. The printed challans could include information like:

Challan number	Challan date	Purchase Order number
Supplier number	Supplier name	Supplier address

as well as item details like:

Raw Material number	Raw Material name
Raw Material unit price	Quantity delivered

The analyst designer could creates a single table whose structure is as follows:

Table Name: **Challan**

Column Name	**Data Type**	**Size**
ChlnNo (Challan number)	Number	5
ChlnDt (Challan date)	Date	

PONo (Purchase order number)	Number	5
SuplrNo (Supplier number)	Number	5
SuplrName (Supplier name)	Varchar2	20
SuplrAddr (Supplier address)	Varchar2	70
RmNo (Raw Material number)	Number	6
RmName (Raw Material name)	Varchar2	20
UnitPrice (Raw Material unit price)	Number	7,2
QtySupplied (Quantity supplied)	Number	8

Table 4.1

The systems analyst or database designer calls this structure (as shown in Table 8.5) the **Mother Matrix**.

A supplier can be ordered to deliver either a single item or multiple items. Hence in turn a challan can have a single product entry or multiple product entries.

Thus, if a single table is created, there will be **redundant** data in the table **Challan** for ChlnNo, ChlnDt, SuplrNo, SuplrName and SuplrAddr because of these items **repeating** in the table structure and being required to hold **identical** data, which is in fact the **redundant** data.

To convert **Challan** into it's **first normal form**(at) information about the items that a supplier delivers **must be** stored in a separate table.

Thus after applying the **first** normalization rule, the mother matrix will be re-structured as follows:

Table Name: **Chln_Mstr**

Column Name	**Data Type**	**Size**
ChlnNo (Challan number)	Number	5
ChlnDt (Challan date)	Date	
PONo (Purchase order number)	Number	5
SuplrNo (Supplier number)	Number	5
SuplrName (Supplier name)	Varchar2	20
SuplrAddr (Supplier address)	Varchar2	70

Table 4.2

Table Name: Chln_Dtls

Column Name	Data Type	Size
ChlnNo (Challan number)	Number	5
RmNo (Raw Material number)	Number	6
RmName (Raw Material name)	Varchar2	20
UnitPrice (Raw Material unit price)	Number	7,2
QtySupplied (Quantity supplied)	Number	8

Table 4.3

Tip: *When the Mother Matrix (i.e table Challan) is decomposed into multiple related tables and all repeating groups of **business data** are eliminated the table data is said to be in First Normal Form(at).*

This **fully normalizes** the table data of the mother matrix **Challan**.

Challan has been decomposed into two other tables, i.e. **Chln_Mstr** and **Chln_Dtls**.

The column named **ChlnNo** must be added in Chln_Dtls, so that items in the Chln_Dtls **are linked** to Chln_Mstr. The contents of ChlnNo will be identical in both tables hence redundant data cannot be reduced to zero in any relational db schema.

The **relationship** between Chln_Mstr and the Chln_Dtls could be **one to one** or **one to many** (**i.e.** for every Challan in Chln_Mstr there can be one or more items in Chln_Dtls).

Second Normal Form

Table data is said to be in **Second Normal Form**(at) when each record in the table is in first normal form **and** each column in the record is **fully dependent on the primary key**.

To test whether the columns are dependent on the primary key, (i.e. table data is in second normal form (at), an analyst designer needs to identify**:**

- Whether by only knowing a **supplier name**, a **challan number (or numbers)** be identified?

  i.e. Is there a **one to one** relationship between the **supplier name** and the **challan number**?

If the data for the **Chln_Mstr** table is analyzed, Supplier information like Supplier name, Supplier address is **not dependent** on the **ChlnNo**, rather this data is related to **SuplrNo**.

- There is also a **one to many** relationship between supplier name and challan number, **i.e.** multiple challans are bound to a single supplier.

Similarly, if the data of the **Chln_Dtls** table is analyzed, raw material information like raw material name and raw material unit price is **not dependent** on the **ChlnNo**, rather this data is related to RmNo (raw material number).

To convert this table data into **second normal form**(at) **Supplier** information must be stored in separate table. Thus, after applying the rules of second normal form(at), the mother matrix will have to be again re-structured as follows**:**

Table Name: **Suplr_Mstr**

Column Name	**Data Type**	**Size**
SuplrNo (Supplier number)	Number	5
SuplrName (Supplier name)	Varchar2	20
SuplrAddr (Supplier address)	Varchar2	70

Table 4.4

Table Name: **Chln_Mstr**

Column Name	**Data Type**	**Size**
ChlnNo (Challan number)	Number	5
ChlnDt (Challan date)	Date	
PONo (Purchase order number)	Number	5
SuplrNo (Supplier number)	Number	5

Table 4.5

Table Name: **Material_Mstr**

Column Name	**Data Type**	**Size**
RmNo (Raw Material number)	Number	6
RmName (Raw Material name)	Varchar2	20
UnitPrice (Raw Material unit price)	Number	7,2

Table 4.6

Table Name: **Chln_Dtls**

Column Name	**Data Type**	**Size**
ChlnNo (Challan number)	Number	5
RmNo (Raw Material number)	Number	6
QtySupplied (Quantity supplied)	Number	8

Table 4.7

Note: *Table data is said to be in **Second Normal Form(at)** when each record in the table is in first normal form and each column in the record is fully dependent on the primary key.*

Here, it is visible that **all** records in the **master tables:**

- Suplr_Mstr
- Chln_Mstr
- Material_Mstr

Are uniquely defined by their primary keys. Hence the table data is in its second normal form(at).

Third Normal Form

Table data is said to be in **Third Normal Form(at)** when all transitive dependencies are removed from this data.

A general case of transitive dependencies is as follows:

A, **B**, **C** are three columns in a table

If **C** is related to **B**

If **B** is related to **A**

Then **C** is **indirectly related** to **A** .

This is when transitive dependency in table exists.

To convert such table data to third normal form(at) remove transitive dependency by splitting each relation into **two** separate relations. This means that the data in columns A, B, C must be placed in **three separate tables**, which are linked using a **foreign key**.

Consider capturing **Raw Material** information in a table, when the raw material used supplied by different suppliers.

Thus the mother matrix before normalization could be:

Table Name: **Material**

Column Name	**Data Type**	**Size**
RmNo (Material number)	Number	5
RmName (Material name)	Varchar2	20
SuplrNo (Supplier number)	Number	5
SuplrName (Supplier name)	Varchar2	30
SuplrAddr (Supplier address)	Varchar2	70
UnitPrice (Raw Material unit price)	Number	7,2
PartNo (Part number)	Number	5
PartDesc (Part description)	Varchar2	30
Qty (Quantity used)	Number	5

Table 4.8

If the Material table is analyzed, since the raw material is made of **multiple** parts the **raw material** is **dependent** on its **parts**. Since each of part is purchased from a supplier, the suppliers and parts are related.

Thus, if the table is left as is it will result into:

- RmNo (Raw Material number), PartNo (*Part number*) and SuplrNo (*Supplier number*) are three columns in the Material table
- SuplrNo (*Supplier number*) is related to PartNo (*Part number*)
- PartNo (*Part number*) is related to RmNo (*Raw Material number*)
- Thus, RmNo (*Raw Material number*) is indirectly related to SuplrNo (*Supplier number*)

Therefore, a **transitive dependency** exists in the data held in the table **Material**.

To remove transitive dependency (**i.e.** bring table data into its **Third Normal Form(at)** the product table must be divided into following tables:

- **Material_Mstr**
- **Material_Dtls**
- **Part_Mstr**
- **Suplr_Mstr**

Table Name: **Material_Mstr**

Column Name	Data Type	Size
RmNo (Material number)	Number	5
RmName (Material name)	Varchar2	20
UnitPrice (Raw Material unit price)	Number	7,2

Table 4.9

Table Name: **Material_Dtls**

Column Name	Data Type	Size
RmNo (Material number)	Number	5
PartNo (Part number)	Number	5
Qty (Quantity used)	Number	5

Table 4.10

Table Name: **Part_Mstr**

Column Name	Data Type	Size
PartNo (Part number)	Number	5
PartDesc (Part description)	Varchar2	30
SuplrNo (Supplier number)	Number	5

Table 4.11

Table Name: **Suplr_Mstr**

Column Name	Data Type	Size
SuplrNo (Supplier number)	Number	5
SuplrName (Supplier name)	Varchar2	30
SuplrAddr (Supplier address)	Varchar2	70

Table 4.12

As is visible from the above exercise all the transitive dependencies of the data held in the mother matrix **Material** has been completely eliminated. The data in the mother matrix is now said to be in its third normal form(at).

Designing your tables to comply with 3NF (third normal form) is usually sufficient to ensure good design so, most of the time, you can stop right here. The *higher normal forms* address less common data problems. They are included here so you'll know what they are and what to do about them if you come across them. These normal forms do get a bit more complicated.

The truth is there are times when you will want to *denormalize* your data. That means you may sometimes want to put the data in two normalized tables back into one *denormalized* table. The reasons for doing this are usually associated with database performance, for example, the speed at which queries run.

This will always be a thought through, conscious decision, and represents one of the beauties of normalization. Properly normalized tables can always be put back together with no loss or gain of data.

Higher Normal Forms - Boyce-Codd Normal Form:

A table is in third normal form (3NF) and all determinants are candidate keys.

Boyce-Codd normal form (BCNF) can be thought of as a "new" third normal form.

It was introduced to cover situations that the "old" third normal form did not address. Keep in mind the mean of a determinant (determines the value in another field) and candidate keys (qualify for designation as primary key). This normal form applies to situations where you have overlapping candidate keys.

Note: *If a table has no non-key fields, it is automatically in BCNF.*

A Practical Approach

Look for potential problems in updating existing data (modification anomaly) and in entering new data (insertion anomaly) when you are designing a table schema.

For example: Imagine that you were designing a table for a college to hold information about courses, students, and teaching assistants. You have the following business rules.

- Each course can have many students
- Each student can take many courses
- Each course can have multiple Teachers
- Each Teachers is associated with only one course
- For each course, each student has one Teacher

Some sample data:

COURSES_STUDENTS_TEACHERS's		
CourseNum	**Student**	**TEACHERS**
MAT301	Deepak	Hitesh
MAT301	Ashwin	Sara
MAT301	Prerna	Sara
SCI450	Ashwin	Parag
SCI450	Deepak	Arun
SCI450	Seema	Parag

To uniquely identify each record, you could choose CourseNum + Student as a primary key. This would satisfy third normal form also because the combination of CourseNum and Student determines the value in TEACHERS. Another candidate key would be Student + TEACHERS. In this case, you have overlapping candidate keys (Student is in both).

The second choice, however, would not comply with third normal form because the CourseNum is not determined by the combination of Student and TEACHERS; it only depends on the value in TEACHERS (see the business rules). This is the situation that Boyce-Codd normal form addresses; the combination of Student + TEACHERS could not be considered to be a candidate key.

If you wanted to assign a TEACHER to a course before any students enrolled, you couldn't because Student is part of the primary key. Also, if the name of a TEACHER changed, you would have to update it in multiple records.

If you assume you have just these fields, this data would be better stored in three tables:

- One with CourseNum and Student
- Another with Student and TEACHERS
- The third with CourseNum and TEACHERS

COURSES	
***CourseNum**	***Student**
MAT301	Deepak
MAT301	Ashwin
MAT301	Prerna
SCI450	Ashwin
SCI450	Deepak
SCI450	Seema

STUDENTS	
***Student**	***TEACHERS**
Deepak	Hitesh
Ashwin	Sara
Prerna	Sara
Ashwin	Parag
Deepak	Arun
Seema	Parag

TEACHERS's	
***CourseNum**	***TEACHERS**
MAT301	Hitesh
MAT301	Sara
SCI450	Arun
SCI450	Parag

Above, showing tables that comply with BCNF

Fourth Normal Form:

A table is in Boyce-Codd normal form (BCNF) and there are no multi-valued dependencies.

A *multi-valued dependency* occurs when, for each value in field A, there is a set of values for field B and a set of values for field C but fields B and C are not related.

A Practical Approach

Look for repeated or null values in non-key fields.

A multi-valued dependency occurs when the table contains fields that are not logically related. An often used example is the following table:

MOVIES		
***Movie**	***Star**	***Producer**
Badshah	Shahrukh	Bhawar Jain
Badshah	Twinkle Khanna	Bhawar Jain
Badshah	Shahrukh	Girish Jain
Badshah	Twinkle Khanna	Girish Jain
My name is Khan	Kajol	Karan Johar
My name is Khan	Shahrukh	Karan Johar

A movie can have more than one star and more than one producer. A star can be in more than one movie. A producer can produce more than one movie. The primary key would have to include all three fields and so this table would be in BCNF. However, there will be unnecessarily repeated values. This brings in data maintenance problems, especially data deletion anomalies.

The Star and the Producer really are not logically related. The Movie determines the Star and the Movie determines the Producer. The answer is to have a separate table for each of those logical relationships - one holding Movie and Star and the other with Movie and Producer, as shown below:

STARS	
***Movie**	***Star**
Badshah	Shahrukh
Badshah	Twinkle Khanna
My name is Khan	Kajol
My name is Khan	Shahrukh

PRODUCERS	
***Movie**	***Producer**
Badshah	Bhawar Jain
Badshah	Girish Jain
My name is Khan	Karan Johar

Above, showing tables that comply with 4NF

Below is another example of a common design error, and it's easily spotted by all the missing or blank values.

PROJECTS_EQUIPMENT				
DeptCode	**ProjectNum**	**ProjectMgrID**	**Equipment**	**PropertyID**
IS	36-272-TC	EN1-15	CD-ROM	657
IS			VGA desktop monitor	305
AC	35-152-TC	EN1-15		
AC			Dot-matrix printer	358
AC			Calculator with tape	239
TW	30-452-T3	EN1-10	486 PC	275
TW	30-457-T3	EN1-15		
TW	31-124-T3	EN1-15	Laser printer	109
TW	31-238-TC	EN1-15	Hand-held scanner	479
RI			Fax machine	775
MK			Laser printer	858
MK			Answering machine	187
TW	31-241-TC	EN1-15	Standard 19200 bps modem	386
SL			486 Laptop PC	772
SL			Electronic notebook	458

Above, a table with many null values (NOTE: it also does not comply with 3NF and BCNF)

It's the same problem here because not all of the data is logically related. As usual, the answer is more tables - one to hold the information on the equipment assigned to departments (with PropertyID as the primary key) and another with projects and departments.

You'd have to know the business rules to know whether a project might involve more than one department or manager and be able to figure out the primary key. Assuming a project can have only one manager and be associated with only one department, the tables would be as follows:

EQUIPMENT		
***PropertyID**	**Equipment**	**DeptCode**
657	CD-ROM	IS
305	VGA desktop monitor	IS
358	Dot-matrix printer	AC
239	Calculator with tape	AC
275	486 PC	TW
109	Laser printer	TW
479	Hand-held scanner	TW
775	Fax machine	RI
858	Laser printer	MK
187	Answering machine	MK
386	Standard 19200 bps modem	TW
772	486 Laptop PC	SL
458	Electronic notebook	SL

PROJECTS_EQUIPMENT		
***ProjectNum**	**ProjectMgrID**	**DeptCode**
36-272-TC	EN1-15	IS
35-152-TC	EN1-15	AC
30-452-T3	EN1-10	TW
30-457-T3	EN1-15	TW
31-124-T3	EN1-15	TW
31-238-TC	EN1-15	TW
31-241-TC	EN1-15	TW

Above, tables that eliminate the null values and comply with 4NF

Fifth Normal Form:

A table is in fourth normal form (4NF) and there are no cyclic dependencies.

A *cyclic dependency* can occur only when you have a multi-field primary key consisting of three or more fields. For example, let's say your primary key consists of fields A, B, and C. A cyclic dependency would arise if the values in those fields were related in pairs of A and B, B and C, and A and C.

Fifth normal form is also called projection-join normal form. A *projection* is a new table holding a subset of fields from an original table. When properly formed projections are joined, they must result in the same set of data that was contained in the original table.

A Practical Approach

Look for the number of records that will have to be added or maintained

Following is some sample data about buyers, the products they buy, and the companies they buy from on behalf of MegaMall, a large department store.

BUYING		
***Buyer**	***Product**	***Company**
Kavita	jeans	Levi
Kavita	jeans	Wrangler
Kavita	shirts	Levi
Meher	jeans	Levi

Above, a table with cyclic dependencies

The primary key consists of all three fields. One data maintenance problem that occurs is that you need to add a record for every buyer who buys a product for every company that makes that product or they can't buy from them. That may not appear to be a big deal in this sample of 2 buyers, 2 products, and 2 companies (2 X 2 X 2 = 8 total records). But what if you went to 20 buyers, 50 products, and 100 companies (20 X 50 X 100 = 100,000 potential records)? It quickly gets out of hand and becomes impossible to maintain.

You might be tempted to solve this by dividing this into the following two tables:

BUYERS	
***Buyer**	***Product**
Kavita	jeans
Kavita	shirts
Meher	jeans

PRODUCTS	
***Product**	***Company**
Jeans	Wrangler
Jeans	Levi
Shirts	Levi

However, if you joined the two tables above on the Product field, it would produce a record not part of the original data set (it would say that Lori buys jeans from Wrangler). This is where the projection-join concept comes in.

The correct solution would be three tables:

BUYERS	
***Buyer**	***Product**
Kavita	jeans
Kavita	shirts
Meher	jeans

PRODUCTS	
***Product**	***Company**
Jeans	Wrangler
Jeans	Levi
Shirts	Levi

COMPANIES	
***Buyer**	***Company**
Kavita	Levi
Kavita	Wrangler
Meher	Levi

Above, tables that comply with 5NF

When the first two tables are joined by Product and the result joined to the third table by Buyer and Company, the result is the original set of data.

In our scenario of 20 buyers, 50 products, and 100 companies, you would have, at most, 1000 records in the Buyers table (20 X 50), 5000 records in the Products table (50 X 100), and 2000 records in the Companies table (20 X 100). With a maximum of 8000 records, these tables would be much easier to maintain than the possible 100,000 records we saw earlier.

Self Review Questions

Fill In The Blanks

1. Data integrity constraints can be ________ level or ________ level constraints.
2. While DB designing ensures that all ____________ between table data columns are represented.
3. In RDBMS the space on a hard disk where data is stored permanently is always at a ___________.
4. No table column should be flagged as _______ _______ unless the data being entered is considered as absolutely mandatory for the system.
5. All the attributes of the original schema must appear in the __________ tables.
6. ____________ is a process that helps analyst or database designers to design table structures for an application.
7. Normalization is a technique that decomposes data into ________ dimensional tables.
8. When table data is decomposed into two-dimensional tables with all repeating groups of data eliminated, the table data is said to be in _________ _________ Form.
9. Table data is said to be in _________ ________ Form when all transitive dependencies are removed from this data.
10. ________ ___________ constrain the set of legal relations over a schema to those relations for which a given decomposition is a lossless-join decomposition.
11. Normalization can improve the quality of design for an application by rationalization of _________ _________.
12. The portion of data record that is repeated is termed as ___________ _________.

True Or False

13. While DB designing avoids redundant data by proper denormalization of tables.
14. Designer goals should apply proper data integrity constraints that check data being stored in tables during inserts or updates.
15. Often all the table columns are flagged as NULL.
16. All the table columns of the original schema must appear in the decomposed tables.
17. The focus of normalization is to reduce redundant table data to the very minimum.
18. Normalization is a technique that eliminates any relationships in which table data fully depends upon the primary key of a record.
19. In the second Normal form, the columns in the data table are fully dependent on the primary key.
20. It is always possible to decompose a relation into relations in 3NF and the decomposition is lossless.

21. There are database schemas in BCNF that do not seem to be sufficiently normalized.
22. All key declarations are functional dependencies and all functional dependencies are key declarations.
23. Redundant data can be reduced to zero in any database management system.
24. Normalization is carried out to reduce the need to restructure tables as new application requirements arise.

Objective Questions

1. What are the pitfalls when in relational database design?
2. What is normalization and de-normalization?
3. Describe with and simple example when table data is in first normal form?
4. Describe with and simple example when table data is in second normal form?
5. Describe with and simple example when table data is in third normal form?

5. Query Processing And Query Optimization

What Is A Query?

RDBMS engines are listener / talkers in a computer's memory. Any user can communicate with the RDBMS engine using its natural language ANSI SQL. Hence a query is an ANSI SQL command sentence delivered to an RDBMS engine normally via a character based client. The query sentence normally instructs the RDBMS engine to retrieve specific table data.

The table data retrieved by the RDBMS engine is normally sent directly to the VDU from where the query originated, i.e. to the character based client used to fire the query to the RDBMS engine.

In some cases the output of a query can be sent to a printer, or stored in a file or used as input data to another command or process.

What Is Optimization?

ANSI SQL sentences can trigger table read or write operations. The ANSI SQL SELECT query triggers a table read operation. The ANSI SQL INSERT, UPDATE or DELETE query triggers a table write operation.

Whenever any such queries are received by the RDBMS engine it must first determine **how** to execute the query so that the least internal resources such as CPU clock cycles, memory buffers, hard disk reads and so on are used. A part of the RDBMS engine itself, called the **query optimizer,** actually chooses the way in which a query will be executed so that it loads system resources the very least.

ANSI SQL SELECT queries are probably the most frequently used type of SQL queries. There is a category of SQL users who are actually not authorized to use any other type of query. As a result of this, most RDBMS engines give the highest priority to controlling computer resources used for executing SELECT queries (**i.e.** user defined SELECT statements).

The goal of the query optimizer is to choose the most **efficient** way to execute an SQL statement by deciding on the best possible way to extract the table data specified in the SELECT using the least system resources and at the highest possible speed.

The query optimizer considers a number of factors and makes the best choice from among multiple alternatives.

How is a Query Executed?

The ANSI SQL SELECT statement issued via the character based client is delivered via the network to the RDBMS engine normally resident on the RDBMS server.

The ANSI SQL SELECT is placed in a **P**ublic **G**lobal **A**rea (**i.e.** PGA), a place in the Server's memory where all queries reside. The SELECT is then processed by the RDBMS **parser** and which segments the SELECT query into **three** parts, **WHERE**, **FROM** and **SELECT.**

Subsequent to the parsing the RDBMS engine will:

- Identify the table specified in the **FROM** clause
- Open this table in an **implicit** cursor in the Server's **S**hared **G**lobal **A**rea (**i.e.** SGA)
- Next, the RDBMS engine looks at the WHERE clause and **filters** the active data set in the implicit cursor depending on the conditions specified
- After which columns **not specified** in the SELECT clause are eliminated
- The final resultant data set is returned to the client's (i.e. requestors) VDU

The RDBMS's tables reside on the Server's hard disk drive. User data resides within the tables. It is the RDBMS's **query optimizer**, that has specific built in algorithms, which automatically decide on the best way to retrieve user data from the table specified in the ANSI SQL SELECT.

> **Note:** *When these techniques are understood a programmer can apply them when writing ANSI SQL queries.*
>
> *If queries are carefully written using good query optimization techniques by programmers, they will run like lightning on the Server and deliver their output to the requesting client.*

When well optimized queries are fired to the RDBMS engine and executed on the RDBMS Server they consume the least Server resources, such as memory, CPU clock cycles, RDBMS processes, SGA space, hard disk accesses and so on.

Since the RDBMS Server actually services several clients on a network, writing well optimized queries helps the commercial application to run efficiently **i.e.** consume the least Server's resources and produce useful output.

Hence an understanding of how the built-in query optimizer of the RDBMS engine works will help in writing efficient queries. The query optimizer can also be programmer controlled. This indicates the level of flexibility built into the query optimizer.

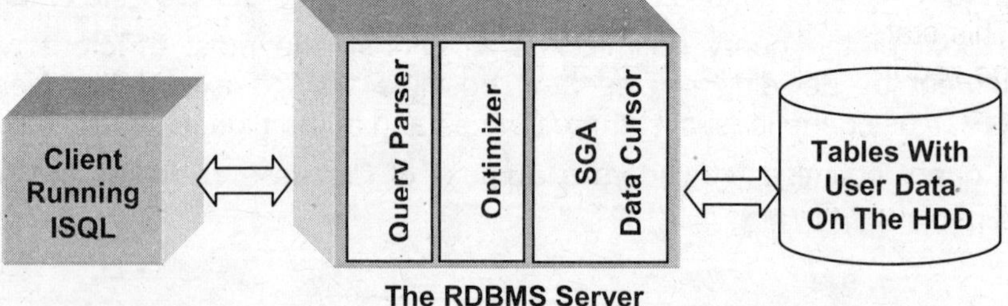

Diagram 5.1 A brief outline of the RDBMS engine on a Server.

Example:

SELECT SuplrNo, SuplrName FROM Suplr_Mstr WHERE SuplrNo = '1';

All the data in **SuplrMstr** table is opened in the SGA using an implicit cursor as follows:

SuplrNo	SuplrName	Addr	City	Pincode	Phone
1	Universal Computers	15/13, Lamington Rd	Mumbai	400001	22555786
2	Byte Systems	IV floor, Pratap	Mumbai	400096	26434058
3	Ayus System	105/E, Moti Market	Mumbai	400066	25656214
4	Techno Sys	23/152 Sea view, 15th Cross Rd	Calcutta	220034	25678495
5	MegaByte	Shop 2, Nehru Rd	New Delhi	110003	22536894

Table 5.1

Next referencing the **WHERE** clause (i.e. - SuplrNo = '1') the implicit cursor is filtered and the first target table is created in the SGA.

SuplrNo	SuplrName	Addr	City	Pincode	Phone
1	Universal Computers	15/13, Lamington Rd	Mumbai	400001	22555786

The RDBMS engine will then use the **column list** specified in the SELECT clause to create the second target table, which in this case is the final active data set returned to the client.

SuplrNo	SuplrName
1	Universal Computers

Query Execution Plans

There are several steps that the RDBMS engine goes through to execute any ANSI SQL, DML statement. Each of these steps either physically **retrieves** rows of data from a table or **manipulates** the retrieved data in some way on behalf of the requestor. All the steps followed by the query optimizer to execute an ANSI SQL query are called its query **execution plan**.

Example:

```
SELECT suplrname, city FROM suplr_mstr
    WHERE city NOT IN(SELECT city FROM country WHERE countryname = 'India');
```

This statement selects the supplier **name** and **city** from the **suplr_mstr** table for which there is **no record** of an associated city in the **country** table.

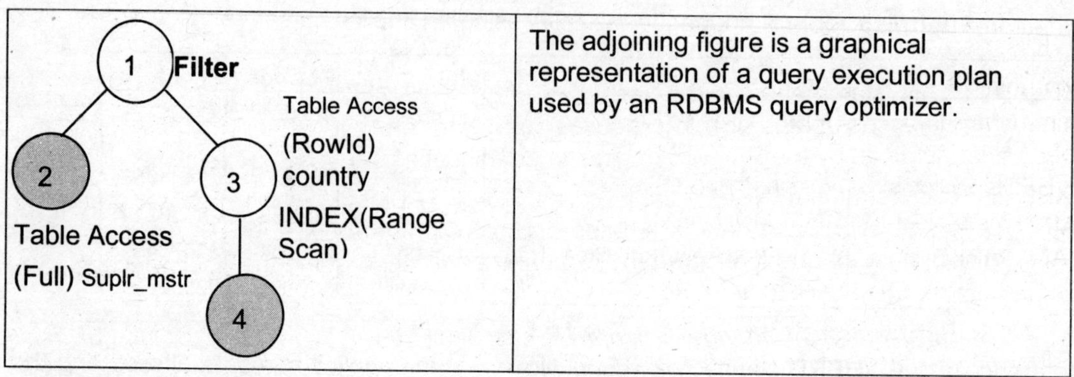

Diagram 5.2

Steps Of The Execution Plan

Each step of a query execution plan returns data rows that are either used by another step or returned to the requestor. The **set** of data rows returned by any step in query execution is called a **row source**.

Each step in a query execution plan therefore either retrieves rows from a table **or** accepts rows from one or more row sources as its input.

The steps indicated by the gray circles in diagram 5.2 physically retrieve data from an object in the database. Such steps are called **access paths:**

- Step 2 reads all the rows of the suplr_mstr table.
- Step 3 performs an Index Range Scan on the country table, to find the ROWID's of the rows in the country table matching the condition specified in the WHERE clause. idx_country is an index defined on the country table which has country_name as its key-field. This index is **not a unique index** and hence a Range Scan is performed on the table.

Steps indicated by clear circles operate on **data row sources:**

- Step 1 performs a filter operation receiving row sources from Steps 2 and 3, eliminating rows from Step 2 based on the presence of a corresponding row in Step 3, and returning the remaining rows to the requestor.

Note:	*The steps of the query execution plan are **not performed** exactly in the order in which they are numbered. The RDBMS engine first performs the steps that are associated with the access paths appear as shaded nodes in the graphical representation in diagram 5.2. The data rows returned by the access paths are then returned to each parent step. Then the RDBMS engine performs the parent steps.*

On many occasions parent steps require only a single data row from the access paths before they complete execution. For such a parent step, the RDBMS engine executes the parent step the rest of the execution plan **as soon as** a single row has been returned from the child step.

Some parent steps require all data rows from their child steps before they can complete execution. In such a case, the RDBMS engine **cannot perform** the parent step until **all data rows** have been returned from the child step. Such parent steps can include sorts, sort-merge joins, and group functions or aggregates.

The Explain Plan Command

An EXPLAIN PLAN statement can be included with an ANSI SQL SELECT statement to determine what its access paths are. The **access path /s** of an SQL SELECT statement is the order of operations, used by the RDBMS engine when executing any ANSI SQL, DML.

The EXPLAIN PLAN statement uses a table called PLAN_TABLE, in which data generated by EXPLAIN PLAN is stored. Once data is created and stored by the EXPLAIN PLAN statement, the PLAN_TABLE must be queried **manually** to analyze and understand the query access path /s.

Note:	*All RDBMS products provide a script file to create the PLAN_TABLE. Although the name of the file is system dependent, it is probably called utlxplan.sql. This script must be run first to caret the PLAN_TABLE and only then should the EXPLAIN PLAN statement be used.*

Example:

EXPLAIN PLAN SET statement_id = 's1' INTO PLAN_TABLE FOR

SELECT suplrname, city FROM suplr_mstr WHERE city NOT IN (SELECT city FROM country

WHERE countryname = 'India');

Here the results of the SELECT query are **not shown** because the **purpose** of the EXPLAIN PLAN statement is **not to display** the output of a query, but to **analyze how the SELECT query executes**.

What follows is a SELECT statement which displays information from PLAN_TABLE in an easy-to-read format.

SELECT lpad(' ',2*(level-1))||OPERATION||' '|| OPTIONS "QUERY PLAN", OBJECT_NAME

FROM plan_table START WITH id = 0 AND statement_id = '&statement_id'

CONNECT BY prior id = parent_id AND statement_id = statement_id

The output of the above SELECT statement from PLAN_TABLE with reference to the example above is as shown in Table 5.2:

QUERY PLAN	OBJECT_NAME
SELECT STATEMENT	
FILTER	
TABLE ACCESS FULL	SUPLR_MSTR
INDEX RANGE SCAN	IDX_COUNTRY

Table 5.2

The query traverses the tree-structured data created in PLAN_TABLE.

Line 1 uses the LPAD function to indent the records returned, based on their level in the tree. The LEVEL pseudo-column contains the depth of the record within the tree structure. The OPERATION column contains the operation performed by the execution step. When present, the OPTIONS column contains the options of the operations.

Referring to the above example, OPERATIONS would be INDEX, TABLE ACCESS, FILTER, SELECT STATEMENT, whereas OPTIONS would be RANGE SCAN and FULL. It also provides an alias for the calculated column and returns the OBJECT_NAME column containing the database object the operation effects. In this particular case, the objects effected are idx_country (**i.e.** an index) and Suplr_Mstr (**i.e.** a base table).

Line 2 contains the FROM clause specifying the PLAN_TABLE as the source of data.

The CONNECT BY PRIOR statement in **Line 3,** and the START WITH clause in **Line 2** are used to navigate the tree-structure. The &STATEMENT_ID substitution variable contained in **Line 2** allows the user to specify a statement to query.

Caution: *When attempting to understand query optimization of a generic ANSI SQL SELECT, the query optimization must be understood with reference to a specific RDBMS product. This is because all RDBMS products* ***do not*** *implement query optimization in exactly the same way.*

However, that there is no huge difference in the way RDBMS engines perform query optimization. Since most Universities chose ***Oracle*** *as the RDBMS product while studying database management systems, all further information on query optimization contained in this chapter is strictly bound to the Oracle RDBMS product from Oracle Corporation.*

Oracle's Approaches To Optimization

To choose an execution plan for an SQL statement, the Oracle's query optimizer uses one of these two approaches:

Approach	Description
Rule-based	Using the rule-based approach, the query optimizer chooses an execution plan based on a default set of rules built into the query optimizer. Additionally, the Oracle **D**ata**B**ase **A**dministrator (**i.e.** the DBA) has the power to manually modify the default set of rules of the query optimizer to fit the behavior and technical specifications of the server hardware used by the Database Engine.
Cost-based	Using the cost-based approach, the query optimizer considers various table data access paths available and determines which access path is most efficient based on statistics in the data dictionary for the table/s accessed by the statement and their associated clusters and indexes. It then builds its query execution plan based on this information. The cost-based approach also considers **hints**, (or optimization suggestions) directly embedded within an ANSI SQL statement. A programmer is responsible for embedding appropriate hints within the ANSI SQL statement. This is because the programmer who writes the ANSI SQL statement most likely knows the hardware and behavior of the database Server intimately on which the query will execute.

Table 5.3

The Rule-Based Approach

The rule-based approach chooses query execution plans based on **heuristically** ranked operations. If there is more than one way to execute an SQL statement, the rule-based approach always uses an operation with the lower rank.

In most cases, operations with the **lower rank execute faster** than those associated with constructs of a higher rank.

The following, is a list of access paths and their associated ranks:

Rank	Access Path
1	Single row by ROWID
2	Single row by cluster join
3	Single row by hash cluster key with unique or primary key
4	Single row by unique or primary key
5	Cluster join
6	Hash cluster key
7	Indexed cluster key
8	Composite index
9	Single-column indexes
10	Bounded range search on indexed columns
11	Unbounded range search on indexed columns
12	Sort-merge join
13	MAX or MIN of indexed column
14	ORDER BY on indexed columns
15	Full table scan

Table 5.4

Basic Access Methods

Full Table Scan

A full table scan retrieves all rows from a table. To perform a full table scan, ORACLE reads all rows in a table, examining each row to determine whether it satisfies the query's WHERE clause. ORACLE reads every data block allocated to a table sequentially, so a full table scan can be performed very efficiently using multi-block reads. ORACLE reads each data block only once.

This access path is available for any ANSI SQL SELECT statement, regardless of the conditions specified in its WHERE clause.

Example:

```
SELECT * FROM suplr_mstr;
```

Table Access by ROWID

A table access by ROWID retrieves data rows from a table. The ROWID of a row specifies the **data file** and **data block** containing the row and the location of the actual **data row** in the data block. Locating a row by its ROWID is the fastest way for ORACLE to find a single row.

To access a table by ROWID, ORACLE first obtains the ROWIDs of the selected rows, either from the statement's WHERE clause **or** through an index scan of one or more of the table's indexes. ORACLE then locates each selected row on the Server's hard disk based on its ROWID.

Retrieval of a **Single Row** by the ROWID access path is only possible if the SELECT statement's WHERE clause identifies the selected rows **by ROWID**.

Example:

SELECT * FROM suplr_mstr WHERE ROWID = '00000DC5.0000.0001';

Index Scans

An index scan retrieves data from an index based on the value of one or more columns of the index. To perform an index scan, ORACLE searches the indexed column for values which are demanded by the ANSI SQL SELECT statement WHERE clause. If the SELECT statement accesses user data which is contained in the columns of the index, ORACLE reads the indexed column values directly, rather than use the index and then link to table data and read it from there.

In addition to each indexed value, an index also contains the ROWIDs of data rows in the table containing the same data values. Hence, if the SELECT statement accesses other data columns in addition to the indexed columns, ORACLE then locates the data rows in the base table using ROWID values and subsequently reads the data required directly from the base table.

An index scan can be one of these types:

Unique	A scan of a unique index returns only a single ROWID. ORACLE performs a unique scan if there is a unique or primary key index available for the column /s mentioned in the WHERE clause of the Select statement. This guarantees that the ANSI SQL SELECT statement accesses only a single row in the base table.
Range	A range scan of an index can return one or more ROWIDs depending on how many rows are being accessed by the range specified in the WHERE clause of the ANSI SQL SELECT statement.

Table 5.5

Example:

SELECT * FROM Suplr_Mstr WHERE SuplrNo = 1;

In the above example, ORACLE performs a scan on the primary key (i.e. SuplrNo is the primary key columns) retrieves a single ROWID from the primary key index and then accesses base table data on the Server's hard disk using that ROWID.

Choosing Access Paths

The query optimizer needs to make several choices when formulating its execution plan on **how** to retrieve base table data. For any row in any table accessed by an ANSI SQL SELECT query, there may be many access paths by which that row can be accessed and retrieved from the hard disk drive. The optimizer chooses **one** access path using:

The Cost-Based Approach

Conceptually, the cost-based approach consists of the following steps:

- The query optimizer generates a **set** of **potential** execution plans for the ANSI SQL SELECT statements based on **available access paths** and **any hints** included in the SELECT statement
- The query optimizer **estimates the cost** of each execution plan based on the statistics of data distribution and storage characteristics for the tables, clusters and indexes in the data dictionary
- The cost is an estimated value proportional to the **expected elapsed time** needed to execute the ANSI SQL statement using the execution plan
- The optimizer calculates the cost based on the estimated use of computer resources (including but not limited to) such as I/O, CPU cycles, and memory (RAM) required to execute the statement using the plan. Execution plans with greater costs take more time to execute than those with smaller costs
- The optimizer compares the costs of the execution plans and chooses the one with the smallest cost.

By default, the goal of the cost-based approach is the best throughput, **or** minimal elapsed time necessary to process all rows accessed by the ANSI SQL SELECT statement. ORACLE can also optimize a statement with the goal of best response time, **or** minimal elapsed time necessary to process only the **first row** accessed by an ANSI SQL statement.

Statistics Used For The Cost-Based Approach

The cost-based approach uses statistics to estimate the cost of each execution plan. These statistics quantify the data distribution and storage characteristics of tables, column and indexes. Using these statistics, the optimizer estimates how much I/O, CPU time and memory are required to execute an SQL statement using a particular execution plan.

The statistics are visible through the following data dictionary views:

- USER_TABLES, ALL_TABLES, and DBA_TABLES
- USER_TAB_COLUMNS, ALL_TAB_COLUMNS, and DBA_TAB_COLUMNS
- USER_INDEXES, ALL_INDEXES, and DBA_INDEXES
- USER_CLUSTERS and DBA_CLUSTERS

Choosing An Optimization Approach And Goal

The Oracle query optimizer's behavior when choosing an optimization approach and goal for an ANSI SQL SELECT statement is affected by these factors:

- The OPTIMIZER_MODE initialization parameter
- Statistics in the data dictionary
- The OPTIMIZER_GOAL parameter of the ALTER SESSION command
- Hints embedded in the ANSI SQL query statement

Optimizer_Mode Initialization Parameter

This parameter establishes the **default** behavior for choosing an optimization approach by the Oracle database engine. This parameter can have these values:

COST	This value causes the query optimizer to choose between the rule based approach and the cost based approach for an ANSI SQL SELECT statement based on the presence of statistics for the tables accessed by the statement or not. If the data dictionary contains statistics for at least **one** of these tables, the query optimizer uses the cost-based approach. This is the **default** value for the parameter.
RULE	This value causes the query optimizer to choose the rule-based approach for all ANSI SQL SELECT statements issued to the Oracle RDBMS engine regardless of the presence of statistics.

Table 5.6

Note: *If the query optimizer is using the cost-based approach for deciding on a query execution plan for an ANSI SQL SELECT statement and some tables accessed y the statement have no statistics, the optimizer uses internal information such as the number of data blocks allocated to these tables and then estimates other statistics for these tables.*

Optimizer_Goal Parameter

This parameter of the ALTER SESSION command can override the optimization approach and goal established in the OPTIMIZER_MODE initialization parameter for an individual session. This parameter can have these values:

CHOOSE	This value causes the query optimizer to choose between the rule-based approach and the cost-based approach for an ANSI SQL SELECT statement based on the presence of statistics for the tables accessed by the statement. If the data dictionary contains statistics for at least one of these tables, the optimizer uses the cost-based approach and optimizes with the goal of best throughput. If the data dictionary contains no statistics for any of these tables, the optimizer uses the rule-based approach.
ALL_ROWS	This value causes the optimizer to use the cost-based approach for all ANSI SQL SELECT statements in the session regardless of the presence of statistics and to optimize with a goal of best throughput.
FIRST_ROWS	This value causes the optimizer to use the cost-based approach for all ANSI SQL SELECT statements in the session regardless of the presence of statistics and to optimize with a goal of best response time.
RULE	This value causes the optimizer to use the rule-based approach for all ANSI SQL SELECT statements in a session regardless of the presence of statistics.

Table 5.7

The value of this parameter does affect the optimization of ANSI SQL SELECT statements issued by stored procedures and functions called during the session, and it does not affect the optimization of recursive ANSL SQL SELECT statements that ORACLE issues during the session.

The optimization for recursive ANSI SQL SELECT statements is only affected by the value of the OPTIMIZER_MODE initialization parameter. When the optimizer uses the cost-based approach for recursive ANSI SQL SELECT statements, the goal is **always best throughput**.

The FIRST_ROWS, ALL_ROWS, and RULE hints can override the effects of the OPTIMIZER_MODE initialization parameter and the OPTIMIZER_GOAL parameter of the ALTER SESSION command for an individual ANSI SQL SELECT statement.

Passing Hints To The Query Optimizer

Hints are suggestions given to the query optimizer for optimizing an ANSI SQL SELECT statement. Hints allow the programmer to make decisions usually made by the query optimizer.

Hints can be used to specify the:

- Optimization approach for an ANSI SQL SELECT statement
- Goal of the cost-based approach for an ANSI SQL SELECT statement
- Access path for a table accessed by the statement
- Join order for a join statement

Hints are passed to the query optimizer inside **comments**. When a hint is passed to the query optimizer, it attempts to change the query execution plan of the ANSI SQL SELECT statement based on the hint.

Syntax

/*+hint text*/

+	Is a **plus sign** that causes ORACLE to interpret the comments as a list of hints. The plus sign must follow immediately after the comment delimiter (**no space** is permitted).
hint	Is one of the hints provided by ORACLE (refer to table 5.9). If the comment contains multiple hints, each hint must be separated from the other by at least one space.
text	Is other commenting text that can be interspersed within the hints.

Table 5.8

If hints are specified incorrectly, the ORACLE engine ignores them, **but does not return an error**.

- ORACLE ignores hints if the comment containing them does not follow a DELETE, SELECT, or UPDATE keyword.
- ORACLE ignores hints containing syntax errors, **but considers** other correctly specified hints within the same comments.

It's in cost based query optimization that the query optimizer only recognizes hints. If a programmer has included a hint in a statement block, the optimizer automatically uses the cost-based approach to query optimization.

A statement block can have only **one comment**, containing hints. The comment containing hints can only be used with SELECT, UPDATE, or DELETE ANSI SQL keyword not with an INSERT.

A list of hints, which can be passed to the query optimizer are shown in table 5.9:

HINT	DESCRIPTION
all_rows	Optimize the statement for the best total throughput.
and_equal	Use index merging on the specified table
cluster	Use a cluster scan
cost	Use cost-based optimization
first_row	Optimize the SQL statement for best response time.
full	Use a full table scan on the specified table.
hash	Use a hash search on the specified table.
index	Use the specified index on te specified table.
index_asc	Use the specified index in ascending order.
index_desc	Use the specified index in descending order.
ordered	Use the join sequence from the FROM clause.
rowid	Use the ROWID access method.
rule	Use rule-based optimization.
user_merge	Use sort-merge join techniques on the specified table.
use_nl	Use nested-loop join techniques on the specified table.

Table 5.9

Each hint described in table 5.9 suggests an access method for a table. Specifying one of these hints causes the query optimizer to choose the specified access path **only if** an access path is available based on the existence of an index or cluster index associated with the ANSI SQL constructs.

Note: *After hints the statement block are provided to the query optimizer, EXPLAIN PLAN can be used to determine how the execution of the ANSI SQL statement changed because of the hint.*

Example:

SELECT suplrname, city FROM suplr_mstr WHERE city NOT IN(SELECT /*+ Full(country) */ city

FROM country WHERE countryname = 'India');

When the above ANSI SQL SELECT query is being executed, **assume** that a unique index exists on **city** bound to the **country** table. Normally, the query optimizer would perform a unique index scan to process the nested query. But since a hint (/*+Full(country) */) is specified, the query optimizer will now perform a **full table scan** on the country table.

The INDEX Hint

An INDEX hint explicitly point to an index scan for a specified table. This hint may optionally specify one or more indexes:

- If this hint specifies a single available index, the query optimizer performs a scan on this index. The query optimizer does not consider a full table scan or a scan on any other index bound to the table.

- If a hint specifies multiple indexes, the query optimizer considers the cost of a data scan on each index in the list. Then performs the index scan with the lowest cost. The query optimizer may also choose to scan multiple indexes from this list and merge the results, if such an access path **has the lowest cost** to acquire the requestor's table data.
- If a hint specifies no indexes, the query optimizer considers the cost of a scan on each available index on the table. Then performs the index scan with the lowest cost. The query optimizer may also choose to scan multiple indexes and merge the results, if such an access path has the lowest cost to acquire the requestor's table data. The query optimizer **does not consider** a full table scan.

Example:

SELECT suplrname, pincode, phone FROM suplr_mstr WHERE city = 'Mumbai';

This query selects the supplier name, pincode, and phone number from the supplier master table.

Assume that there is an index on the **city** column and that this column contains the values Mumbai and Delhi.

If there are equal number of Mumbai and Delhi suppliers, the ANSI SQL SELECT query will return a relatively large percentage of the table's rows and a **full table scan** is likely to be **faster** than the index scan.

However, if a very small percentage of the suppliers are from Mumbai, the query returns a very small percentage of the table's rows and an index scan is likely to be faster than a full table scan.

The cost-based approach assumes that each value has an equal probability of appearing in each row. For a column having two distinct values, the query optimizer assumes each value appears in 50% of the rows, so the cost based approach is **likely to choose a full table scan** rather than an **index scan**.

If the programmer knows that the value in the WHERE clause of the ANSI SQL SELECT query appears in a very small percentage of the rows, an INDEX hint can be used to force the query optimizer to choose an INDEX scan.

```
SELECT /*+INDEX(suplr_mstr city_index) */ suplrname, pincode, phone FROM suplr_mstr
    WHERE city = 'Mumbai';
```

In Conclusion

These are the basics of query optimization. To strengthen these concepts self review questions follow immediately along with their solutions.

Self Review Questions

Fill In The Blanks

1. A __________ is an ANSI SQL command given to an RDBMS engine, telling it to retrieve certain specified table data.
2. A part of the RDBMS engine, called the __________ __________, chooses one from the many ways in which ANSI SQL statements can be executed.
3. ______________ is an important step in the processing of any ANSI SQL statement.
4. The ANSI SQL statement issued from the client using SQL*Plus is picked up by __________.
5. A place in the Server's memory where all queries reside is called __________ __________ __________.
6. Writing optimized queries helps the commercial application to run most __________.
7. The combination of all steps followed by the query optimizer to execute an ANSI SQL statement is called its query __________ __________.
8. A set of rows returned by a step is called a ________ ________ ________.
9. Parent steps include ________, ________ ________, and group functions or aggregates.
10. The ________ ________ statement can be included with an ANSI SQL statement to determine its access path.
11. The ________ path /s of an SQL statement is the order of operations, used by the RDBMS engine when executing any ANSI SQL statement.
12. The EXPLAIN PLAN statement uses a table called __________, in which data generated by EXPLAIN PLAN is stored.
13. The name of the script file to create the PLAN_TABLE is system dependent, and is usually called __________.
14. Using the __________ approach, the query optimizer chooses an execution plan based on a default set of rules built into the query optimizer.
15. The __________ approach also considers hints, (or optimization suggestions) directly embedded within an ANSI SQL statement.
16. If there is more than one way to execute an SQL statement, the rule-based approach always uses an operation with the ________ rank.
17. A ________ ________ scan retrieves all rows from a table.
18. ORACLE reads every data block allocated to a table sequentially, so a full table scan can be performed very efficiently using __________ reads.
19. The ROWID of a row specifies the ________ ________ and ________ ________ containing the row and the location of the actual data row in the data block.

20 The Single Row by ROWID access path is only available if the Select statement's WHERE clause identifies the selected rows by ________.

21. An __________ __________ retrieves data from an index based on the value of one or more columns of the index.

22. A ________ scan of an index can return one or more ROWIDs.

23. The cost is an estimated value proportional to the _________ _________ _________ needed to execute the ANSI SQL statement using the execution plan.

24 By default, the goal of the ____________ approach is the best throughput, or minimal elapsed time necessary to process all rows accessed by the ANSI SQL statement.

25. The _____________ approach uses statistics to estimate the cost of each execution plan.

26. The _____________ initialization parameter establishes the default behavior for choosing an optimization approach by the Oracle database engine.

27. The _________ value in the OPTIMIZER_MODE initialization parameter causes the query optimizer to choose between the rule based approach and the cost based approach for an ANSI SQL statement based on the presence of statistics for the tables accessed by the statement.

28. The _________ value causes the query optimizer to choose the rule-based approach for all ANSI SQL statements issued to the Oracle RDBMS engine regardless of the presence of statistics.

29. The ________________ parameter of the ALTER SESSION command can override the optimization approach.

30. In a OPTIMIZER_GOAL Parameter, the ___________ value causes the optimizer to use the rule-based approach for all ANSI SQL statements in a session regardless of the presence of statistics.

31. A statement block can have only ________ comment, containing hints.

True Or False

32. ANSI SQL queries are the less frequently used type of SQL statements.

33. Most RDBMS engines give the highest priority to controlling computer resources used for executing queries. The ANSI SQL statement issued from the client using SQL*Plus is picked up by SQL *Net.

34. The query is picked up by the RDBMS parser and is segmented by the parser into four parts.

35. User data resides outside the tables.

36. It is the RDBMS's query optimizer that automatically decides on the best way to retrieve user data from the table /s specified in the ANSI SQL query.

37. When fully optimized queries are fired against the RDBMS engine and executed on the RDBMS Server they consume maximum Server resources.

38. Each of these steps either physically retrieves rows of data from a database/table or manipulates the retrieved data for the requestor.
39. An understanding of how the built-in query optimizer of the DBMS engine works will provide a means to writing efficient queries.
40. The RDBMS's tables reside on the Server's hard disk drive.
41. Each step of the execution plan returns columns.
42. The RDBMS engine cannot perform the parent step until all rows have been returned from the child step.
43. The EXPLAIN PLAN statement cannot be included with an ANSI SQL statement.
44. The access path /s of an SQL statement is the order of operations, used by the RDBMS engine when executing any ANSI SQL statement.
45. The results of the query plan are shown in SQL*Plus because the purpose of the EXPLAIN PLAN statement is to display the results of the query, but to analyze its execution.
46. Once data is created and stored by the EXPLAIN PLAN statement, the PLAN_TABLE gets queried automatically.
47. Using the rule-based approach, the query optimizer chooses an execution plan based on a default set of rules built into the query optimizer.
48. All RDBMS products implement query optimization in exactly the same way.
49. Using the rule-based approach, the query optimizer considers various table data access paths available and determines which access path is most efficient.
50. A programmer is responsible for embedding appropriate hints within the ANSI SQL statement.
51. If there is more than one way to execute an SQL statement, the rule-based approach always uses an operation with the lower rank.
52. In most cases, operations with the lower rank get executed slowly.
53. A table access by ROWID cannot retrieve rows from a table.
54. Locating a row by its ROWID is the fastest way for ORACLE to find a single row.
55. The Single Row by ROWID access path is only available if the Select statement's WHERE clause identifies the selected rows by ROW COUNT.
56. If the statement accesses only columns of the index, ORACLE reads the indexed column values directly from the index, rather than from the table.
57. In a OPTIMIZER_GOAL Parameter, the ALL_ROWS value causes the optimizer to use the cost-based approach for all ANSI SQL statements in the session regardless of the presence of statistics and to optimize with a goal of best throughput.
58. In a OPTIMIZER_GOAL Parameter, the RULE value causes the optimizer to use the rule-based approach for all ANSI SQL statements in a session regardless of the presence of statistics.

59. The optimization for recursive SQL statements is not affected by the value of the OPTIMIZER_MODE initialization parameter.
60. ORACLE ignores hints containing syntax errors, but considers other correctly specified hints within the same comments.

Objective Questions

1. What is a query?
2. What is query optimization?
3. Describe with a simple example how a query is executed?
4. What is Rule based and Cost based optimization?
5. What is a Hint when used with a query?
6. How is a Hint used with a query?

6. Transaction Management

Oracle Transactions

A series of one or more SQL statements that are logically related **or** a series of operations performed on Oracle table data is termed as a **Transaction**. Oracle treats this logical unit as a single entity. Oracle treats changes to table data as a two-step process. First, the changes requested are done. To make these changes **permanent** a **COMMIT** statement has to be given at the SQL prompt. A **ROLLBACK** statement given at the SQL prompt can be used to **undo** a part of **or** the entire transaction.

A transaction begins with the **first** executable SQL statement after a **commit, rollback** or **connection** made to the Oracle engine. All changes made to an Oracle table data via a transaction are made or undone at one instance.

Specifically, a transaction is a group of events that occur between any of the following events:

- Connecting to Oracle
- Disconnecting from Oracle
- Committing changes to the database table
- Rollback

Closing Transactions

A transaction can be closed by using either a **commit** or a **rollback** statement. By using these statements, table data can be changed **or** all the changes made to the table data undone.

Using COMMIT

A **COMMIT** ends the current transaction and makes permanent any changes made during the transaction. All transactional locks acquired on tables are released.

Syntax:

```
COMMIT;
```

Using ROLLBACK:

A **ROLLBACK** does exactly the opposite of **COMMIT**. It ends the transaction but undoes any changes made during the transaction. All transactional locks acquired on tables are released.

Syntax:

```
ROLLBACK [WORK] [TO [SAVEPOINT] <SavePointName>];
```

where,

WORK	Is optional and is provided for ANSI compatibility
SAVEPOINT	Is optional and is used to rollback a transaction partially, as far as the specified savepoint
SAVEPOINTNAME	Is a savepoint created during the current transaction

Creating A SAVEPOINT

SAVEPOINT marks and saves the current point in the processing of a transaction. When a **SAVEPOINT** is used with a **ROLLBACK** statement, parts of a transaction can be undone. An active **SAVEPOINT** is one that is specified since the last **COMMIT** or **ROLLBACK**.

Syntax:

```
SAVEPOINT <SavePointName>;
```

ROLLBACK can be fired from the SQL prompt **with or without** the **SAVEPOINT** clause. The implication of each is described below.

A **ROLLBACK** operation performed **without** the **SAVEPOINT** clause amounts to the following:

- Ends the transaction
- Undoes all the changes in the current transaction
- Erases all savepoints in that transaction
- Releases the transactional locks

A **ROLLBACK** operation performed **with** the **TO SAVEPOINT** clause amounts to the following:

- A predetermined portion of the transaction is rolled back
- Retains the save point rolled back to, but loses those created after the named savepoint
- Releases all transactional locks that were acquired since the savepoint was taken

The Concept Of ANSI SQL Transactions

A transaction is a single unit of work done by an RDBMS engine under user instructions. The unit of work usually accesses and possibly updates the data in various tables. For a transaction to be deemed successful it must leave the database in a **consistent** state.

During actual time when transaction is executing the database may be inconsistent. However, when a transaction is committed, the data within the database returns to its consistent state.

There are **two** main concerns that must be dealt with during any transaction.

1) **Failures** of various kinds, such as hardware and/or a system crash during transaction execution.
2) **Concurrent** execution of transactions fired by multiple users to the RDBMS engine.

ACID Properties

To preserve the integrity of table data during any transaction, the RDBMS engine must ensure:

Atomicity Of The Transaction

All operations of a transaction are correctly reflected in the database or none are reflected in the database (**i.e.** the transaction is automatically rolled back).

Consistency Of The Transaction

All transactions must execute in isolation which helps preserves the consistency of the transaction, thus the consistency of the database.

Isolation Of The Transaction

Although multiple transactions may execute concurrently, each transaction must be completely unaware of other concurrently executing transactions. Intermediate transaction results must be hidden from other concurrently executing transactions.

Durability Of The Transaction

After a transaction completes successfully, the changes made to the database **must persist**, inspite of system failures.

Example Of Funds Transfer

A transaction to transfer INR500 from bank account A to bank account B:

1. **read**(A)
2. A:= A-500
3. **write**(A)
4. **read**(B)
5. B:= B+500
6. **write**(B)

Consistency Requirement

The individual values of account A and account B are **changed** by the execution of this transaction only if both read / write operations are successful.

Atomicity Requirement

If the transaction fails after step 3 and before step 6, the RDBMS should ensure that none of the updates are reflected in the database, otherwise the database will be inconsistent.

Durability Requirement

Once the user has been notified that the transaction has completed (**i.e.** the transfer of the INR500 has taken place form account A to account B), the updates to the database by the transaction **must persist** despite failures of any kind.

Isolation Requirement

If between steps 3 and 6, another transaction is allowed to access the partially updated database, it will see an inconsistent database (the sum A+B will be different from what it should be).

This can be ensured at a very cheap cost by running transactions **serially**, (**i.e.** one after the other). However, executing multiple transactions concurrently has significant benefits.

Transaction States

Active

This is the state of any transaction while it executes.

Partially committed

This is the state a transaction reaches after the final ANSI SQL statement of the transaction block has been executed. The memory buffers have been updated but they have not yet been written out to the hard disk.

Failed

This is the state a transaction reaches after the RDBMS engine discovers that normal execution of the transaction can no longer proceed for any reason whatsoever.

Aborted

This is the status of a transaction after the transaction has been rolled back and the database restored to its original state prior to the start of the transaction.

There are two options available to the RDBMS engine after a transaction has aborted:

- Restart the transaction – (only if there has been no internal logical error)

Or

- Kill the transaction

Committed

The state of a transaction after its successful completion and all changes have to be written to database tables.

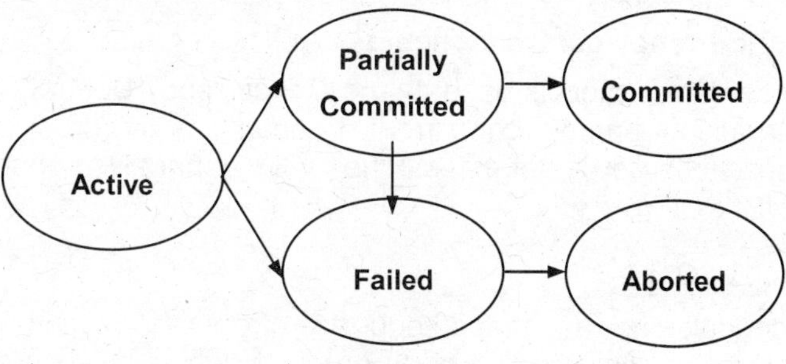

Diagram 6.1

Diagram 6.1 displays all the states of an ANSI SQL transaction fired against an RDBMS engine.

Implementation - Atomicity & Durability

The **Recovery Manager**, an internal component of all RDBMS engines implements the atomicity and durability of all ANSI SQL transactions.

A shadow database schema for query transaction execution:

- Assume that only one transaction is active at a time
- A pointer called **db pointer** always points to the current consistent copy of the database
- All updates are made on a **shadow copy** of the database held in memory. The **db pointer** is made to point to the updated shadow copy only after the transaction reaches its partial commit and all updated pages have been flushed to hard disk redo log buffers

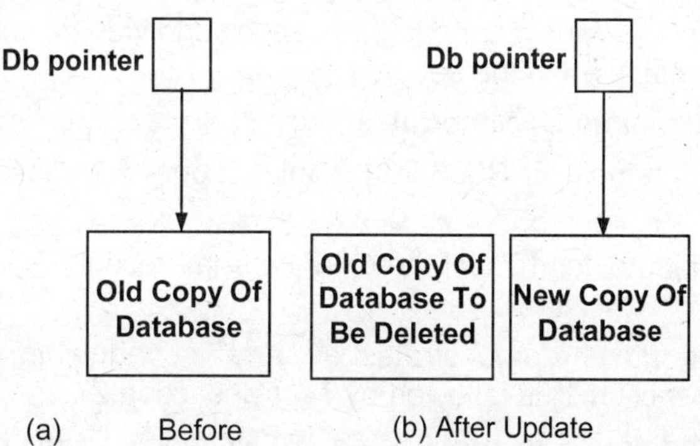

Diagram 6.2

- In case the transaction fails, the old, but consistent, copy pointed out by **db pointer** can be reused, and the shadow copy is deleted.
- This approach assumes that hard disks do not fail
- Is fairly useful technique when used with **text editors**, but extremely inefficient for large databases. This is because executing a single transaction requires copying the entire database into memory.

Concurrent Transactions

Multiple transactions can be allowed to run concurrently in the system. The advantages are:

- Increased processor and hard disk utilization, leading to better transaction throughput. **i.e.** One transaction can be using the CPU while another is being read from or written to the hard disk.
- Reduced average response time for transactions. Short transactions need not wait behind long ones.

Concurrency control schemes

These are protocols used by the **C**oncurrency **C**ontrol **M**anager (CCM) of an RDBMS to control interaction among concurrent transactions in order to prevent them from destroying the consistency of a database. The CCM generally produces a schedule for the execution of an ANSI SQL query.

Schedules

Schedules are a planned sequence of operations, carried out by the CCM of the RDBMS which determine the chronological order in which the operations of concurrent transactions are executed.

- A schedule for a **set** of transactions must consist of **all** instructions of those transactions
- The schedule must preserve the **order** in which the instructions appear in each individual transaction belonging to the set

An Example Of Schedules

Let **T_1** transfer INR500 from bank account A to bank account B.

Let **T_2** transfer 10% of the balance from account A to account B.

Schedule 1 demonstrates a **serial** schedule in which **T_1** (transaction 1) is followed by **T_2** (transaction 2).

Schedule 2 is **not a serial** schedule, but does the **equivalent** to Schedule 1.

In both Schedules 1 and 2, even though the transaction does not run serially the essence of the transaction remains exactly the same. The bank account A is depleted correctly and the bank account B is increased correctly.

T_1	T_2
read(A)	
A:= A- 500	
write(A)	
read(B)	
B:= B+ 500	
write(B)	
	read(A)
	temp:= A* 0.1;
	A:= A- temp
	write(A)
	read(B)
	B:= B+ temp
	write(B)

Schedule 1

Schedule 3, which follows, a concurrent schedule, but **does not** preserve the serializability of the transaction.

Serializability

The basic assumption is that each transaction preserves database consistency. Thus serial execution of a set of transactions preserves database consistency. A concurrent schedule is serializable if it is exactly the equivalent of a serial schedule.

Different forms of scheduling gives rise to the notions of:

1. Conflict of serializability
2. View of serializability

Simplified schedules consist of only **read** and **write** instructions.

Those Transactions which perform arbitrary computations on data in local buffers in between reads and writes are ignored.

Conflict Serializability

Instructions Ii and Ij, of transactions Ti and Tj respectively, conflict only if there exists some item Q accessed by both Ii and Ij, and at least one of these instructions wrote Q.

Ii = **read**(Q), Ij = **read**(Q). Ii and Ij do not conflict.

Ii = **read**(Q), Ij = **write**(Q). They conflict.

Ii = **write**(Q), Ij = **read**(Q). They conflict.

Ii = **write**(Q), Ij = **write**(Q). They conflict.

Intuitively, a conflict between Ii and Ij forces a (logical) temporal order between them. If Ii and Ij are consecutive in a schedule and they do not conflict, their results would remain the same even if they had been interchanged in the schedule.

Thus if a schedule S can be transformed into a schedule Z by a series of swaps of non-conflicting instructions, then S and Z are conflict equivalent.

Schedule S is conflict serializable if it is conflict equivalent to a serial schedule.

Example of a schedule that is **not** conflict serializable:

Swapping instructions in Schedule 4 to obtain either the serial schedule <T_3, T_4>, or the serial schedule <T_4, T_3> is **not** possible.

T_1	T_2
read(A)	
A:= A- 500	
write(A)	
	read(A)
	temp:= A* 0.1;
	A:= A- temp
	write(A)
read(B)	
B:= B+ 500	
write(B)	
	read(B)
	B:= B+ temp
	write(B)

Schedule 2

T_1	T_2
read(A)	
A:= A- 500	
	read(A)
	temp:= A* 0.1;
	A:= A- temp
	write(A)
	read(B)
write(A)	
read(B)	
B:= B+ 500	
write(B)	
	B:= B+ temp
	write(B)

Schedule 3

Schedule 5 below can be transformed into Schedule 1, a serial schedule where T2 follows T1, by a series of swaps of non-conflicting instructions.

T_3	T_4
read(Q)	
	write(Q)
write(Q)	

Schedule 4

T_1	T_2
read(A)	
write(A)	
	read(A)
	write(A)
read(B)	A:= A- temp
write(B)	
	read(B)
	write(B)

Schedule 5

Recoverability

Is the need to address the effect of ANSI SQL transaction failures on concurrently running transactions.

Recoverable Schedule

If a transaction Tj reads data items previously written by a transaction Ti, the commit operation of Ti must appear before the commit operation of Tj.

Schedule 6 is **not recoverable** if T_9 commits immediately after the read.

If T_8 should abort, T_9 would have read (and possibly shown to the user) an inconsistent database state. Hence RDBMS engines must ensure that ANSI SQL, transaction schedules, are recoverable.

T_8	T_9
read(A)	
write(A)	
	read(A)
read(B)	

Schedule 6

Cascading Rollback

A single transaction failure can lead to a series of transaction rollbacks. Consider the following schedule where none of the transactions have yet been committed (so the schedule is recoverable).

In Schedule 7, if T_{10} fails, T_{11} and T_{12} must also be rolled back.

T_{10}	T_{11}	T_{12}
read(A)		
read(B)		
write(A)		
	read(A)	
	write(A)	
		read(A)

Schedule 7

Cascadeless Schedules

Cascading rollbacks cannot occur for each pair of transactions Ti and Tj such that Tj reads a data item previously written by Ti, since the commit operation of Ti appears before the read operation of Tj.

Every a cascadeless schedule must also be recoverable. It is a good idea to restrict transaction schedules to those that are cascadeless.

Transaction schedules must be conflict or view serializable, **and** recoverable, for the sake of database consistency. Finally, transaction schedules should preferably be cascadeless.

A policy in which only one transaction can execute at a time generates serial schedules, but provides a poor degree of concurrency.

The **C**oncurrency **C**ontrol **M**anager (CCM), in any RDBMS engine has built in artificial intelligence that trades off between the amount of concurrency allowed and the amount of **overhead** that concurrent transactions incur.

Some CCM schemes allow only conflict-serializable schedules to be generated, while others allow view serializable schedules that are not conflict-serializable.

Transaction Definition In ANSI SQL

ANSI SQL, the table data manipulation language, **must** include a construct for specifying the set of actions that comprise a transaction.

In SQL, a transaction begins implicitly. A transaction in SQL ends by:

- **Commit work** commits the current active transaction and begins a new one
- **Rollback work** causes the current active transaction to abort

Levels of consistency specified by ANSI SQL-92:

- Serializable — default
- Repeatable read
- Read committed
- Read uncommitted

Serializable

Default, all transactions must preserve database consistency.

Repeatable Read

Only committed records can be read, repeated reads of the same record must return the same value.

Read Committed

Only committed records can be read. Successive reads of a record may return different (*but committed*) values.

Read Uncommitted

Even uncommitted records *may be read.*

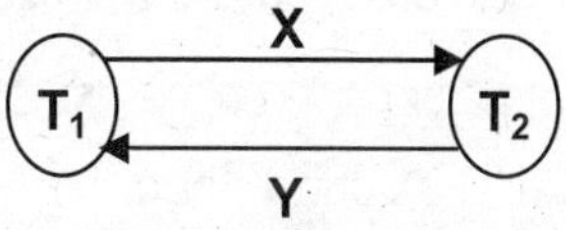

X

T_1 T_2

Y

Diagram 6.3

Testing for Serializability

- Consider some schedules of a set of transactions T_1, T_2, ..., T_n
- Diagram 6.3 Precedence graph, a directed graph where the vertices are the transactions (names)
- Draw an arc from T1 to T5 to check if the two transactions conflict, and Ti accessed the data item on which the conflict arose earlier
- Then label the arc by the item that was accessed

Precedence Graph For Schedule A

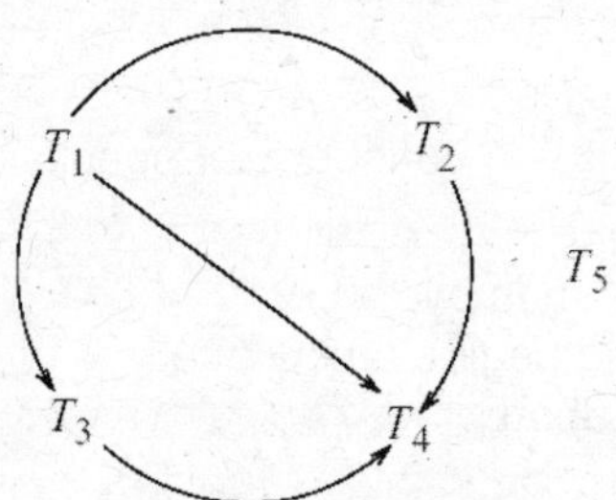

Diagram 6.4

T_1	T_2	T_3	T_4	T_5
read(Y)	read(X)			
read(Z)				
				read(V)
				read(W)
				write(W)
	read(Y)			
	write(Y)			
		write(Z)		
read(U)				
			read(Y)	
			write(Y)	
			read(Z)	
			write(Z)	
read(U)				
write(U)				

Schedule A

A schedule is conflict serializable only if its precedence graph is cyclic.

Cycle-detection algorithms exist which take order $\mathbf{n^2}$ times, where **n** is the number of vertices in the graph. (Better algorithms take order n+e where e is the number of edges).

If the precedence graph is cyclic, the serializability order can be obtained by a topological sorting of the graph.

For example, a serializability order for Schedule A would be $\mathbf{T_5 \rightarrow T_1 \rightarrow T_3 \rightarrow T_2 \rightarrow T_4}$.

Concurrency Control vs. Serializability Tests

Testing a schedule for serializability after it has executed is a little too late.

Goal

To develop concurrency control protocols that will assure serializability.

Concurrency control protocols will generally not examine the precedence graph **as it is** being created. Instead a protocol will impose a set of rules that avoids nonserializable schedules.

Tests for serializability helps understand why a concurrency control protocol is correct.

The real great thing about the Atomicity, Consistency, Isolation, Durability, Scheduling and so on of ANSI SQL transactions is that its all done **automatically** and **transparently** by the built in transaction processor sub-system of the RDBMS engine.

To understand ANSI SQL transactions a few examples have to be worked out. These examples require an RDBMS to execute against.

What Is Concurrency Control

Business data is a very valuable business resource. Business managers who use timely and accurate business data, to make informed business decisions, consistently make profit for a business.

With the advent of networks, Business data perhaps the most valuable of all business resources, needs to be shared just like any other valuable resource.

Prior networking, business data was replicated on every computer used by business managers. This gave rise to a huge amount of redundant (duplicate) data. More importantly, if there was an error in updating data on a computer, the business manager using that computer to make a business decision was definitely misinformed. This could very well lead to erroneous business decisions. This was largely because the updation of business data was a **manual** process prior the existence of networks.

One way to get rid of inconsistent data being handled by a business manger was to treat business data as a centralized resource. This requires business data to be held on a Server where multiple users could access it, **concurrently**.

Once business data is treated as a shared, global resource, its concurrent access by multiple users is mandatory. The RDBMS engine is used as the intermediary between the user who requests for data and the data itself. Hence, its mandatory that all RDBMS engines should deal with **concurrent multiuser requests** for business data held in tables under the RDBMS's control.

For an RDBMS engine to implement multiuser, concurrent, access to business data held within its table's data access rules must be defined. Concurrent data access rules must be simple and straightforward, otherwise implementing concurrent business data access via the RDBMS engine would simply fail.

The Simple Rules For Concurrent Business Data Access are:

1. **Writing** business data to a table must wait for any **Reader** reading the same data to finish first, before getting access to write data.
2. **Writing** table data must wait till all previous data writing processes have c**ompleted writing** their data before getting access to the table.
3. Multiple **Readers** of table data **need not wait** at all.

If these rules are thought through they really are both simple and fair.

Rule 1:

It would make table data inconsistent if table data was changed (i.e. updated) **while** someone was reading the same data.

Rule 2:

It would make no sense at all if two different individuals were permitted to update the same table data at exactly the same time. The RDBMS would simply not be able to decide on whose data must be saved to the table thereby giving rise to data inconsistencies.

Rule 3:

If table data is being read (**i.e.** not changed in any way) then it does not matter how many readers have access the same data block at all.

After these rules for concurrent data access were frozen, a technique was required by which an RDBMS applied these rules to table data.

The technique used by the RDBMS engine is called **Locking**.

RDBMS engines implement a built-in default locking strategy to their table data by implementing lock based protocols on table data.

Lock-Based Protocols

A **lock** is a **mechanism** to **control concurrent access** to an item of data held within a database table.

Data items can be locked in one of two modes:

- Exclusive (**X**) mode: The data item can be both **read** as well as **written** to by the individual who locked it in Exclusive mode. X-locks are requested using **lock-X** instructions built into the RDBMS engine.
- Shared (**S**) mode: The data item can **only be read** (**i.e.** cannot be updated), by the individual who locked it in Shared mode. S-locks are requested using **lock-S** instructions built into the RDBMS engine.

	S	**X**
S	**true**	**false**
X	**false**	**false**

Table 6.1

Lock requests are made to the **C**oncurrency-**C**ontrol **M**anager (CCM), built into the RDBMS engine. A ANSI SQL transaction can proceed **only after** the concurrency-control manager **grants** such requests.

Lock-compatibility Matrix

With reference to the lock-compatibility matrix:

A transaction may be granted a lock on a data item if the requested lock is compatible with locks already held on the item by other transactions. (**i.e. multiple** shared locks can be granted on a data item)

The matrix allows any number of transactions to hold shared locks on a data item, but if any transaction holds an exclusive lock on a data item **no other** transaction may hold any lock on the data item until the exclusive lock is either automatically (or manually) released.

If a lock cannot be granted on a data item due to a lock request incompatibility, (**i.e.** requesting an exclusive lock on a data item already locked exclusively) the requesting transaction is made to wait till all incompatible locks held by other transactions have been released. Only then does the concurrency control manager grant the lock.

T_2:	**lock-S**(A);
	read(A);
	unlock(A);
	lock-S(B);
	read(B);
	unlock(B);
	display(A+B).

Schedule 8

Example of a transaction performing locking:

The above type of locking is not sufficient to guarantee serializability, if A and B get updated in-between the read of A and B, the displayed sum **would be wrong**.

> **Note:** *A locking **protocol** is a **set of rules** followed by all ANSI SQL transactions while requesting and releasing locks.*

Pitfalls Of Lock-Based Protocols

Consider The Following Locking Schedule

Neither T_3 (transaction 3) nor T_4 (transaction 4) can make progress. Executing **lock-S**(B) causes T_4 to wait for T3 to release its lock on B, while executing **lock-X**(A) causes T_3 to wait for T_4 to release its lock on A.

Such a situation is called a **DEADLOCK**. To handle a deadlock either T_3 **or** T_4 must be **rolled back** and its locks released. The potential for a deadlock exists in most locking protocols.

Starvation is also possible if a concurrency control manager is badly designed.

T_3	T_4
lock-X(B)	
read(B)	
B:= B- 500	
write(B)	
	lock-S(A)
	read(A)
	lock-S(B)
lock-X(A)	

Schedule 9

Example:

A transaction may be waiting for an X-lock on an item, while a sequence of other transaction requests are granted a S-lock on the same item. The transaction will be repeatedly rolled back due to deadlocks. The repeated rolling back of a transaction is called starvation.

All concurrency control managers must be designed to **prevent** starvation.

The Two-Phase Locking Protocol

This is a protocol, which tries to ensure that conflict-serializable locking schedules **do not** occur.

Phase 1: Growing Phase

- A transaction may obtain locks
- A transaction may not release locks

Phase 2: Shrinking Phase

- A transaction may release locks
- A transaction may not obtain locks

The two-phase locking protocol assures serializability to a large extent. Two-phase locking **does not** guarantee freedom from deadlocks.

Cascading rollbacks tend to occur under two-phase locking. To avoid this, a modified protocol called **strict** two-phase locking is followed. Here a transaction **must hold all** its **exclusive** locks till it is either committed or aborted.

Rigorous two-phase locking is even stricter. Here **all locks** are held till a transaction is either committed or aborted. Two-phased locking protocol transactions can be serialized in the order in which they are committed.

Automatic Acquisition Of Locks

A transaction Ti issues the standard read/write instruction, without implicit locking calls to the concurrency control manager.

The operation **read**(D) is processed as:

```
if Ti has a lock on D then
    read(D)
else
    begin
        If necessary wait until no other transaction has a
        lock-X on D
        grant Ti a lock-S on D;
        read(D)
    end
end If;
```

by the CCM.

write(D) is processed as:

```
if Ti has a lock-X on D then
    write(D)
else
    begin
        if necessary wait until no other transaction has any lock on D,
        if Ti has a lock-S on D then
            upgrade lock on D to lock-X
        else
            grant Ti a lock-X on D
        write(D)
    end
end if;
```

by the CCM.

All locks (*of any type*) are released after commit or rollback is fired as part of the ANSI SQL transaction.

Intention Lock Modes

Apart from the **S** and **X** lock modes, which is part of the locking protocol, there are three additional lock modes with multiple granularity.

Intention-shared (IS): Indicates explicit locking at a lower level of the tree but only with shared locks.

Intention-exclusive (IX): Indicates explicit locking at a lower level with exclusive or shared locks.

Shared and intention-exclusive (SIX): The sub tree rooted by that node is locked explicitly in shared mode and explicit locking is being done at a lower level with exclusive-mode locks.

Intention locks allow a higher-level node to be locked in S or X mode **without** having to check all descendent nodes.

Compatibility Matrix with Intention Lock Modes

The compatibility matrix for all lock modes is:

	IS	IX	S	SIX	X
IS	✓	✓	✓	✓	**X**
IX	✓	✓	**X**	**X**	**X**
S	✓	**X**	✓	**X**	**X**
SIX	✓	**X**	**X**	**X**	**X**
X	**X**	**X**	**X**	**X**	**X**

Note: ✓= true, and **X** = false

Table 6.2

Multiple Granularity Locking Scheme

Transaction Ti can lock a node Q, using the following rules:

- The lock compatibility matrix must be observed. The root of the tree must be locked first, and may be locked in any mode
- A node Q can be locked by Ti in S or IS mode only if the parent of Q is currently locked by Ti in either IX or IS mode
- A node Q can be locked by Ti in X, or IX mode only if the parent of Q is currently locked by Ti in either X or IX mode
- Ti can lock a node only if it has not previously unlocked any node (that is, Ti is two-phase)
- Ti can unlock a node Q only if none of the children of Q are currently locked by Ti

Note: *Observe that locks are acquired in root-to-leaf order, whereas they are released in leaf-to-root order.*

Deadlock Handling

Consider the following two transactions:

T_1:	**write(X)**	T_2:	**write(Y)**
	write(Y)		**write(X)**

Schedule 10

Schedule with deadlock

T_1	T_2
lock-X on X	
write(X)	
	lock-X on Y
	write(Y)
	wait for **lock-X** on X
wait for **lock-X** on Y	

Schedule 11

The system is deadlocked if there is a set of transactions such that **every** transaction in the set is waiting for another transaction in the set. This will result in all transactions entering an indefinite wait state.

Deadlock prevention protocols ensure that transactions will never enter into such a deadlock state.

Some prevention strategies require that:

- Each transaction lock all its data items before it begins execution (pre-declaration)
- Impose partial ordering of all data items
- That a transaction can lock data items only in the order specified by the partial order (graph-based protocol)

Other Deadlock Prevention Strategies

The following schemes use transaction timestamps for the sake of deadlock prevention alone.

Wait-die scheme -- non-preemptive.

An older transaction may wait for younger one to release a data item. Younger transactions **never** wait for older ones, they are rolled back instead.

A transaction may die several times before acquiring a required data item

Wound-wait scheme -- preemptive.

An older transaction wounds (*forces rollback*) of a younger transaction instead of waiting for it. Younger transactions may wait for older ones.

May be fewer rollbacks than wait-die scheme.

Both in wait-die and in wound-wait schemes, a rolled back transaction is restarted with its original timestamp. Older transactions thus have precedence over newer ones, and starvation is avoided.

Timeout-Based Schemes

A transaction waits for a lock only for a specified amount of time. After that, the wait times out and the transaction is rolled back

Thus deadlocks are not possible. This locking protocol is simple to implement in an RDBMS concurrency control manager, but time starvation is an issue that can and does occur.

It is also difficult to determine a good value for the timeout interval on a case to case basis.

Deadlock Detection

Deadlocks can be described as a wait-for graph, which consists of a pair G=(V, E),

- V is a set of vertices (all the transactions in the system)
- E is a set of edges. Each data element is an ordered pair Ti → Tj

If Ti → Tj is in E, then there is a directed edge from Ti to Tj, implying that Ti is waiting for Tj to **release** a data item.

When Ti requests a data item currently being held by Tj, then the edge Ti → Tj is inserted in the wait-for graph. This edge is removed only when Tj is no longer holding a data item needed by Ti.

The system is in a deadlock state if **and only if** the wait-for graph has a cycle. The concurrency control manager must invoke a deadlock-detection algorithm periodically to identify such cycles.

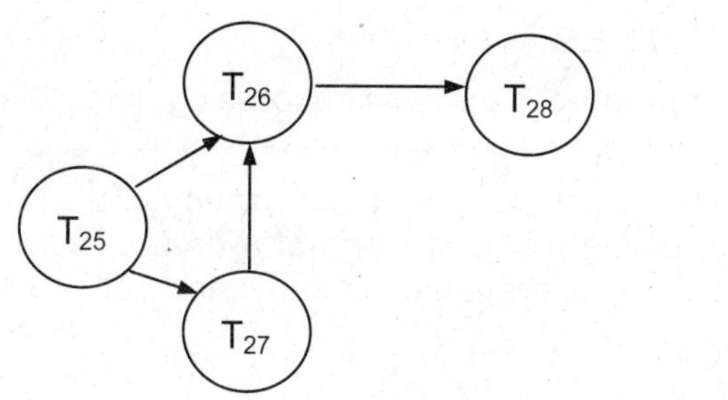

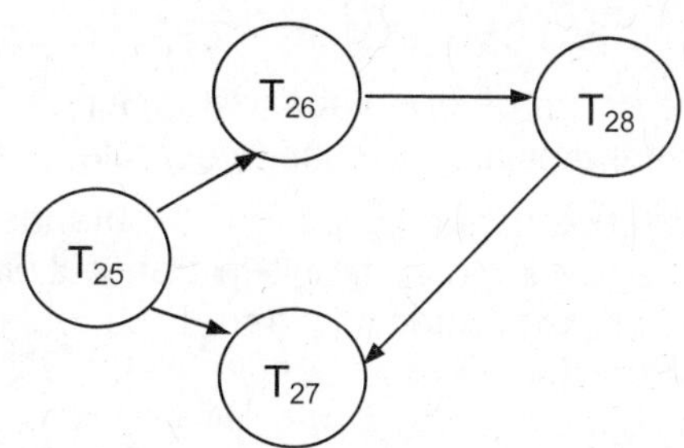

Diagram 6.5: Wait-for graph with no cycle. **Diagram 6.6:** Wait-for graph with a cycle.

Deadlock Recovery

When a deadlock is detected:

Some transactions will have to be rolled back (made a victim) to break deadlock. That transaction selected to be rolled back by the CCM is the one that will have minimum cost to the running transaction.

- Rollback: Determine how far to roll back transaction
- Total rollback: Abort the transaction and then restart it

It's a lot more effective to roll back a transaction only as far as necessary to break a deadlock.

Starvation happens if same transaction is always chosen as victim. Include the number of rollbacks in the cost factor to avoid starvation.

Insert and Delete Operations

If two-phase locking is used:

- A **DELETE** operation may be performed only if the transaction deleting the record has an X lock on the record to be deleted
- A transaction that **INSERTS** a new record into the database is given an automatic X lock on the record

Index Locking Protocol

Every relation must have at least one index. Access to a relation must be made only through one of the indices of the relation. A transaction T_i that performs a lookup (*a data read operation*) must lock all the index buckets that it accesses, in S-mode.

A transaction **Ti** may not insert a record **ti** into a relation **r** without updating all indices of **r**. Ti must perform a lookup on every index to find all index buckets that could have possibly contained a pointer to record Ti, had it existed already, and obtain X locks on all these index buckets. Ti must also obtain X locks on all index buckets that it modifies.

The rules of the two-phase locking protocol are thus observed.

Concurrency in Index Structures

Indices are unlike other database items in that their only job is to help in accessing data. Index-structures are typically accessed very often, much more than other database items.

Treating index-structures like other database items leads to **low concurrency**. Two-phase locking on an index may result in transactions executing practically **one-at-a-time**. There are index concurrency protocols where locks on internal nodes are released early, and not in a two-phase fashion.

In Conclusion

The **great thing** about Lock Control Managers is that they have all the above logic built into them by the creators of the RDBMS to which they belong. The RDBMS engine applies this logic automatically and transparently. In fact most RDBMS engines indicate that their default locking strategy is generally superior to user defined locking.

Only under exceptional conditions, should user defined locking be used. All RDBMS provide syntax that permits user defined locking to be specified to the RDBMS's concurrency control manager and override it's built in locking protocols.

Concurrency Control In Oracle

Having learned about the concepts, and type of locking protocols this needs to be mapped to a few data models and a RDBMS product. This mapping is done using an appropriate business model, an RDBMS and suitable ANSI SQL syntax.

Then examples that follow use Oracle as the RDBMS engine of choice. This material binds its model and syntax mapping to the default locking strategy of Oracle.

Users manipulate Oracle table data via SQL or PL/SQL sentences. An Oracle transaction can be made up of a single SQL sentence or several SQL sentences. This gives rise to Single Query Transactions and Multiple Query Transactions i.e. SQT and MQT.

These transactions (whether SQT or MQT) access an Oracle table or tables. Since Oracle works on a multi-user platform, it is more than likely that several people will access data either for viewing or for manipulating (inserting, updating and deleting records) from the same tables at the same time via different SQL statements. The Oracle table is therefore a **global resource**, i.e. it is shared by several users.

Tables (i.e. global resource) contain valuable data on which business decisions are based. There is a definite need to ensure that the integrity of data in a table is maintained each time its data is accessed. The Oracle Engine has to allow simultaneous access to table data without causing damage to the data.

The technique employed by the Oracle engine to protect table data when several people are accessing it is called **Concurrency Control**.

Oracle uses **Locking** to implement concurrency control when multiple users access a table to manipulate its data concurrently.

Locks

Locks are mechanisms used to ensure data integrity while allowing maximum concurrent access to data. Oracle's locking is fully automatic and requires no user intervention. The Oracle engine automatically locks table data while executing SQL statements. This type of locking is called **Implicit** Locking.

Oracle's Default Locking Strategy - Implicit Locking

Since the Oracle engine has a fully automatic locking strategy, it has to decide on two issues:

- Type of Lock to be applied
- Level of Lock to be applied

Types Of Locks

The type of lock to be placed on a resource depends on the operation being performed on that resource. Operations on tables can be distinctly grouped into the following two categories:

- **Read Operations :** SELECT statements
- **Write Operations :** INSERT, UPDATE, DELETE statements

Since Read operations make no changes to data in a table and are meant only for viewing purposes, simultaneous **read** operations can be performed on a table without any danger to the table's data. Hence, the Oracle engine places a **Shared** lock on a table when its data is being viewed.

On the other hand, **write** operations cause a change in table data i.e. any insert, update or delete statement affects table data directly and hence, simultaneous write operations can adversely affect table data integrity. Simultaneous write operation will cause **Loss of data consistency** in the table. Hence, the Oracle engine places an **Exclusive** lock on a table or specific sections of the table's resources when data is being written to a table.

The rules of locking can be summarized as:

- DATA being CHANGED cannot be READ
- Writers wait for other writers, **if** they attempt to update the same rows at the same time

The two **Types** of locks supported by Oracle are:

Shared Locks

- Shared locks are placed on resources whenever a **Read** operation (SELECT) is performed
- Multiple shared locks can be simultaneously set on a resource

Exclusive Locks

- Exclusive locks are placed on resources whenever **Write** operations (INSERT, UPDATE and DELETE) are performed
- Only **one** exclusive lock can be placed on a resource at a time i.e. the first user who acquires an exclusive lock will continue to have the sole ownership of the resource, and no other user can acquire an exclusive lock on that resource

Note:	*In the absence of explicit user defined locking being defined to the Oracle engine, if a default Exclusive lock is taken on a table a Shared lock on the very same data is permitted.*

Automatic application of locks on resources by the Oracle engine results in a high degree of data consistency.

Levels Of Locks

A table can be decomposed into rows and a row can be further decomposed into fields. Hence, if an automatic locking system is designed so as to be able to lock the fields of a record, it will be the most flexible locking system available.

It would mean that more than one user could be working on a single record in a table i.e. each on a different field of the same record in the same table. **Oracle does not provide a field level lock**.

Oracle provides the following three levels of locking:

- Row level
- Page level
- Table level

The Oracle engine decides on the **level of lock** to be used by the **presence** or **absence** of a **WHERE** condition in the SQL sentence.

- If the **WHERE** clause evaluates to only one row in the table, a **row level** lock is used
- If the **WHERE** clause evaluates to a set of data, a **page level** lock is used
- If there is no **WHERE** clause, (i.e. the query accesses the entire table,) a **table level** lock is used

Although the Oracle engine, has a default locking strategy in commercial applications, explicit user defined locking is often required. Consider the example below:

If two client computers (Client A and Client B) are entering sales orders, each time a sales order is prepared, the **quantity on hand** of the product for which the order is being generated needs to be updated in the **PRODUCT_MSTR** table.

Now, if Client A fires an update command on a record in the **PRODUCT_MSTR** table, then Oracle will **implicitly** lock the record so that no further data manipulation can be done by any other user till the lock is released. The lock will be released only when Client A fires a **commit** or **rollback**.

In the meantime, if Client B tries to view the same record, the Oracle engine will display the old set for values for the record as the transaction for that record has not been completed by Client A. This leads to wrong information being displayed to Client B.

In such cases, Client A must explicitly lock the record such that, no other user can access the record **even for viewing purposes** till Client A's transaction is completed.

A Lock so defined is called **Explicit Lock**. User defined explicit locking always overrides Oracle's default locking strategy.

Explicit Locking

The technique of lock taken on a table or its resources by a user is called **Explicit Locking**.

Who Can Explicitly Lock?

Users can lock tables they own or any tables on which they have been granted table privileges (such as select, insert, update, delete).

Oracle provides facilities by which the default locking strategy can be overridden. Table(s) or row(s) can be explicitly locked by using either the **SELECT ... FOR UPDATE** statement, or **LOCK TABLE** statement.

The SELECT ... For UPDATE Statement

It is used for acquiring exclusive row level locks in anticipation of performing updates on records. This clause is generally used to signal the Oracle engine that data currently being used needs to be updated. It is often followed by one or more **update** statements with a **where** clause.

Example 1:

Two client machines Client A and Client B are recording the transactions performed in a bank for a particular **account number** simultaneously.

Client A fires the following select statement:

Client A> SELECT * FROM ACCT_MSTR **WHERE** ACCT_NO = 'SB9' **FOR UPDATE;**

When the above **SELECT** statement is fired, the Oracle engine locks the record **SB9**. This lock is released when a **commit** or **rollback** is fired by Client A.

Now Client B fires a **SELECT** statement, which points to record **SB9**, which has already been locked by Client A:

Client B> SELECT * FROM ACCT_MSTR **WHERE** ACCT_NO = 'SB9' **FOR UPDATE;**

The Oracle engine will ensure that Client B's SQL statement waits for the lock to be released on ACCT_MSTR by a **commit** or **rollback** statement fired by Client A forever.

In order to avoid unnecessary waiting time, a **NOWAIT** option can be used to inform the Oracle engine to terminate the SQL statement if the record has already been locked. If this happens the Oracle engine terminates the running DML and comes up with a message indicating that the **resource** is **busy**.

If Client B fires the following select statement now with a **NOWAIT** clause:

Client B> SELECT * FROM ACCT_MSTR **WHERE** ACCT_NO = 'SB9' **FOR UPDATE NOWAIT;**

Output:

Since Client A has already locked the record SB9 when Client B tries to acquire a shared lock on the same record the Oracle Engine displays the following message:

```
SQL> 00054: resource busy and acquire with nowait specified.
```

The **SELECT ... FOR UPDATE** cannot be used with the following:

- Distinct and the Group by clause
- Set operators and Group functions

Using Lock Table Statement

To manually override Oracle's default locking strategy by creating a data lock in a specific mode.

Syntax:

```
LOCK TABLE <TableName> [,<TableName>] ...
    IN {ROW SHARE|ROW EXCLUSIVE|SHARE UPDATE|
    SHARE|SHARE ROW EXCLUSIVE|EXCLUSIVE }
    [NOWAIT]
```

where,

TableName	Indicates the name of table(s), view(s) to be locked. In case of views, the lock is placed on underlying tables.
IN	Decides what other locks on the same resource can exist simultaneously. For example, if there is an exclusive lock on the table no user can update rows in the table. It can have any of the following values:
	Exclusive: They allow query on the locked resource but prohibit any other activity. **Share :** It allows queries but prohibits updates to a table. **Row Exclusive:** Row exclusive locks are the same as row share locks, also prohibit locking in shared mode. These locks are acquired when updating, inserting or deleting. **Share RowExclusive:** They are used to look at a whole table, to selective updates and to allow other users to look at rows in the table but not lock the table in share mode or to update rows.
NOWAIT	Indicates that the Oracle engine should immediately return to the user with a message, if the resources are busy. If omitted, the Oracle engine will wait till resources are available forever.

Example 2:

Two client machines Client A and Client B are performing data manipulation on the table **EMP_MSTR**.

Table Name: EMP_MSTR

EMP _NO	BRANCH _NO	FNAME	MNAME	LNAME	DEPT	DESIG	MNGR _NO
E1	B1	Ivan	Nelson	Bayross	Administration	Managing Director	
E2	B2	Amit		Desai	Loans & Financing	Finance Manager	
E3	B3	Maya	Mahima	Joshi	Client Servicing	Sales Manager	
E4	B1	Peter	Iyer	Joseph	Loans & Financing	Clerk	E2
E5	B4	Mandhar	Dilip	Dalvi	Marketing	Marketing Manager	

E6	B6	Sonal	Abdul	Khan	Administration	Admin. Executive	E1
E7	B4	Anil	Ashutosh	Kambli	Marketing	Sales Asst.	E5
E8	B3	Seema	P.	Apte	Client Servicing	Clerk	E3
E9	B2	Vikram	Vilas	Randive	Marketing	Sales Asst.	E5
E10	B6	Anjali	Sameer	Pathak	Administration	HR Manager	E1

Client A has locked the table in exclusive mode (i.e. only querying of records is allowed on the **EMP_MSTR** table by Client B):

Client A> LOCK TABLE EMP_MSTR **IN EXCLUSIVE Mode NOWAIT;**

Output:

```
Table(s) Locked.
```

Client A performs an insert operation but does not commit the transaction:

Client A> INSERT INTO EMP_MSTR
(EMP_NO, BRANCH_NO, FNAME, MNAME, LNAME, DEPT, DESIG, MNGR_NO)
VALUES('E100', 'B1', 'Vishal', 'Kishore', 'Joshi', 'Administration', 'Project Leader', NULL**);**

Output:

```
1 row created.
```

Client B performs a view operation:

Client B> SELECT EMP_NO, FNAME, MNAME, LNAME **FROM** EMP_MSTR;

Output:

```
EMP_NO FNAME    MNAME    LNAME
-----------------------------------
E1     Ivan     Nelson   Bayross
E2     Amit              Desai
E3     Maya     Mahima   Joshi
E4     Peter    Iyer     Joseph
E5     Mandhar Dilip     Dalvi
E6     Sonal    Abdul    Khan
E7     Anil     Ashutosh Kambli
E8     Seema    P.       Apte
E9     Vikram   Vilas    Randive
E10    Anjali   Sameer   Pathak
```

Client B performs an insert operation:

Client B> INSERT INTO EMP_MSTR
(EMP_NO, BRANCH_NO, FNAME, MNAME, LNAME, DEPT, DESIG, MNGR_NO)
VALUES('E101', 'B1', 'Seema', Vishal, 'Joshi', 'Tech Team', 'Programmer', 'E100'**);**

Output:

```
Client B's SQL DML enters into a wait state waiting for Client A to
release the locked resource by using a Commit or Rollback statement.
```

Inferences:

- When Client A locks the table EMP_MSTR in exclusive mode the table is available only for querying to other users. No other data manipulation (i.e. Insert, Update and Delete operation) can be performed on the EMP_MSTR table by other users
- Since Client A has inserted a record in the EMP_MSTR table and not committed the changes when Client B fires a select statement the newly inserted record is not visible to Client B
- As the EMP_MSTR table has been locked when Client B tries to insert a record, the system enters into an indefinite wait period till all locks are released by Client A taken on EMP_MSTR table

Releasing Locks

Locks are released under the following circumstances:

- The transaction is committed successfully using the **Commit** verb
- A **rollback** is performed
- A **rollback to a savepoint** will release locks set after the specified **savepoint**

> **Note:** *All locks are released on **commit** or **unqualified Rollback**.*
> *Table locks are released by rolling back to a **savepoint**.*
> *Row-level locks are not released by rolling back to a **savepoint**.*

Explicit Locking Using SQL And The Behavior Of The Oracle Engine

The locking characteristics for the **insert, update, delete** SQL statements in a multi user environment where real time processing takes place, is explained by taking an example of two client computers (Client A and Client B in our example) talking to the same **BRANCH_MSTR** table via the Oracle Engine.

Example 3:

The BRANCH_MSTR table will be used to check the behavior of the Oracle Engine in multi-user environment when an insert operation is performed.

Table Name: BRANCH_MSTR

BRANCH_NO	NAME
B1	Vile Parle (HO)
B4	Mahim

BRANCH_NO	NAME
B2	Andheri
B5	Borivali

BRANCH_NO	NAME
B3	Churchgate
B6	Darya Ganj

Client A performs an insert operation on the **BRANCH_MSTR** table:

Client A> INSERT INTO BRANCH_MSTR **(**BRANCH_NO, NAME**) VALUES(**'B7', 'Dahisar'**);**

Output:

```
1 row created.
```

Client A fires a SELECT statement on the **BRANCH_MSTR** table:

Client A> SELECT * FROM BRANCH_MSTR;

Output:

```
BRANCH_NO  NAME
--------------------------------
B1         Vile Parle (HO)
B2         Andheri
B3         Churchgate
B4         Mahim
B5         Borivali
B6         Darya Ganj
B7         Dahisar
7 rows selected.
```

Client B fires a SELECT statement on the **BRANCH_MSTR** table:

Client B> SELECT * FROM BRANCH_MSTR;

Output:

```
BRANCH_NO  NAME
--------------------------------
B1         Vile Parle (HO)
B2         Andheri
B3         Churchgate
B4         Mahim
B5         Borivali
B6         Darya Ganj
6 rows selected.
```

Observation:

- Client A can see the newly inserted record B7
- Client B cannot see the newly inserted record, as Client A has not committed it

Inferences:

Since Client A has not fired a commit statement for permanently saving the newly inserted record in the **BRANCH_MSTR** table, Client B cannot access the newly inserted record or manipulate it any way

Note:	*Client A can view, update or delete the newly inserted record since it exists in the buffer on the Client A's computer. However, this record does not exist in the Server's table, because Client A has not committed the transaction.*

Example 4:

The ACCT_MSTR table will be used to check the behavior of the Oracle Engine in multi-user environment when an update operation is performed.

Table name: ACCT_MSTR (Partials Extract)

ACCT_NO	CURBAL	ACCT_NO	CURBAL	ACCT_NO	CURBAL	ACCT_NO	CURBAL
SB1	500	CA2	3000	SB3	500	CA4	12000
SB5	500	SB6	500	CA7	22000	SB8	500
SB9	500	CA10	32000	SB11	500	CA12	5000
SB13	500	CA14	10000	SB15	500		

Client A performs an update operation on A/c. No. SB9 in the ACCT_MSTR table:

Client A> UPDATE ACCT_MSTR **SET** CURBAL = CURBAL + 5000 **WHERE** ACCT_NO = 'SB9';

Output:

```
1 row updated.
```

Client A fires a SELECT statement on the ACCT_MSTR table:

Client A> SELECT ACCT_NO, CURBAL FROM ACCT_MSTR;

Output:

```
ACCT_NO   CURBAL
-------------------
SB1          500
CA2         3000
SB3          500
CA4        12000
SB5          500
SB6          500
CA7        22000
SB8          500
SB9         5500
CA10       32000
SB11         500
CA12        3000
SB13         500
```

Output: (Continued)

```
ACCT_NO   CURBAL
----------------
CA14       12000
SB15         500
15 rows selected.
```

Client B fires a SELECT statement on the ACCT_MSTR table:

Client B> SELECT ACCT_NO, CURBAL **FROM** ACCT_MSTR;

Output:

```
ACCT_NO   CURBAL
----------------
SB1          500
CA2         3000
SB3          500
CA4        12000
SB5          500
SB6          500
CA7        22000
SB8          500
SB9          500
CA10       32000
SB11         500
CA12        3000
SB13         500
CA14       12000
SB15         500
15 rows selected.
```

Observation:

- Client A can see the changes made to the record SB9 that was updated
- Client B continues to see the old values of the updated record, as Client A has not committed the transaction

Inferences:

- Client A has updated the record 'SB9' and not committed it. Hence, when Client B fires a select statement, Client B cannot see the changes made to record SB9

Example 5:

The ACCT_MSTR table will be used to check the behavior of the Oracle Engine in a multi-user environment. An update operation is performed after specifying the FOR UPDATE clause.

Table name: ACCT_MSTR (Partials Extract)

ACCT_NO	CURBAL	ACCT_NO	CURBAL	ACCT_NO	CURBAL	ACCT_NO	CURBAL
SB1	500	CA2	3000	SB3	500	CA4	12000
SB5	500	SB6	500	CA7	22000	SB8	500
SB9	500	CA10	32000	SB11	500	CA12	5000
SB13	500	CA14	10000	SB15	500		

Client A selects all the records from the ACCT_MSTR table with the **FOR UPDATE** clause**:**

Client A> SELECT ACCT_NO, CURBAL **FROM** ACCT_MSTR **FOR UPDATE;**

Client A performs an update operation on the record SB9 in the ACCT_MSTR table:

Client A> UPDATE ACCT_MSTR **SET** CURBAL = CURBAL + 5000 **WHERE** ACCT_NO = 'SB9';

Output:

```
1 row updated.
```

Client A fires a SELECT statement on the ACCT_MSTR table:

Client A> SELECT ACCT_NO, CURBAL **FROM** ACCT_MSTR;

Output:

```
ACCT_NO   CURBAL
----------------
SB1          500
CA2         3000
SB3          500
CA4        12000
SB5          500
SB6          500
CA7        22000
SB8          500
SB9         5500
CA10       32000
SB11         500
CA12        3000
SB13         500
CA14       12000
SB15         500
15 rows selected.
```

Client B fires a SELECT statement with a **FOR UPDATE** clause on the ACCT_MSTR table:

Client B> SELECT ACCT_NO, CURBAL **FROM** ACCT_MSTR **FOR UPDATE;**

Output:

```
Client B's SQL DML enters into an indefinite wait state waiting for Client A to release the locked resource by using a Commit or Rollback statement.
```

Observation:

- Client A can see the changes made to the record SB9 that was updated
- When Client B fires a select command with for update clause, Oracle enters a **wait** state till Client A releases the locks on the ACCT_MSTR table

Inferences:

- The select for update fired by Client A acquires an exclusive lock on the records of the ACCT_MSTR table
- Client A has not committed the record SB9 that was updated
- The select statement fired by Client B tries to acquire a lock on all the records of the ACCT_MSTR table
- Since these records are already locked by Client A, Client B enters into a Wait state
- When Client A fires a Commit or Rollback, all locks are released by Client A. The records are now available to Client B for locking
- The select statement processing executed by Client B will now be completed, as Client B would see all the records and lock them

Example 6:

The ACCT_MSTR table will be used to check the behavior of the Oracle Engine in multi-user environment. An update operation is performed after specifying the FOR UPDATE clause, but the other user executes SQL commands with the NOWAIT options.

Table name: ACCT_MSTR (Partials Extract)

ACCT_NO	CURBAL	ACCT_NO	CURBAL	ACCT_NO	CURBAL	ACCT_NO	CURBAL
SB1	500	CA2	3000	SB3	500	CA4	12000
SB5	500	SB6	500	CA7	22000	SB8	500
SB9	500	CA10	32000	SB11	500	CA12	5000
SB13	500	CA14	10000	SB15	500		

Client A selects all the records from the ACCT_MSTR table with the **FOR UPDATE** clause**:**

Client A> SELECT ACCT_NO, CURBAL **FROM** ACCT_MSTR **FOR UPDATE;**

Client A performs an update operation on the record SB9 in the ACCT_MSTR table:

Client A> UPDATE ACCT_MSTR **SET** CURBAL = CURBAL + 5000 **WHERE** ACCT_NO = 'SB9';

Output:

```
1 row updated.
```

Client A fires a SELECT statement on the ACCT_MSTR table:

Client A> SELECT ACCT_NO, CURBAL **FROM** ACCT_MSTR;

Output:

```
ACCT_NO  CURBAL
---------------
SB1         500
CA2        3000
SB3         500
CA4       12000
SB5         500
SB6         500
CA7       22000
SB8         500
SB9        5500
CA10      32000
SB11        500
CA12       3000
SB13        500
CA14      12000
SB15        500
15 rows selected.
```

Client B fires a SELECT command also with a **FOR UPDATE** and **NOWAIT** clause on the ACCT_MSTR table:

Client B> SELECT ACCT_NO, CURBAL **FROM** ACCT_MSTR **FOR UPDATE NOWAIT;**

Output:

```
SELECT ACCT_NO, CURBAL FROM ACCT_MSTR
                                  *

ERROR at line 1:
ORA-00054: resource busy and acquire with NOWAIT specified
```

Observation:

- Client A can see the changes made to the record SB9 that was updated
- When Client B fires a select command, Oracle checks to find if the record SB9 is available for a lock to be taken. Since the record has already been locked by Client A the Oracle engine displays an appropriate error message

Inferences:

- The select **for update** fired by Client A acquires an exclusive lock on all the records the ACCT_MSTR table
- Client A has not committed the record SB9 that was updated. Hence, when Client B fires a select statement **for update** and **nowait** clause, the Oracle engine returns a message that the resource is in use by another user and terminates Client B's SQL sentence

- The SQL prompt returns on Client B's VDU
- Only when Client A fires a Commit or a Rollback, will all locks taken be released and the records available to Client B

Example 7:

The BRANCH_MSTR table will be used to check the behavior of the Oracle Engine in multi-user environment when a delete operation is performed.

Table Name: BRANCH_MSTR

BRANCH_NO	NAME	BRANCH_NO	NAME
B1	Vile Parle (HO)	B2	Andheri
B3	Churchgate	B4	Mahim
B5	Borivali	B6	Darya Ganj

Client A performs a delete operation on a record B5 in the BRANCH_MSTR table:

Client A> DELETE FROM BRANCH_MSTR **WHERE** BRANCH_NO = 'B5';

Output:

```
1 row deleted.
```

Client A fires a SELECT statement on the ACCT_MSTR table:

Client A> SELECT * FROM BRANCH_MSTR;

Output:

```
BRANCH_NO  NAME
---------------------------------
B1         Vile Parle (HO)
B2         Andheri
B3         Churchgate
B4         Mahim
B6         Darya Ganj
5 rows selected.
```

Client B fires a SELECT statement on the BRANCH_MSTR table:

Client B> SELECT * FROM BRANCH_MSTR;

Output:

```
BRANCH_NO  NAME
---------------------------------
B1         Vile Parle (HO)
B2         Andheri
B3         Churchgate
B4         Mahim
B5         Borivali
B6         Darya Ganj
6 rows selected.
```

Observation:

- Client A does not see the record B5 any more as it has been deleted
- Client B continues to see the record B5, as Client A has not committed the delete operation

Inferences:

- Client A has deleted the record B5 and not committed the same
- Hence, when Client B fires a select statement, Client B can still see record B5

Example 8:

The BRANCH_MSTR table will be used to check the behavior of the Oracle Engine in multi-user environment. A delete operation is performed after specifying the FOR UPDATE clause.

Table Name: BRANCH_MSTR

BRANCH_NO	NAME	BRANCH_NO	NAME
B1	Vile Parle (HO)	B2	Andheri
B3	Churchgate	B4	Mahim
B5	Borivali	B6	Darya Ganj

Client A selects a record from the BRANCH_MSTR table with the for update clause:

Client A> SELECT * FROM BRANCH_MSTR **FOR UPDATE;**

Client A performs a delete operation on the record B5 in the BRANCH_MSTR table:

Client A> DELETE FROM BRANCH_MSTR **WHERE** BRANCH_NO = 'B5';

Output:

```
1 row deleted.
```

Client A fires a SELECT on the BRANCH_MSTR table:

Client A> SELECT * FROM BRANCH_MSTR;

Output:

```
BRANCH_NO  NAME
---------------------------
B1         Vile Parle (HO)
B2         Andheri
B3         Churchgate
B4         Mahim
B6         Darya Ganj
5 rows selected.
```

Client B fires a SELECT command with **FOR UPDATE** clause on the BRANCH_MSTR table:

Client B> SELECT * FROM BRANCH_MSTR **FOR UPDATE;**

Output:

```
Client B's SQL DML enters into a wait state waiting for Client A to
release the locked resource by using a Commit or Rollback statement.
```

Observation:

- Client A can no longer see the record as it has been deleted
- When Client B fires a **select** command, Oracle enters a **wait** state till Client A releases the lock on the record

Inferences:

- Since Client A has fired a select statement with a **for update** clause, all the records of the BRANCH_MSTR table have been **exclusively** locked by Client A
- The record B5 is deleted by Client A, no locks have been released
- When Client B fires a SELECT statement and tries to acquire a lock on all the records of BRANCH_MSTR table, Client B enters into a wait state
- Only when Client A fires a Commit or a Rollback, will all locks on the records be released and the records will be available to Client B for locking
- The SELECT statement processing executed by Client B will now be completed as Client B would see all the records and lock them

Example 9:

The BRANCH_MSTR table will be used to check the behavior of the Oracle Engine in multi-user environment. An update operation is performed after specifying the FOR UPDATE clause, but the other user executes SQL commands with the NOWAIT options.

Table Name: BRANCH_MSTR

BRANCH_NO	NAME	BRANCH_NO	NAME
B1	Vile Parle (HO)	B2	Andheri
B3	Churchgate	B4	Mahim
B5	Borivali	B6	Darya Ganj

Client A selects records from the BRANCH_MSTR table with the **FOR UPDATE** clause:

Client A> SELECT * FROM BRANCH_MSTR **FOR UPDATE;**

Client A performs a delete operation on the record in the BRANCH_MSTR table:

Client A> DELETE FROM BRANCH_MSTR **WHERE** BRANCH_NO = 'B5';

Output:

```
1 row deleted.
```

Client A fires a select statement on the BRANCH_MSTR table:

Client A> SELECT * FROM BRANCH_MSTR;

Output:

```
BRANCH_NO NAME
------------------------------------
B1        Vile Parle (HO)
B2        Andheri
B3        Churchgate
```

Output: (Continued)

```
B4          Mahim
B6          Darya Ganj
5 rows selected.
```

Client B fires a select statement on the BRANCH_MSTR table:

Client B> SELECT * FROM BRANCH_MSTR **FOR UPDATE NOWAIT;**

Output:

```
SQL> 00054: resource busy and acquire with nowait specified.
no rows selected
```

Observation:

- Client A can no longer see the record B5 as it has been deleted
- When Client B fires a select command, Oracle checks to find if the record B5 is available for a lock to be taken. Since Client A has already locked the record the Oracle engine displays an appropriate message

Inferences:

- The select for update fired by Client A acquires an exclusive lock on all the records of the BRANCH_MSTR table
- Client A has not committed the record B5 that was deleted
- When Client B fires a **SELECT ... FOR UPDATE** and **NOWAIT** clause, the Oracle engine displays the message that the resource is in use by another user and returns Client B to the SQL prompt.
- Only when Client A fires a Commit or a Rollback, will all locks on the records be released

Explicit Locking Using PL/SQL And The Oracle Engine

The manner in which explicit locking can be used in a PL/SQL block of code and functionality of the Oracle engine in processing the code block in a multi-user environment is explained with the help of the following example.

Example 10:

Write a PL/SQL code block that will accept:

- An account number, the type of transaction, the amount involved and whether the amount to be debited to or credited to an account number
- The balance in the **account** table for the corresponding account number is updated

Before the update is fired, the record is viewed in the **FOR UPDATE NOWAIT mode** so that a lock can be acquired on the record to be updated and no other user has access to the same record till the transaction is completed.

Table name: ACCT_MSTR (Partials Extract)

ACCT_NO	CURBAL	ACCT_NO	CURBAL	ACCT_NO	CURBAL	ACCT_NO	CURBAL
SB1	500	CA2	3000	SB3	500	CA4	12000
SB5	500	SB6	500	CA7	22000	SB8	500
SB9	500	CA10	32000	SB11	500	CA12	5000
SB13	500	CA14	10000	SB15	500		

```
DECLARE
/* Declaration of memory variables and constants to be used in the
Execution section. */
   ACCT_BALANCE NUMBER (11,2);
   ACCT_NUM VARCHAR2(10);
   TRANS_AMT NUMBER(11,2) ;
   OPER CHAR(1);
BEGIN
/* Accept an ACCT_NO,OPER and the TRANS_AMT from the user. */
   ACCT_NUM := &ACCT_NUM;
   TRANS_AMT := &TRANS_AMT;
   OPER := &OPER;
/* Retrieving the balance from the accounts table where the ACCT_NO in
the table is equal to the ACCT_NUM entered by the user. Also the select
is with a for update and nowait clause in order to acquire a lock on
the record. */
   SELECT CURBAL INTO ACCT_BALANCE FROM ACCT_MSTR
      WHERE ACCT_NO = ACCT_NUM FOR UPDATE NOWAIT;
/* Checking if the operation specified is debit or credit. If the
operation specified is debit then the balance is reduced by the
TRANS_AMT. If the operation specified is credit then the balance is
increased by the TRANS_AMT of the corresponding ACCT_NO. */
   IF OPER= 'D' THEN
      UPDATE ACCT_MSTR SET CURBAL = CURBAL - TRANS_AMT
         WHERE ACCT_NO = ACCT_NUM;
   ELSIF OPER= 'C' THEN
      UPDATE ACCT_MSTR SET CURBAL = CURBAL + TRANS_AMT
         WHERE ACCT_NO = ACCT_NUM;
   END IF;
END;
```

Output:

```
Enter value for acct_num: 'SB1'
old  10:  ACCT_NUM := &ACCT_NUM;
new  10:  ACCT_NUM := 'SB1';
Enter value for trans_amt: 2000
old  11:  TRANS_AMT := &TRANS_AMT;
```

```
new  11:  TRANS_AMT := 2000;
Enter value for oper: 'C'
old  12:  OPER := &OPER;
new  12:  OPER := 'C';
PL/SQL procedure successfully completed.
```

In a scenario, where two users Client A and Client B are accessing the ACCT_MSTR table and Client A first executes the PL/SQL block of code and enters SB1 as the ACCT_NUM, 2000 as the TRANS_AMT and C for OPER:

- The SELECT statement will retrieve the balance amount of 500 from the ACCT_MSTR table that is related to A/c. No. SB1. The Oracle engine will also acquire a lock on the record SB1 as the SELECT statement is with the FOR UPDATE NOWAIT clause.
- The Oracle Engine then checks whether the **OPER** entered is C or D
- Since the **OPER** entered is C the TRANS_AMT of Rs. 2000 will be added to ACCT_NO SB1
- At this point in time, if Client A fires a SELECT sentence:

  SELECT * FROM Accounts;

Output:

```
ACCT_NO  CURBAL
SB1        2500
CA2        3000
SB3         500
CA4       12000
SB5         500
SB6         500
CA7       22000
SB8         500
SB9        5500
CA10      32000
SB11        500
CA12       3000
SB13        500
CA14      12000
SB15        500
15 rows selected.
```

Since Client A has not yet committed the record, the lock on the record still exists.

- Now if Client B fires the PL/SQL block of code for the same record SB1, the SELECT statement will fail to acquire the lock as Client A already locked the record

- Since the NOWAIT clause has been specified in the SELECT sentence, the Oracle engine will come out of the PL/SQL block and display the following message:

```
DECLARE
*
ERROR at line 1:
ORA-00054: resource busy and acquire with NOWAIT specified
ORA-06512: at line 10
```

Thus, by exclusively locking the row just before the UPDATE is fired in a PL/SQL block of code, concurrency control can be maintained in a multi-user environment where multiple users would want to access the same resource at the same time.

Deadlock

In a deadlock, two database operations wait for each other to release a lock. A deadlock occurs when two users have a lock, each on a separate object, and, they want to acquire a lock on each other's object. When this happens, the first user has to wait for the second user to release the lock, but the second user will not release it until the lock on the first user's object is freed. At this point, both the users are at an impasse and cannot proceed with their business. In such a case, Oracle detects the deadlock automatically and solves the problem by aborting one of the two transactions.

Example 11:

Transaction 1

```
BEGIN
    UPDATE ACCT_MSTR SET CURBAL = 500 WHERE ACCT_NO='SB1';
    UPDATE ACCT_MSTR SET CURBAL = 2500 WHERE ACCT_NO='CA2';
END
```

Transaction 2

```
BEGIN
    UPDATE ACCT_MSTR SET CURBAL = 5000 WHERE ACCT_NO='CA2';
    UPDATE ACCT_MSTR SET CURBAL = 3500 WHERE ACCT_NO='SB1';
END
```

Assume that Transaction1 and Transaction2 begin exactly at the same time. By default Oracle automatically places exclusive lock on data that is being updated. This causes Transaction1 to wait for Transaction2 to complete but in turn Transaction2 has to wait for Transaction1 to complete.

This scenario will continue indefinitely and both DML's will enter into an indefinite wait state. This is what is known as a deadlock **i.e.** a lock which the Oracle engine cannot resolve automatically.

When this situation is detected by the Oracle engine both update statements are rolled back automatically and the Deadlock resolved.

Self Review Questions

Fill In The Blanks

1. A series of one or more SQL statements that are logically related, or a series of operations performed on Oracle table data is termed as a ___________.
2. To make the changes permanent a ___________ statement has to be given at the SQL prompt.
3. A __________ ends the current transaction and makes permanent any changes made during the transaction.
4. ___________ marks and saves the current point in the processing of a transaction.
5. The technique employed by the Oracle engine to protect table data when several people are accessing it is called _____________ ____________.
6. Oracle uses a method called ____________ to implement concurrency control.
7. Operations on tables can be distinctly grouped into ______________ and ____________ operations.
8. The Oracle engine places an ______________ lock on a table or specific sections of the table's resources when data is being written to a table.
9. Only one _____________ lock can be placed on a resource at a time.
10. If the WHERE clause evaluates to a set of data, a _________________ lock is used.
11. The technique of lock taken on a table or its resources by a user is called ______________ __________.
12. A ____________ option can be used to inform the Oracle engine to terminate the SQL statement if the record has already been locked.
13. All locks are released on ___________________ or ______________________.
14. ________ level locks are not released by rolling back to a savepoint.
15. In a ____________ two database operations wait for each other to release a lock.
16. A ___________ is a mechanism to control concurrent access to an item of data held within a database table.
17. In an ___________ __________ the data item can be both read as well as written to by the individual who locked it.
18. A __________ may be granted a lock on a data item if the requested lock is compatible with locks already held on the item by other transactions.
19. The _________ allows any number of transactions to hold shared locks on a data item.
20. A locking __________ is a set of rules followed by all ANSI SQL transactions while requesting and releasing locks.
21. The two-phase locking protocol assures _____________ to a large extent.
22. Two-phase locking does not guarantee freedom from __________.

23. Cascading __________ tend to occur under two-phase locking.
24. _________ locks allow a higher-level node to be locked in S or X mode without having to check all descendent nodes.
25. A transaction waits for a ________ only for a specified amount of time.
26. Treating index-structures like other database items leads to ________ __________.
27. ________ are mechanisms used to ensure data integrity while allowing maximum concurrent access to data.
28. The Oracle engine automatically locks table data while executing SQL statements which is called _________ _________.
29. A table can be decomposed into rows and a row can be further decomposed into ________.
30. A transaction can be closed by using either a __________ or a __________ statement.
31. An _________ savepoint is one that is specified since the last COMMIT or ROLLBACK.
32. A ROLLBACK operation performed _________ the SAVEPOINT clause ends the transaction.
33. A ROLLBACK operation performed _______ the TO SAVEPOINT clause rolls back a predetermined portion of the transaction.

True Or False

34. A ROLLBACK statement at the SQL prompt is used to make permanent changes.
35. The SAVEPOINT attribute in the ROLLABACK statement is optional and is used to rollback a partial transaction, as far as the specified savepoint.
36. A Rollback statement cannot be used to close a transaction.
37. ROLLBACK cannot be fired from the SQL prompt without the SAVEPOINT clause.
38. In Real time processing records are gathered in a table and at regular intervals manipulated.
39. COMMIT can be fired upto a savepoint.
40. The Oracle engine automatically locks table data while executing SQL statements.
41. The type of lock to be placed on a resource depends on the operation being performed on that resource.
42. The Oracle engine places shared lock on a table or specific sections of the table's resources when data is being written to a table.
43. Multiple shared locks cannot be set simultaneously on a resource.
44. Only one exclusive lock can be placed on a resource at a time.
45. If the WHERE clause evaluates to a set of data, a table level lock is used.
46. User defined explicit locking always overrides Oracle's default locking strategy.

47. The select... for update can be used with set operators and group by clause.
48. Locks are released when the transaction is committed successfully using the Commit verb.
49. Oracle detects the deadlock automatically and solves the problem by aborting one of the two transactions.
50. A series of one or more SQL statements that are logically related, or a series of sequential operations performed on table data is termed as a Transaction.
51. A ROLLBACK ends the current transaction and makes permanent any changes in table data made during the transaction.
52. SAVEPOINTNAME is optional and is used to rollback a partial transaction, as far as the specified savepoint.
53. When a SAVEPOINT is used with a ROLLBACK statement, specific parts of a transaction can be undone.
54. In a Shared mode, the data item can be both read as well as written to by the individual who locked it.
55. A transaction can proceed only after the concurrency-control manager grants such requests.
56. Multiple shared locks cannot be granted on a data item.
57. The matrix disallows any number of transactions to hold shared locks on a data item.
58. Locking schedules not possible under two-phase locking are possible under tree protocol.
59. Two-phase locking guarantees freedom from deadlocks.
60. In the read and execution phase, the transaction performs a validation test to determine if local variables can be written without violating serializability.
61. Deadlock prevention protocols ensure that the system will never enter into a deadlock state.
62. The Oracle engine automatically locks table data while executing SQL statements which is called Implicit Locking.
63. Multiple shared locks cannot be simultaneously set on a resource.
64. Automatic application of locks on resources by the Oracle engine results in a high degree of data consistency.
65. The technique of lock taken on a table or its resources by a user is called Explicit Locking.
66. Row exclusive locks prohibit locking in shared mode.
67. Row-level locks are released by rolling back to a SAVEPOINT.

Objectives Questions

1. What is a transaction?
2. What is COMMIT?
3. What is ROLLBACK?
4. What is concurrency control?
5. How is a dead lock handled?
6. What are the different types of Locks?
7. What are the different levels of Locks?
8. Describe with a simple example explicit user defined locking?

7. Security

Discretionary Access Control

An access control system is a system that that permits specific entities (people, processes, or hardware devices) to access system resources based on the a set of permissions granted to that particular entity.

In database security **discretionary access control** (**DAC**), is a kind of access control defined by the owner of all the database resources (i.e. **root**) that restricts access to database objects based on the identity of individual(s) and/or groups.

These access controls are discretionary in the sense that an individual is capable of passing their access permission (perhaps indirectly) on to any other individuals, unless restrained by the database resources owner when their identities were initially created.

Access control can be handled at operating system levels, especially if a Multi user, **N**etwork **O**perating **S**ystem (NOS) is in use. Since the operating system is the only media via which all other system resources can be accessed (such as folders with files in them on a hard disk) it does make a great deal of sense to enforce first level discretionary access control at operating system level itself.

The security policy of Unix / Linux modeled operating systems prescribes a relationship between access rules and access attributes. The access attributes allow the system to define several distinct levels of authorization, and the access rules provide the mechanism for the system to prevent unauthorized access to sensitive information.

Normally access to a file is determined by the file's absolute pathname.

The operating system kernel (irrespective which O/S it belongs to) generally determines whether or not to allow a read, write, execute / search process to run on folders and files based on the:

- User and Group IDs associated with the process
- Privileges (if any) associated with the process
- Discretionary controls (in the form of permission bits, and, possibly, **A**ccess **C**ontrol **L**ists (ACLs) associated with the file and all the directories that make up the absolute pathname of the file

These access checks are performed at the time the file is opened, rather than at the time a read or write is actually attempted.

For example, if the file `/usr/src/cmd/clientmaster.c` is readable by a user, but the directory `/usr/src/cmd` (or any other directory in the path) is not searchable by that user (that is, the user does not have search permission on `/usr/src/cmd`), then `clientmaster.c` cannot be read.

The system enforces access control by means of the Discretionary Access Control (DAC) mechanism.

Users on a computer system typically share commands, programs, library routines, and files. For example, all users need to share the user-level commands in the operating system, such as **ls, ls –al, mkdir,** and so on.

Also, users in the same group or in related groups often may want to share some of the same data or text files. Object sharing introduces some potential security violations. To maintain security, the security policy requires that the system oversee object sharing in a known and controlled manner.

DAC provides for the controlled sharing of objects among individuals. DAC is part of the - *who can access what* - mechanism of any NOS. With DAC, the owner of an object can choose to grant access permissions to other users, that is - the segregation of information and the prevention of unauthorized access to information is set according to the discretion of the **owner of the information**.

Mandatory Access Control

Mandatory **A**ccess **C**ontrol (MAC) is a system of access control that assigns security labels or classifications to system resources and allows access only to entities (people, processes, devices) with distinct levels of authorization or clearance. These controls are enforced by the operating system or security kernel. For example, the operating system will not convert a top secret document to a lower classification without a formal, documented process of declassification.

A database management system, in its access control mechanism, can also apply mandatory access control. In this case, the objects are tables, views, procedures, and so on.

With mandatory access control, this security policy is centrally controlled by a security policy administrator, normally the owner of all the DBMS resources i.e. the **root** user. Other users do not have the ability to override the policy and, for example, grant access to files that would otherwise be restricted.

Data Encryption

Data encryption is a process in which plaintext data is converted into ciphertext so that it cannot be read. Generally known as encryption, this process can be accomplished in a wide variety of ways, and with varying degrees of success. Some of the best data encryption can last for centuries, while other types of decryption can be broken in minutes or even seconds by people who are skilled at such tasks.

In today's digital age, people rely heavily on data encryption on a daily basis. Chances are high that you have received or sent encrypted data at some point today, for example if you've made a purchase via any Internet portal and payment gateway. This is true even if you did not directly perform the encryption or decryption of the data personally yourself.

An alphabetic substitution is usually fairly easy to break; in fact, many major newspapers have a simple substitution encryption on their puzzles page for people to solve every day.

More complex methods of data encryption can be used to make data encryption breaking a more challenging task.

Hackers can try to use brute force algorithms to crack encryption, and they may eventually succeed, but it should take a long time. Many methods of encryption focus on keeping the key secure, and allowing the encrypted data to be freely seen, based on the argument that once encrypted, the data is harmless, as long as people do not obtain the key.

There are a number of reasons to need to encrypt data, most of which rely on shielding data from the eyes of other people. Banks, for example, send encrypted data about their clients back and forth, while governments rely on encryption to get secure messages to overseas embassies. Most email programs offer data encryption while sending and receiving so that emails cannot be read by third parties, as do sites which handle personal information like addresses and credit card numbers.

Some encryption protocols are standardized so that people can easily communicate with each other, while in other cases, a key may be developed specifically for use by particular people, and the key is not standardized to make it harder to crack. Personalized keys were once the only way to encrypt data, until shared key encryption allowed people to exchange information about a key across an open network without disclosing the contents of the key itself.

Relational Database Management Systems Security

Today almost all data management is done using **R**elational **D**atabase **M**anagement **S**ystems (**RDBMS**). Data management is a domain that exists within the business domain. What this means that business generally uses and RDBMS to help manage business data in real time.

Business data is sensitive. Competition in the business domain ensures this. If business data were to fall into a compsetitor's hands this could sharply impact the growth of a business. Hence an important facet of any RDBMS is **data security**.

An RDBMS needs to provide features that when applied properly (and in combination) will help ensure that there is no unauthorized access to the data held within a database.

Deciding On A Security Policy

Before any specific security features of an RDBMS are used a company needs to develop and document a **security policy**. The DBA, management, application support team members, application development team members and other users of the database have to decide **how open** the database and its data will be.

Security policies vary widely across companies and generally depend upon the specifics of an application and the requirements of the organization.

Security policies can range from read-only databases that can be queried by anyone in the organization to companies who are carrying data so sensitive that access is through restricted terminals, which in turn are placed in level VI type security enclosures where access is via retinal scanning and finger print checking.

Developing a sound security policy depends on answering the kind of questions listed below. The analysis of the answers indicates the kind of security that has to be applied to the database.

Once this has been established the various features of the RDBMS can be used separately and in combination to help ensure the level of data security required by the organization and the commercial application via which business data is being manipulated.

Security Policy creation - (Questions Asked)

User Access To The Database

Will users share one or more common userids?

Or

Will each user have unique userid?

Should user access passwords expire after a pre-determined period of time?

Should passwords be of a minimum length?

Must password be alpha numeric? Pure alphabet based passwords will then be rejected.

Should the number of concurrent sessions of a user be limited?

Will users be allowed to create their own database objects?

Will the DBA and other such privileged accounts have restricted access?

Will remote users be able to connect to the database via SQL*Net?

Will the database be accessible for distributed queries?

Read Sensitivity Of Data

Will application data be accessible to all users of the database?

Will different levels of access be granted to different users of the database?

Will users with rights to create database objects have the right in turn to grant others right of access to the object they create?

Write Sensitivity Of Data

Can table data be changed only the table owner or by non-owners as well?

Will some tables contain data that can be updated?

Should some tables be used only as audit tables with insert-only rights granted to users?

Will some tables have data that can never be deleted? The data held within them can only be marked as deleted but never physically deleted.

Will some tables have data that can never be updated? The data held within them can only be marked as replaced with new rows.

A Data Audit Policy

A data audit policy is required when the company needs to know

- Which user manipulated table data
- On what data and at which time this occurred
- From what terminal and with which UserId
- The actual data manipulation that occurred

The following questions would need to be answered.

Is there a need to know who has selected from, inserted into, updated, or deleted from tables?

Is this information to be colleted based on each user session?

Is there a need to pinpoint the exact time when the above manipulation takes place on the data held within a database table?

Is it enough to know that someone accessed the table?

Is it necessary to know exactly which row was accessed?

Is it necessary to know exactly what was changed a row when it was accessed?

When answers to the above type of questions are obtained this has to be analyzed and the highest level of RDBMS security determined.

The highest level of security must be determined. This has to be in turn colored by specific application requirements. Applications that manipulate critical data will have critical data security applied. Applications whose data needs to be made available to a broader spectrum of users will have lower levels of security applied.

Some applications belonging to critical domains (such as defense, police, medical research and so on) would probably have critical security applied right across the application irrespective which user access the application. Additionally, this will almost always be bound to a stringent data audit policy.

The RDBMS model used is Oracle, hence a brief look at the techniques provided by Oracle (these techniques are generally available across all commercial strength RDBMS) to enforce data security follows.

Creating Users:

Each person accessing a database must have an Oracle **Userid**. Userid's are normally created by a DBA. However, any person with the CREATE ANY USER system privilege can create users. As a general rule do not bind a number of users to a single userid but have each user bound to a single, unique userid.

When each Userid is created it has to be bound to a set of attributes that give the user access to system resources.

It can get very tedious for a DBA to create a single Userid and bind this id to a number of specific system resources.

User Profiles:

Oracle provides a solution to this. A DBA can create a **named** user profile. Attach several pre-determined, system privileges, to the profile and then simply bind the Userid being created to the profile. The Userid will then have access to system resources as assigned to the profile.

This reduces the work of a DBA when creating Userids. Several profiles can be pre-created by the DBA with different levels of access to system resources assigned to them. Then when a new Userid is being created the id can simply be bound to an appropriate profile.

When required, specific users may have special access to system resources individually set by the DBA.

There are a number of system resources assignable by the DBA. The possible values to these parameters are an **INTEGER** or the keywords **DEFAULT** or **UNLIMITED**.

Some of the parameters are described below:
COMPOSITE_LIMIT
CPU_PER_SESSION
CPU_PER_CALL
CONNECT_TIME
IDLE_TIME
LOGICAL_READS_PER_SESSION
LOGICAL_READS_PER_CALL
PRIVATE_SGA
SESSIONS_PER_USER

Some Password Control Parameters

FAILED_LOGIN_ATTEMPTS
PASSWORD_GRACE_TIME
PASSWORD_LIFE_TIME
PASSWORD_LOCK_TIME
PASSWORD_REUSE_MAX
PASSWORD_REUSE_TIME
PASSWROD_VERIFY_FUNCTION

Note: *At the time when the database is created, an initial profile named DEFALUT is established. This profile will act as the default profile for a user when no profile is specified. It can also act as a definition of the default values for any other profile.*

System Privileges:

System privileges allow a user of the database to perform specific actions within the database. In Oracle 8 (and above) there are 90 system privileges that can be assigned to a **user** or a **role**.

Object Privileges:

Object privileges allow a user to access or manipulate objects in a database. Depending upon the type of database object different privileges will apply. By default only the owner of an object automatically has all the privileges for the object.

Additionally, anyone who is the DBA or has DBA privileges can manipulate any object in any schema.

Roles:

Roles are a mechanism used by Oracle to facilitate the granting of system and object privileges to users. The granting of roles is multi step process:

1. The role is created by someone with the CREATE ROLE privilege
2. System or object privileges are granted to the role by anyone with proper authorization
3. The role is grated to a user by anyone who has the GRANT ANY ROLE system privilege or by anyone who has been granted the role via the WITH ADMIN OPTION

Default Role:

Normally when a role is granted to a user it becomes the role that is automatically active when the user connects to a database i.e. the **default role**.

Auditing Activity Within A Database:

Once a database is operational, the DBA may want to track the kind of activity within the database. This kind of internal activity tracking is known as **auditing**. Using the AUDIT SQL statement access to individual database objects, the use of specific SQL statements, or the use of system resources can be tracked.

Oracle's auditing is action oriented. When an SQL statement is processed the Oracle engine writes a record to an audit trail. The record in the audit trail table, registers details such as

- Userid
- Time action performed
- Database object against which the action was performed
- Whether the action was successful or not

And so on.

Reading the contents of the audit table will inform the DBA about all the transactions performed against database objects, whether these were successful or not, and who performed these transactions.

In Conclusion:

An appropriate mix and match of User control and audit trails mapped to a database and its objects offer excellent database security.

Self Review Questions

Fill In The Blanks

1. ________________ is a domain that exists within the business domain.
2. Before any specific security features of an RDBMS are used a company needs to develop and document a ________________.
3. A ________________ is required when the company needs to know which user manipulated table data.
4. Any person with the ________________ system privilege can create users.
5. ________________ allow a user of the database to perform specific actions within the database.
6. __________ are a mechanism used by Oracle to facilitate the granting of system and object privileges to users.

True Or False

7. Applications that manipulate critical data will have minimum data security applied.
8. Applications whose data needs to be made available to a broader spectrum of users will have lower levels of security applied.
9. When each Userid is created it has to be bound to a set of attributes that give the user access to system resources.
10. Several profiles can be pre-created by the DBA with different levels of access to system resources assigned to them.
11. System privileges allow a user to access or manipulate objects in a database.

Objective Questions

1. What is discretionary access control?
2. What is mandatory access control?
3. Why is data encryption used?
4. How do you decide on a security policy?
5. Write down at least eight security questions that must be asked?
6. When is a data audit policy used?

8. SQL Concepts

Basics Of SQL

Structured Query Language (SQL) is a language that provides an interface to relational database systems. SQL was developed by IBM in the 1970s for use in System R, and is a de facto standard, as well as an ISO and ANSI standard. SQL is often pronounced SEQUEL.

In common usage SQL also encompasses DML (Data Manipulation Language), for INSERTs, UPDATEs, DELETEs and DDL (Data Definition Language), used for creating and modifying tables and other database structures.

The development of SQL is governed by standards. The **A**merican **N**ational **S**tandards **I**nstitute (**ANSI**) is an organization that approves certain standards in many different industries. SQL has been deemed the standard language in relational database communication, originally approved in 1986 based on IBM's implementation. In 1987, the **I**nternational **S**tandards **O**rganization (**ISO**) accepted the **ANSI SQL** standard as the international standard. The standard was revised again in 1992 and was called **SQL-92**. The newest standard is now called **SQL-99**, it is also referred to as **SQL3**. **SQL3** support object extensions and are partially implemented in **Oracle8 and 9**.

SQL has been a command language for communication with the Oracle 9i Server from any tool or application. Oracle SQL contains many extensions. When an SQL statement is entered, it is stored in a part of memory called the SQL buffer and remains there until a new SQL statement is entered.

Features Of SQL

1. SQL can be used by a range of users, including those with little or no programming experience
2. It is a non procedural language
3. It reduces the amount of time required for creating and maintaining systems
4. It is an English-like language

Components Of SQL

1. **DDL (Data Definition Language)** – It is a set of SQL commands used to create, modify and delete database structures but not data. These commands are normally not used by a general user, who should be accessing the database via an application. They are normally used by the DBA to a limited extent, a database designer or application developer. These statements are immediate i.e. they are not susceptible to ROLLBACK commands. It should also be noted that if several DML statements for example updates are executed then issuing any DDL command would COMMIT all the updates as every DDL command implicitly issues a COMMIT command to the database. Anybody using DDL must have the CREATE object privilege and a Tablespace area in which to create objects.
2. **DML (Data Manipulation Language)** –It is the area of SQL that allows changing data within the database.

3. **DCL (Data Control Language)** - It is the component of SQL statement that control access to data and to the database. Occasionally DCL statements are grouped with DML statements.

Examples of DDL, DML and DCL commands

DDL: Data Definition Language statements

Examples:

- **CREATE** To create objects in the database
- **ALTER** Alters the structure of the database
- **DROP** Delete objects from the database
- **TRUNCATE** Remove all records from a table, including ail spaces allocated for the records are removed
- **COMMENT** Add comments to the data dictionary
- **GRANT** Gives user's access privileges to database
- **REVOKE** Withdraw access privileges given with the GRANT command

DML: Data Manipulation Language statements

Examples:

- **INSERT** Insert data into a table
- **UPDATE** Updates existing data within a table
- **DELETE** Deletes all records from a table, the space for the records remain
- **CALL** Call a PL/SQL or Java subprogram
- **EXPLAIN PLAN** Explain access path to data
- **LOCK** TABLE Control concurrency

DCL: Data Control Language statements

Examples:

- **COMMIT** Save work done
- **SAVEPOINT** Identify a point in a transaction to which you can later roll back
- **ROLLBACK** Restore database to original since the last COMMIT
- **SET TRANSACTION** Change transaction options like what rollback segment to use
- **GRANT / REVOKE** Grant or take back permissions to or from the oracle users

Data Manipulation In Database Management Systems

All organizations need to collect process and store data for its human, financial, material needs. For example, an organization could store information for Payroll, Accounts Receivable and Payable, Sales Receivable and Forecast or Design and Manufacturing.

Table / Entity

To represent this information one can use DBMS modeling. In a DBMS a group of similar information or data, which is of interest to an organization, is called an **Entity**. Entity information is stored in an object called **Table**. For example, a **client** is considered an entity. Information about the client entity can be stored in a ***client_master*** table. A **table** is really a two dimensional matrix that consists of rows and columns.

The table must have a unique name (i.e. ***client_master***) via which it can be referred to, after its creation. The Oracle engine can manipulate data stored in such an object, (i.e. a table) at very high speed.

The Component Parts Of A Two Dimensional Matrix:

Attributes / Columns / Fields

Each entity can have a number of characteristics. A client can have characteristics like name, address, telephone number, fax number, balance due etc. The characteristics of an entity are called **Attributes**. The values for these characteristics are called **Attribute values**.

When entity information is stored in a table, the attributes associated with the entity are stored in the table columns / table fields. The client_master table can have columns like name, address, telephone_number, fax_number, bal_due in which the user can store attributes values like 'Datamatics', 'Vile Parle (E)', '6124571', '6111646', '4500.00'.

Thus information in the client_master table will be

Name	Address	Telephone Number	Fax Number	Balance Due
Datamatics	Vile Parle (E)	6123456	6454567	4500.00

Tuple / Record / Row

An organization will deal with many clients and the same information must be recorded for each client. Multiple fields placed in a horizontal plane, is called a **Record** or **Row** or **Tuple**.

Thus information in the client_master table will be:

Name	Address	Telephone Number	Fax Number	Balance Due
Datamatics	Vile Parle (E)	6124571	6111646	4500.00
Sampoorna	Santacruz	5755342	7456443	90.00
Videocon	Fort	7977353	5745342	7000.00
Citicorp	Seepz	34364754	6007734	300.00

To create a column / field, to store, maintain and manipulate data, the engine requires a minimum of three parameters to be passed by the creator. These parameters are column name, column size and column data type. These parameters are passed to the engine, via its natural language, SQL. The tool used is SQL*Plus.

The field 'Name' is of type **char** (character) with size 20, the field 'address' is of type **char** with size 100 and the field 'balance_due' is of type **number** with size 8 and so on.

There are several other parameters that a creator can pass to the engine at column creation time. Some of these parameters will place 'constraints' on the data that a user can load into the column.

The various data types, recognized by the Oracle engine and permitted to be used for creating an Oracle table column are defined below.

The Data Types That A Cell Can Hold

Data Type	Description
CHAR(size)	This data type is used to store character strings values of fixed length. The size in brackets determines the number of characters the cell can hold. The maximum number of characters (i.e. the size) this data type can hold is 255 characters. ORACLE compares CHAR values using blank-padded comparison semantics i.e. if a value that is inserted in a cell of CHAR datatype is shorter than the size it is defined for then it will be padded with spaces on the right until it reaches the size characters in length.
VARCHAR (size) / VARCHAR2 (size)	This data type is used to store variable length alphanumeric data. The maximum this data type can hold is 2000 characters. One difference between this data type and the CHAR data type is ORACLE compares VARCHAR values using non-padded comparison semantics ' e. the inserted values will not be padded with spaces.
NUMBER(P, S)	The NUMBER data type is used to store numbers (fixed or floating point). Numbers of virtually any magnitude maybe stored up to 38 digits of precision. Numbers as large as 9.99 * 10 to the power of 124, i.e. 1 followed by 125 zeros can be stored. The precision, (P), determines the maximum length of the data, whereas the scale, (S), determines the number of places to the right of the decimal. If scale is omitted then the default is zero. If precision is omitted, values are stored with their original precision upto the maximum of 38 digits.
DATE	This data type is used to represent date and time. The standard format is DD-MON-YY as in 21-JUN-98. To enter dates other than the standard format, use the appropriate functions. DateTime stores date in the 24-hour format. By default, the time in a date field is 12:00:00 am, if no time portion is specified. The default date for a date field is the first day of the current month.
LONG	This data type is used to store variable length character strings containing upto 2GB. LONG data can be used to store arrays of binary data in ASCII format. LONG values cannot be indexed, and the normal character functions such as SUBSTR cannot be applied to LONG values.

Data Type	Description
RAW/ LONG RAW	The RAW /LONG RAW data type is used to store binary data, such as digitized picture or image. Data loaded into columns of these data types are stored without any further conversion. RAW data type can have a maximum length of 255 bytes. LONG RAW data type can contain up to 2GB. Values stored in columns having LONG RAW data type cannot be indexed.

Two Dimension Matrix Creation

One needs to communicate with the Oracle engine to create a **two dimensional matrix** (i.e. a table) for the storage and manipulation of data. This must be done using the natural language of the Oracle Engine i.e. SQL.

A Table can be created with cell parameters by using an SQL sentence. Hence, it is necessary to understand how to construct standard SQL sentences. A look at a ***generic SQL*** sentence will help understand SQL syntax.

The Generic SQL Sentence Construct:

Verb

[Clause 1]<para1:1 para1:2 para1:n>,

[Clause 2]<para2:1 para2:2 para2:n>, ... [Clause n];

> **Note:** ***The rules of (grammar) SQL syntax***
>
> *An SQL statement starts with a* ***verb****. This verb may have additional* ***nouns*** *and* ***adjectives****.*
>
> *Each* ***verb*** *is followed by a number of* ***clauses****.*
> *Each* ***clause*** *has one or more* ***parameters****. Beyond this no further decomposition is allowed i.e. parameters cannot in turn have sub-parameters.*
> *A* ***space*** *separates* ***clauses*** *within an SQL statement.*

Data Constraints

All businesses of the world run on business data being gathered, stored and analyzed. Business managers determine a set of business rules that must be applied to their data prior to it being stored in the database/table to ensure its integrity.

For instance, no employee in the sales department can have a salary of less than Rs.1000/-.

Such rules have to be enforced on data stored. Only data, which satisfies the conditions set, should be stored for future analysis.

If the data gathered fails to satisfy the conditions set, it must be rejected. This ensures that the data stored in a table will be valid, and have integrity.

Business rules that are applied to data are completely **System dependent**. The rules applied to data gathered and processed by a **Savings bank system** will be very different, to the business rules applied to data gathered and processed by an **Inventory system**, which in turn will be very different, to the business rules applied to data gathered and processed by a **Personnel management system**.

Business rules, which are enforced on data being stored in a table, are called **Constraints**. Constraints, **super control** the data being entered into a table for permanent storage.

To understand the concept of data constraints, several tables will be created and different types of constraints will be applied to table columns **or** the table itself. The set of tables are described below. Appropriate examples of data constraints are bound to these tables.

Applying Data Constraints

Oracle permits data constraints to be attached to table columns via SQL syntax that checks data for integrity prior storage. Once data constraints are part of a table column construct, the Oracle database engine checks the data being entered into a table column against the data constraints. If the data passes this check, it is stored in the table column, else the data is rejected. Even if a single column of the record being entered into the table fails a constraint, the **entire record is rejected and not stored in the table**.

Both the **Create Table** and **Alter Table** SQL verbs can be used to write SQL sentences that attach constraints (i.e. Business / System rules) to a table column.

Caution:	*Until now tables created in this material have not had any data constraints attached to their table columns. Hence the tables have not been given any instructions to filter what is being stored in the table. This situation can and does, result in erroneous data being stored in the table.*

Once a constraint is attached to a table column, any SQL **INSERT** or **UPDATE** statement automatically causes these constraints to be applied to data prior it is being inserted into the table column for storage.

Note:	*Oracle also permits applying data constraints at Table level. More on table level constraints later in this material.*

Types Of Data Constraints

There are two types of data constraints that can be applied to data being inserted into an Oracle table. One type of constraint is called an **I/O** constraint (**i**nput / **o**utput). This data constraint determines the speed at which data can be inserted or extracted from an Oracle table. The other type of constraint is called a **business rule** constraint.

I/O Constraints

The input/output data constraints are further divided into **two** distinctly different constraints.

The PRIMARY KEY Constraint

A primary key is one or more column(s) in a table used to uniquely identify **each row** in the table. None of the fields that are part of the primary key can contain a null value. A table can have only one primary key. A **primary key column** in a table has special attributes:

- It defines the column, as a mandatory column (**i.e.** the column cannot be left blank). As the NOT NULL attribute is active
- The data held across the column MUST be UNIQUE

A single column primary key is called a **Simple** key. A multicolumn primary key is called a **Composite** primary key. The only function of a primary key in a table is to **uniquely identify a row**. When a record cannot be uniquely identified using a value in a simple key, a composite key must be defined. A primary key can be defined in either a **CREATE TABLE** statement or an **ALTER TABLE** statement.

For example, a **SALES_ORDER_DETAILS** table will hold multiple records that are sales orders. Each such sales order will have multiple products that have been ordered. Standard business rules do not allow multiple entries for the same product. However, multiple orders will definitely have multiple entries of the same product.

Under these circumstances, the only way to uniquely identify a row in the **SALES_ORDER_DETAILS** table is via a composite primary key, consisting of **ORDER_NO** and **PRODUCT_NO**. Thus the combination of order number and product number will uniquely identify a row.

Features of Primary key

1. Primary key is a column or a set of columns that uniquely identifies a row. Its main purpose is the **Record Uniqueness**
2. Primary key will not allow duplicate values
3. Primary key will also not allow null values
4. Primary key is not compulsory but it is recommended
5. Primary key helps to identify one record from another record and also helps in relating tables with one another
6. Primary key cannot be LONG or LONG RAW data type
7. Only one Primary key is allowed per table
8. Unique Index is created automatically if there is a Primary key
9. One table can combine upto 16 columns in a Composite Primary key

PRIMARY KEY Constraint Defined At Column Level

Syntax:

```
<ColumnName> <Datatype>(<Size>) PRIMARY KEY
```

Example:

Drop the CUST_MSTR table, if it already exists. Create a table CUST_MSTR such that the contents of the column CUST_NO is unique and not null.

```
DROP TABLE CUST_MSTR;
CREATE TABLE CUST_MSTR (
    "CUST_NO" VARCHAR2(10) PRIMARY KEY,
    "FNAME" VARCHAR2(25), "MNAME" VARCHAR2(25),
    "LNAME" VARCHAR2(25), "DOB_INC" DATE,
    "OCCUP" VARCHAR2(25), "PHOTOGRAPH" VARCHAR2(25),
    "SIGNATURE"  VARCHAR2(25), "PANCOPY" VARCHAR2(1),
    "FORM60" VARCHAR2(1));
```

Output:

```
Table created.
```

For testing purpose, execute the following **INSERT INTO** statement:

```
INSERT INTO CUST_MSTR (CUST_NO, FNAME, MNAME, LNAME, DOB_INC, OCCUP, PHOTOGRAPH,
                       SIGNATURE, PANCOPY, FORM60)
    VALUES('C1', 'Ivan', 'Nelson', 'Bayross', '25-JUN-1952', 'Self Employed', 'D:/ClntPht/C1.gif',
       'D:/ClntSgnt/C1.gif', 'Y', 'Y');
```

Output:

```
1 row created.
```

To verify whether the Primary Key Constraint is functional, reissue the same **INSERT INTO** statement. The result is the following error:

Output:

```
INSERT INTO CUST_MSTR (CUST_NO, FNAME, MNAME, LNAME, DOB_INC, OCCUP,
PHOTOGRAPH, SIGNATURE, PANCOPY,
*
ERROR at line 1:
ORA-00001: unique constraint (DBA_BANKSYS.SYS_C003009) violated
```

PRIMARY KEY Constraint Defined At Table Level

Syntax:

```
PRIMARY KEY (<ColumnName>, <ColumnName>)
```

Example:

Drop the FD_MSTR table, if it already exists. Create a table FD_MSTR where there is a composite primary key mapped to the columns FD_SER_NO and CORP_CUST_NO.

Since this constraint spans across columns, it must be described at table level.

```
DROP TABLE FD_MSTR;
CREATE TABLE "DBA_BANKSYS"."FD_MSTR"(
    "FD_SER_NO" VARCHAR2(10), "SF_NO" VARCHAR2(10),
    "BRANCH_NO" VARCHAR2(10), "INTRO_CUST_NO" VARCHAR2(10),
```

```
"INTRO_ACCT_NO" VARCHAR2(10), "INTRO_SIGN" VARCHAR2(1),
"ACCT_NO" VARCHAR2(10), "TITLE" VARCHAR2(30),
"CORP_CUST_NO" VARCHAR2(10), "CORP_CNST_TYPE" VARCHAR(4),
"VERI_EMP_NO" VARCHAR2(10), "VERI_SIGN" VARCHAR2(1),
"MANAGER_SIGN" VARCHAR2(1), PRIMARY KEY(FD_SER_NO, CORP_CUST_NO));
```

Output:

```
Table created.
```

For testing purpose, execute the following **INSERT INTO** statement:

```
INSERT INTO FD_MSTR (FD_SER_NO, SF_NO, BRANCH_NO, ACCT_NO, TITLE, CORP_CUST_NO,
                     CORP_CNST_TYPE, INTRO_CUST_NO, INTRO_ACCT_NO, INTRO_SIGN,
                     VERI_EMP_NO, VERI_SIGN, MANAGER_SIGN)
   VALUES ('FS1', 'SF-0011', 'B1', 'CA2', 'Uttam Stores', 'O11', '1C', null, null, 'N', 'E1', 'Y', 'Y');
```

Output:

```
1 row created.
```

To verify whether the Composite Primary Key Constraint is functional, reissue the same **INSERT INTO** statement. The result is the following error:

Output:

```
INSERT INTO FD_MSTR (FD_SER_NO, SF_NO, BRANCH_NO, ACCT_NO, TITLE,
CORP_CUST_NO, CORP_CNST_TYPE, INTR
*
ERROR at line 1:
ORA-00001: unique constraint (DBA_BANKSYS.SYS_C003010) violated
```

Now, simply modify the INSERT INTO statement as show below, to allow the record to pass the composite primary key constraint:

```
INSERT INTO FD_MSTR (FD_SER_NO, SF_NO, BRANCH_NO, ACCT_NO, TITLE, CORP_CUST_NO,
                     CORP_CNST_TYPE, INTRO_CUST_NO, INTRO_ACCT_NO, INTRO_SIGN,
                     VERI_EMP_NO, VERI_SIGN, MANAGER_SIGN)
   VALUES ('FS2', 'SF-0012', 'B1', 'CA4', 'Sun''s Pvt. Ltd.', 'C12', '4C', null, null, 'N', 'E1', 'Y', 'Y');
```

Output:

```
1 row created.
```

The FOREIGN KEY (Self Reference) Constraint

Foreign keys represent relationships between tables. A foreign key is a column (or a group of columns) whose values are derived from the **primary key** or **unique key** of some other table.

The table in which the foreign key is defined is called a **Foreign table** or **Detail table**. The table that defines the **primary** or **unique** key and is referenced by the **foreign key** is called the **Primary table** or **Master table**. A Foreign key can be defined in either a CREATE TABLE statement or an ALTER TABLE statement

The master table can be referenced in the foreign key definition by using the clause **REFERENCES TableName.ColumnName** when defining the foreign key, column attributes, in the detail table.

Features of Foreign Keys

1. Foreign key is a column(s) that references a column(s) of a table and it can be the same table also
2. Parent that is being referenced has to be unique or Primary key
3. Child may have duplicates and nulls but unless it is specified
4. Foreign key constraint can be specified on child but not on parent
5. Parent record can be delete provided no child record exist
6. Master table cannot be updated if child record exist

This constraint establishes a relationship between records (i.e. column data) across a Master and a Detail table. This relationship ensures:

- Records cannot be **inserted** into a **detail table** if corresponding records in the master table do not exist
- Records of the master **table** cannot be **deleted** if corresponding records in the detail table actually exist

Insert Or Update Operation In The FOREIGN KEY Table

The existence of a foreign key implies that the table with the foreign key is **related** to the master table from which the foreign key is derived. A foreign key must have a corresponding primary key or unique key value in the master table.

For example a personnel information system includes two tables (i.e. department and employee). An employee cannot belong to a department that does not exist. Thus the department number specified in the employee table must be present in the department table.

Delete Operation On The PRIMARY KEY Table

Oracle **displays an error message** when a record in the master table is deleted and corresponding records exists in a detail table and **prevents the delete operation** from going through.

> **Note:** *The default behavior of the foreign key can be changed, by using the ON DELETE CASCADE option. When the ON DELETE CASCADE option is specified in the foreign key definition, if a record is deleted in the master table, all corresponding records in the detail table along with the record in the master table will be deleted.*

Principles of **Foreign Key/References** constraint:

- Rejects an **INSERT** or **UPDATE** of a value, if a corresponding value does not currently exist in the master key table
- If the **ON DELETE CASCADE** option is set, a **DELETE** operation in the master table will trigger a **DELETE** operation for corresponding records **in all** detail tables

- If the **ON DELETE SET NULL** option is set, a **DELETE** operation in the master table will set the value held by the foreign key of the detail tables to null
- **Rejects** a **DELETE** from the Master table if **corresponding records** in the DETAIL table **exist**
- Must reference a **PRIMARY KEY** or **UNIQUE** column(s) in primary table
- Requires that the **FOREIGN KEY** column(s) and the **CONSTRAINT** column(s) have **matching** data types
- Can reference the same table named in the **CREATE TABLE** statement

FOREIGN KEY Constraint Defined At The Column Level

Syntax:

```
<ColumnName> <DataType>(<Size>)
    REFERENCES <TableName> [(<ColumnName>)]
        [ON DELETE CASCADE]
```

Example:

Drop the table EMP_MSTR, if it already exists. Create a table EMP_MSTR with its primary as EMP_NO referencing the foreign key BRANCH_NO in the BRANCH_MSTR table.

```
DROP TABLE EMP_MSTR;
CREATE TABLE "DBA_BANKSYS"."EMP_MSTR"(
    "EMP_NO" VARCHAR2(10) PRIMARY KEY,
    "BRANCH_NO" VARCHAR2(10) REFERENCES BRANCH_MSTR,
    "FNAME" VARCHAR2(25), "MNAME" VARCHAR2(25),
    "LNAME" VARCHAR2(25), "DEPT" VARCHAR2(30),
    "DESIG" VARCHAR2(30));
```

Output:

```
Table created.
```

The **REFERENCES** key word points to the table **BRANCH_MSTR**. The table **BRANCH_MSTR** has the column **BRANCH_NO** as its primary key column. Since no column is specified in the foreign key definition, Oracle applies an automatic (default) link to the primary key column i.e. **BRANCH_NO** of the table **BRANCH_MSTR**.

The foreign key definition is specified as

```
"BRANCH_NO" VARCHAR2(10) REFERENCES BRANCH_MSTR
```

FOREIGN KEY Constraint Defined At The Table Level

Syntax:

```
FOREIGN KEY (<ColumnName> [,<ColumnName>] )
    REFERENCES <TableName> [(<ColumnName>,<ColumnName>)
```

Example:

Drop the table ACCT_FD_CUST_DTLS, if it already exists. Create a table ACCT_FD_CUST_DTLS with CUST_NO as foreign key referencing column CUST_NO in the CUST_MSTR table

```
DROP TABLE ACCT_FD_CUST_DTLS;
CREATE TABLE "DBA_BANKSYS"."ACCT_FD_CUST_DTLS"(
    "ACCT_FD_NO" VARCHAR2(10), "CUST_NO" VARCHAR2(10),
    FOREIGN KEY (CUST_NO) REFERENCES CUST_MSTR(CUST_NO));
```

Output:

```
Table created.
```

FOREIGN KEY Constraint Defined With ON DELETE CASCADE

Example:

Drop the table FD_MSTR, if it already exists. Create a table FD_MSTR with its primary key as FD_SER_NO.

Drop the table FD_DTLS, if it already exists. Create a table FD_DTLS with its foreign key as FD_SER_NO with the ON DELETE CASCADE option. The foreign key is FD_SER_NO and is available as a primary key column named FD_SER_NO in the FD_MSTR table.

Insert some records into both the tables.

```
DROP TABLE FD_MSTR;
CREATE TABLE "DBA_BANKSYS"."FD_MSTR"(
    "FD_SER_NO" VARCHAR2(10) PRIMARY KEY,
    "SF_NO" VARCHAR2(10), "BRANCH_NO" VARCHAR2(10),
    "INTRO_CUST_NO" VARCHAR2(10), "INTRO_ACCT_NO" VARCHAR2(10),
    "INTRO_SIGN" VARCHAR2(1), "ACCT_NO" VARCHAR2(10),
    "TITLE" VARCHAR2(30), "CORP_CUST_NO" VARCHAR2(10),
    "CORP_CNST_TYPE" VARCHAR(4), "VERI_EMP_NO" VARCHAR2(10),
    "VERI_SIGN" VARCHAR2(1), "MANAGER_SIGN" VARCHAR2(1));
```

Output:

```
Table created.
```

```
DROP TABLE FD_DTLS;
CREATE TABLE "DBA_BANKSYS"."FD_DTLS"(
    "FD_SER_NO" VARCHAR2(10), "FD_NO" VARCHAR2(10),
    "TYPE" VARCHAR2(1), "PAYTO_ACCTNO" VARCHAR2(10),
    "PERIOD" NUMBER(5), "OPNDT" DATE,
```

```
"DUEDT" DATE, "AMT" NUMBER(8,2),
"DUEAMT" NUMBER(8,2), "INTRATE" NUMBER(3),
"STATUS" VARCHAR2(1) DEFAULT 'A', "AUTO_RENEWAL" VARCHAR2(1) ,
CONSTRAINT f_FDSerNoKey
    FOREIGN KEY (FD_SER_NO) REFERENCES FD_MSTR(FD_SER_NO)
    ON DELETE CASCADE);
```

Output:

```
Table created.
```

Now delete a record from the FD_MSTR table as:

DELETE FROM FD_MSTR **WHERE** FD_SER_NO = 'FS1';

Output:

```
1 row deleted.
```

Query the table FD_DTLS for records:

SELECT * FROM FD_DTLS;

Notice the deletion of the records belonging to **FS1**.

Explanation:

In this example, a primary key is created in the FD_MSTR table. It consists of only **one field** i.e. FD_SER_NO field. Then a foreign key is created in the FD_DTLS table that references the FD_MSTR table based on the contents of the FD_SER_NO field.

Because of the **cascade delete**, when a record in the FD_MSTR table is deleted, all records in the FD_DTLS table will also be deleted that have the same FD_SER_NO value.

FOREIGN KEY Constraint Defined With ON DELETE SET NULL:

A FOREIGN key with a **SET NULL ON DELETE** means that if a record in the parent table is deleted, then the corresponding records in the child table will have the foreign key fields set to **null**. The records in the child table **will not** be deleted.

A FOREIGN key with a **SET NULL ON DELETE** can be defined in either a CREATE TABLE statement or an ALTER TABLE statement.

Example:

Drop the table FD_MSTR, if it already exists. Create a table FD_MSTR with its primary key as FD_SER_NO.

Drop the table FD_DTLS, if it already exists. Create a table FD_DTLS with its foreign key as FD_SER_NO with the ON DELETE SET NULL option. The foreign key is FD_SER_NO and is available as a primary key column named FD_SER_NO in the FD_MSTR table.

Insert some records into both the tables.

```
DROP TABLE FD_MSTR;
CREATE TABLE "DBA_BANKSYS"."FD_MSTR"(
    "FD_SER_NO" VARCHAR2(10) PRIMARY KEY, "SF_NO" VARCHAR2(10),
    "BRANCH_NO" VARCHAR2(10), "INTRO_CUST_NO" VARCHAR2(10),
    "INTRO_ACCT_NO" VARCHAR2(10), "INTRO_SIGN" VARCHAR2(1),
    "ACCT_NO" VARCHAR2(10), "TITLE" VARCHAR2(30), "CORP_CUST_NO" VARCHAR2(10),
    "CORP_CNST_TYPE" VARCHAR(4), "VERI_EMP_NO" VARCHAR2(10),
    "VERI_SIGN" VARCHAR2(1), "MANAGER_SIGN" VARCHAR2(1));
```

Output:

```
Table created.
```

```
DROP TABLE FD_DTLS;
CREATE TABLE "DBA_BANKSYS"."FD_DTLS"(
    "FD_SER_NO" VARCHAR2(10), "FD_NO" VARCHAR2(10), "TYPE" VARCHAR2(1),
    "PAYTO_ACCTNO" VARCHAR2(10), "PERIOD" NUMBER(5), "OPNDT" DATE,
    "DUEDT" DATE, "AMT" NUMBER(8,2), "DUEAMT" NUMBER(8,2), "INTRATE" NUMBER(3),
    "STATUS" VARCHAR2(1) DEFAULT 'A', "AUTO_RENEWAL" VARCHAR2(1) ,
    CONSTRAINT f_FDSerNoKey
        FOREIGN KEY (FD_SER_NO) REFERENCES FD_MSTR(FD_SER_NO)
        ON DELETE SET NULL);
```

Output:

```
Table created.
```

Now delete a record from the FD_MSTR table as:

```
DELETE FROM FD_MSTR WHERE FD_SER_NO = 'FS1';
```

Output:

```
1 row deleted.
```

Query the table FD_DTLS for records:

```
SELECT * FROM FD_DTLS;
```

Notice the value held by the field FD_SER_NO.

Explanation:

In this example, a primary key is created in the FD_MSTR table. It consists of only one field i.e. FD_SER_NO field. Then a foreign key is created in the FD_DTLS table that references the FD_MSTR table based on the FD_SER_NO field.

Because of the **cascade set null**, when a record in the FD_MSTR table is deleted, all corresponding records in the FD_DTLS table will have the FD_SER_NO values set to **null**.

Assigning User Defined Names To Constraints

When constraints are defined, Oracle assigns a **unique name** to each constraint. The convention used by Oracle is

SYS_C**n**

where **n** is a **numeric value** that makes the constraint name **unique**.

Constraints can be given a unique user-defined name along with the constraint definition. A constraint can then, be dropped by referring to the constraint by its name. Under these circumstances a user-defined constraint name becomes very convenient.

User named constraints simplifies the task of dropping constraints. A constraint can be given a user-defined name by preceding the constraint definition with the reserved word **CONSTRAINT** and a **user-defined name**.

Syntax:

```
CONSTRAINT <Constraint Name> <Constraint Definition>
```

Example:

Drop the CUST_MSTR table, if it already exists. Create a table CUST_MSTR with a primary key constraint on the column CUST_NO and also define its constraint name.

```
DROP TABLE CUST_MSTR;
CREATE TABLE CUST_MSTR (
    "CUST_NO" VARCHAR2(10) CONSTRAINT p_CUSTKey PRIMARY KEY,
    "FNAME" VARCHAR2(25), "MNAME" VARCHAR2(25),
    "LNAME" VARCHAR2(25), "DOB_INC" DATE,
    "OCCUP" VARCHAR2(25), "PHOTOGRAPH" VARCHAR2(25),
    "SIGNATURE" VARCHAR2(25), "PANCOPY" VARCHAR2(1),
    "FORM60" VARCHAR2(1));
```

Output:

```
Table created.
```

Example:

Drop the table EMP_MSTR, if it already exists. Create a table EMP_MSTR with its foreign key as BRANCH_NO. The foreign key is BRANCH_NO available and as a primary key in the BRANCH_MSTR table. Also define the name of the foreign key.

```
DROP TABLE EMP_MSTR;
CREATE TABLE "DBA_BANKSYS"."EMP_MSTR"(
```

```
    "EMP_NO" VARCHAR2(10), "BRANCH_NO" VARCHAR2(10),
    "FNAME" VARCHAR2(25), "MNAME" VARCHAR2(25),
    "LNAME" VARCHAR2(25), "DEPT" VARCHAR2(30),
    "DESIG" VARCHAR2(30),
    CONSTRAINT f_BranchKey
        FOREIGN KEY (BRANCH_NO) REFERENCES BRANCH_MSTR);
```

Output:

```
Table created.
```

The UNIQUE KEY Constraint

The **Unique** column constraint **permits multiple entries** of NULL into the column. These NULL values are clubbed at the top of the column in the order in which they were entered into the table. This is **the essential difference** between the Primary Key and the Unique constraints when applied to table column(s).

Key point about Unique Constraint:

1. Unique key will not allow duplicate values
2. Unique index is created automatically
3. A table can have more than one Unique key which is not possible in Primary key
4. Unique key can combine upto 16 columns in a Composite Unique key
5. Unique key cannot be LONG or LONG RAW data type

Unique Constraint Defined At The Column Level

Syntax:

```
<ColumnName> <Datatype>(<Size>) UNIQUE
```

Example:

Drop the CUST_MSTR table, if it already exists. Create a table CUST_MSTR such that the contents of the column CUST_NO are unique across the entire column.

```
DROP TABLE CUST_MSTR;
CREATE TABLE CUST_MSTR (
    "CUST_NO" VARCHAR2(10) UNIQUE, "FNAME" VARCHAR2(25), "MNAME" VARCHAR2(25),
    "LNAME" VARCHAR2(25), "DOB_INC" DATE, "OCCUP" VARCHAR2(25),
    "PHOTOGRAPH" VARCHAR2(25), "SIGNATURE"  VARCHAR2(25), "PANCOPY" VARCHAR2(1),
    "FORM60" VARCHAR2(1));
```

Output:

```
Table created.
```

For testing the Unique constraint execute the following INSERT INTO statements:

```
INSERT INTO CUST_MSTR (CUST_NO, FNAME, MNAME, LNAME, DOB_INC, OCCUP,
                       PHOTOGRAPH, SIGNATURE, PANCOPY, FORM60)
```

VALUES('C1', 'Ivan', 'Nelson', 'Bayross', '25-JUN-1952', 'Self Employed', 'D:/ClntPht/C1.gif', 'D:/ClntSgnt/C1.gif', 'Y', 'Y'**);**

INSERT INTO CUST_MSTR (CUST_NO, FNAME, MNAME, LNAME, DOB_INC, OCCUP, PHOTOGRAPH, SIGNATURE, PANCOPY, FORM60**)**

VALUES('C1', 'Chriselle', 'Ivan', 'Bayross', '29-OCT-1982', 'Service', 'D:/ClntPht/C2.gif', 'D:/ClntSgnt/C2.gif', 'N', 'Y'**);**

INSERT INTO CUST_MSTR (CUST_NO, FNAME, MNAME, LNAME, DOB_INC, OCCUP, PHOTOGRAPH, SIGNATURE, PANCOPY, FORM60**)**

VALUES('C2', 'Mamta', 'Arvind', 'Muzumdar', '28-AUG-1975', 'Service', 'D:/ClntPht/C3.gif', 'D:/ClntSgnt/C3.gif', 'Y', 'Y'**);**

Output:

The first INSERT INTO statement will execute without any errors as show below:

```
1 row created.
```

When the second INSERT INTO statement is executed an errors occurs as show below:

```
INSERT INTO CUST_MSTR (CUST_NO, FNAME, MNAME, LNAME, DOB_INC, OCCUP,
PHOTOGRAPH, SIGNATURE, PANCOPY,
*
ERROR at line 1:
ORA-00001: unique constraint (DBA_BANKSYS.SYS_C003007) violated
```

The third INSERT INTO statement rectifies this and the result is as show below:

```
1 row created.
```

When a SELECT statement is executed on the Client_Master table the records retrieved are:

SELECT CUST_NO, FNAME, MNAME, LNAME **FROM** CUST_MSTR;

Output:

CUST_NO	FNAME	MNAME	LNAME
C1	Ivan	Nelson	Bayross
C2	Mamta	Arvind	Muzumdar

UNIQUE Constraint Defined At The Table Level

Syntax:

```
CREATE TABLE TableName
    (<ColumnName1> <Datatype>(<Size>), <ColumnName2> <Datatype>(<Size>),
        UNIQUE (<ColumnName1>, <ColumnName2>));
```

Example:

Drop the CUST_MSTR table, if it already exists. Create a table CUST_MSTR such that the contents of the column CUST_NO are unique across the entire column.

```
DROP TABLE CUST_MSTR;
CREATE TABLE CUST_MSTR (
    "CUST_NO" VARCHAR2(10), "FNAME" VARCHAR2(25),
    "MNAME" VARCHAR2(25), "LNAME" VARCHAR2(25),
    "DOB_INC" DATE, "OCCUP" VARCHAR2(25),
    "PHOTOGRAPH" VARCHAR2(25), "SIGNATURE"  VARCHAR2(25),
    "PANCOPY" VARCHAR2(1), "FORM60" VARCHAR2(1),
    UNIQUE(CUST_NO));
```

Output:

```
Table created.
```

In the case of the table level unique constraints, the result for the following INSERT INTO statement will remain the same as explained earlier.

```
INSERT INTO CUST_MSTR (CUST_NO, FNAME, MNAME, LNAME, DOB_INC, OCCUP,
                       PHOTOGRAPH, SIGNATURE, PANCOPY, FORM60)
    VALUES('C1', 'Ivan', 'Nelson', 'Bayross', '25-JUN-1952', 'Self Employed', 'D:/ClntPht/C1.gif',
        D:/ClntSgnt/C1.gif', 'Y', 'Y');
INSERT INTO CUST_MSTR (CUST_NO, FNAME, MNAME, LNAME, DOB_INC, OCCUP,
                       PHOTOGRAPH, SIGNATURE, PANCOPY, FORM60)
    VALUES('C1', 'Chriselle', 'Ivan', 'Bayross', '29-OCT-1982', 'Service', 'D:/ClntPht/C2.gif',
        'D:/ClntSgnt/C2.gif', 'N', 'Y');
INSERT INTO CUST_MSTR (CUST_NO, FNAME, MNAME, LNAME, DOB_INC, OCCUP,
                       PHOTOGRAPH, SIGNATURE, PANCOPY, FORM60)
    VALUES('C2', 'Mamta', 'Arvind', 'Muzumdar', '28-AUG-1975', 'Service', 'D:/ClntPht/C3.gif',
        'D:/ClntSgnt/C3.gif', 'Y', 'Y');
```

NOT NULL Constraint

NOT NULL Constraint Defined At The Column Level

In addition to Primary key and Foreign Key, Oracle has **NOT NULL** as column constraint. The **NOT NULL** column constraint ensures that a table column cannot be left empty.

When a column is defined as **not null**, then that column becomes a **mandatory** column. It implies that a value must be entered into the column if the record is to be accepted for storage in the table.

Syntax:

```
<ColumnName> <Datatype>(<Size>) NOT NULL
```

Example:

Drop the table CUST_MSTR, if already exists and then create it again making Date of Birth field not null. Refer to the details of table in chapter 6

```
CREATE TABLE "DBA_BANKSYS"."CUST_MSTR"(
    "CUST_NO" VARCHAR2(10), "FNAME" VARCHAR2(25),
    "MNAME" VARCHAR2(25), "LNAME" VARCHAR2(25),
    "DOB_INC" DATE NOT NULL, "OCCUP" VARCHAR2(25),
    "PHOTOGRAPH" VARCHAR2(25), "SIGNATURE"  VARCHAR2(25),
    "PANCOPY" VARCHAR2(1), "FORM60" VARCHAR2(1));
```

Output:

```
Table created.
```

Note:	*The **NOT NULL** constraint can only be applied at column level.*

Execute the following INSERT INTO statements to verify whether mandatory field constraints are applied:

```
INSERT INTO CUST_MSTR (CUST_NO, FNAME, MNAME, LNAME, DOB_INC, OCCUP,
                        PHOTOGRAPH, SIGNATURE, PANCOPY, FORM60)
    VALUES('O14', null, null, null, null, 'Retail Business', null, null, 'N', 'Y');
```

Output:

```
INSERT INTO CUST_MSTR (CUST_NO, FNAME, MNAME, LNAME, DOB_INC, OCCUP,
PHOTOGRAPH, SIGNATURE, PANCOPY,
*
ERROR at line 1:
ORA-01400: cannot insert NULL into
("DBA_BANKSYS"."CUST_MSTR"."DOB_INC")
```

The above **error** message confirms that the mandatory field constraints are applied successfully.

Caution:	*The NOT NULL constraint can only be applied at column level. Although NOT NULL can be applied as a CHECK constraint, Oracle Corp recommends that this should not be done.*

The CHECK Constraint

Business Rule validations can be applied to a table column by using **CHECK** constraint. **CHECK** constraints must be specified as a logical expression that evaluates either to **TRUE** or **FALSE**.

> **Note:** *A CHECK constraint takes substantially longer to execute as compared to NOT NULL,PRIMARY KEY, FOREIGN KEY or UNIQUE. Thus CHECK constraints must be avoided if the constraint can be defined using the Not Null, Primary key or Foreign key constraint.*

CHECK constraint defined at the column level:

Syntax:

<ColumnName> <Datatype>(<Size>) CHECK (<Logical Expression>)

Example:

Drop the table CUST_MSTR, if already exists. Create a table **CUST_MSTR** with the following check constraints:

- Data values being inserted into the column **CUST_NO** must start with the capital letter **C**
- Data values being inserted into the column **FNAME, MNAME and LNAME** should be in **upper case** only

```
CREATE TABLE CUST_MSTR("CUST_NO" VARCHAR2(10) CHECK(CUST_NO LIKE 'C%'),
    "FNAME" VARCHAR2(25) CHECK (FNAME = UPPER(FNAME)),
    "MNAME" VARCHAR2(25) CHECK (MNAME = UPPER(MNAME)),
    "LNAME" VARCHAR2(25) CHECK (LNAME = UPPER(LNAME)), "DOB_INC" DATE,
    "OCCUP" VARCHAR2(25), "PHOTOGRAPH" VARCHAR2(25), "SIGNATURE" VARCHAR2(25),
    "PANCOPY" VARCHAR2(1), "FORM60" VARCHAR2(1));
```

Output:

```
Table created.
```

CHECK Constraint Defined At The Table Level:

Syntax:

CHECK (<Logical Expression>)

Example:

Drop the table CUST_MSTR, if already exists. Create a table **CUST_MSTR** with the following check constraints:

- Data values being inserted into the column **CUST_NO** must start with the capital letter **C**
- Data values being inserted into the column **FNAME, MNAME and LNAME** should be in **upper case** only

```
CREATE TABLE CUST_MSTR("CUST_NO" VARCHAR2(10), "FNAME" VARCHAR2(25),
    "MNAME" VARCHAR2(25), "LNAME" VARCHAR2(25), "DOB_INC" DATE,
    "OCCUP" VARCHAR2(25), "PHOTOGRAPH" VARCHAR2(25), "SIGNATURE" VARCHAR2(25),
```

"PANCOPY" VARCHAR2(1), "FORM60" VARCHAR2(1),
CHECK (CUST_NO LIKE 'C%'), **CHECK** (FNAME = UPPER(FNAME)),
CHECK (MNAME = UPPER(MNAME)), **CHECK** (LNAME = UPPER(LNAME)));

Output:

```
Table created.
```

Execute the following INSERT INTO statements to verify whether check constraints are applied:

INSERT INTO CUST_MSTR (CUST_NO, FNAME, MNAME, LNAME, DOB_INC, OCCUP, PHOTOGRAPH, SIGNATURE, PANCOPY, FORM60**)**
VALUES('O14', 'RAJESH', 'CHAITANYA', 'SHAH', '03-Jan-1981', 'Business', null, null, 'N', 'Y'**);**

Output:

```
INSERT INTO CUST_MSTR (CUST_NO, FNAME, MNAME, LNAME, DOB_INC, OCCUP,
PHOTOGRAPH, SIGNATURE, PANCOPY,
*
ERROR at line 1:
ORA-02290: check constraint (DBA_BANKSYS.SYS_C003055) violated
```

INSERT INTO CUST_MSTR (CUST_NO, FNAME, MNAME, LNAME, DOB_INC, OCCUP, PHOTOGRAPH, SIGNATURE, PANCOPY, FORM60**)**
VALUES('C14', **'Rajesh'**, 'CHAITANYA', 'SHAH', '03-Jan-1981', 'Business', null, null, 'N', 'Y'**);**

Output:

```
INSERT INTO CUST_MSTR (CUST_NO, FNAME, MNAME, LNAME, DOB_INC, OCCUP,
PHOTOGRAPH, SIGNATURE, PANCOPY,
*
ERROR at line 1:
ORA-02290: check constraint (DBA_BANKSYS.SYS_C003056) violated
```

INSERT INTO CUST_MSTR (CUST_NO, FNAME, MNAME, LNAME, DOB_INC, OCCUP, PHOTOGRAPH, SIGNATURE, PANCOPY, FORM60***)***
VALUES('C14', 'RAJESH', **'Chaitanya'**, 'SHAH', '03-Jan-1981', 'Business', null, null, 'N', 'Y'**);**

Output:

```
INSERT INTO CUST_MSTR (CUST_NO, FNAME, MNAME, LNAME, DOB_INC, OCCUP,
PHOTOGRAPH, SIGNATURE, PANCOPY,
*
ERROR at line 1:
ORA-02290: check constraint (DBA_BANKSYS.SYS_C003057) violated
```

INSERT INTO CUST_MSTR (CUST_NO, FNAME, MNAME, LNAME, DOB_INC, OCCUP, PHOTOGRAPH, SIGNATURE, PANCOPY, FORM60**)**
VALUES('C14', 'RAJESH', 'CHAITANYA', **'sHAh'**, '03-Jan-1981', 'Business', null, null, 'N', 'Y'**);**

Output:

```
INSERT INTO CUST_MSTR (CUST_NO, FNAME, MNAME, LNAME, DOB_INC, OCCUP,
PHOTOGRAPH, SIGNATURE, PANCOPY,
*
ERROR at line 1:
ORA-02290: check constraint (DBA_BANKSYS.SYS_C003058) violated
```

The above **error** messages confirm that the check constraints are applied successfully.

When using **CHECK** constraints, consider the ANSI / ISO standard, which states that a CHECK constraint is violated only if the condition evaluates to **False**. A check constraint is not violated if the condition evaluates to **True**.

Note: *If the expression in a check constraint does not return a true / false, the value is Indeterminate or Unknown. Unknown values do not violate a check constraint condition. For example, consider the following CHECK constraint for SellPrice column in the Product_Master table:*

CHECK (SellPrice > 0)

*At first glance, this rule may be interpreted as "do not allow a row in the **Product_Master** table unless **the Sellprice** is greater than 0". However, note that if a row is inserted with a **null SellPrice**, the row **does not violate** the CHECK constraint because the entire check condition is evaluated as **unknown**.*

*In this particular case, prevent such violations by placing the **not null** integrity constraint along with the check constraint on **SellPrice** column of the table **Product_Master**.*

Restrictions On CHECK Constraints

A **CHECK** integrity constraint requires that a condition be **true** or **unknown** for the row to be processed. If an SQL statement causes the condition to evaluate to **false**, an appropriate error message is displayed and processing stops.

A **CHECK** constraint has the following limitations:

- The condition must be a **Boolean** expression that can be evaluated using the values in the row being inserted or updated.
- The condition cannot contain **subqueries** or **sequences**.
- The condition cannot include the SYSDATE, UID, USER or USERENV SQL functions.

The IN and NOT IN Operator:

The arithmetic operator **(=)** compares a single value to another single value. In case a value needs to be compared to a list of values then the **IN** operator is used. The IN operator helps reduce the need to use multiple OR conditions

Example:

List the customer details of the customers named Hansel, Mamta, Namita and Aruna.

Synopsis:

Tables:	CUST_MSTR
Columns:	FNAME, LNAME, DOB_INC
Technique:	**Operators:** IN, **Clauses:** WHERE, **Others:** ALIAS

Solution:

SELECT FNAME, LNAME, DOB_INC "birthday", OCCUP **FROM** CUST_MSTR
WHERE FNAME **IN(**'Hansel', 'Mamta', 'Namita', 'Aruna'**);**

Output:

```
FNAME     LNAME     Birthday   OCCUP
--------------------------------------------------
Mamta     Muzumda   28-AUG-75  Service
          r
Hansel    Colaco    01-JAN-82  Service
Namita    Kanade    10-JUN-78  Self Employed
```

Explanation:

The above example, displays all those records where the FNAME field holds any one of the four specified values.

The **NOT IN** operator is the opposite of the IN operator. This will select all the rows where values **do not** match the values in the list.

Example:

List the customer details of the customers other then Hansel, Mamta, Namita and Aruna.

Synopsis:

Tables:	CUST_MSTR
Columns:	FNAME, LNAME, DOB_INC
Technique:	**Operators:** NOT, IN, **Clauses:** WHERE, **Others:** ALIAS

Solution:

SELECT FNAME, LNAME, DOB_INC "Birthday", OCCUP **FROM** CUST_MSTR
WHERE FNAME **NOT IN(**'Hansel', 'Mamta', 'Namita', 'Aruna'**);**

Output:

```
FNAME      LNAME     Birthday   OCCUP
-----------------------------------------------------
Ivan       Bayross   25-JUN-52  Self Employed
Chriselle  Bayross   29-OCT-82  Service
```

Output: (Continued)

```
Chhaya     Bankar     06-OCT-76 Service
Ashwini    Joshi      20-NOV-78 Business
Anil       Dhone      12-OCT-83 Self Employed
Alex       Fernandes  30-SEP-62 Executive
Ashwini    Apte       19-APR-79 Service
7 rows selected.
```

Explanation:

In the above example by just changing the operator to **NOT IN** the Select statement will now retrieve all the rows where the FNAME is **not in** the values specified. In other words, information about customers whose names are **not Hansel, Mamta, Namita, Aruna** will be displayed.

Aggregate Functions

AVG: Returns an average value of '**n**', **ignoring** null values in a column.

Syntax:

AVG ([<DISTINCT>|<ALL>] <n>)

Example:

SELECT AVG(CURBAL) "Average Balance" **FROM** ACCT_MSTR;

Output:

```
Average Balance
---------------
           1100
```

> **Note:** *In the above SELECT statement, AVG function is used to calculate the average balance of all accounts branch wise. The selected column is renamed as Average Balance in the output.*

MIN: Returns a minimum value of **expr**.

Syntax:

MIN([<DISTINCT>|<ALL>] <expr>)

Example:

SELECT MIN(CURBAL) "Minimum Balance" **FROM** ACCT_MSTR;

Output:

```
Minimum Balance
---------------
            500
```

COUNT(expr): Returns the number of rows where **expr** is not null.

Syntax:

COUNT([<DISTINCT>|<ALL>] <expr>)

Example:

```
SELECT COUNT(ACCT_NO) "No. Of Accounts" FROM ACCT_MSTR;
```

Output:

```
No. Of Accounts
---------------
             10
```

COUNT(*): Returns the number of rows in the table, including duplicates and those with nulls.

Syntax:

COUNT(*)

Example:

```
SELECT COUNT(*) "No. Of Records" FROM ACCT_MSTR;
```

Output:

```
No. of Records
--------------
            10
```

MAX: Returns the maximum value of **expr**.

Syntax:

MAX([<DISTINCT>|<ALL>] <expr>)

Example:

```
SELECT MAX(CURBAL) "Maximum Balance" FROM ACCT_MSTR;
```

Output:

```
Maximum
Balance
--------------
          2000
```

SUM: Returns the sum of the values of **'n'**.

Syntax:

SUM([<DISTINCT>|<ALL>] <n>)

Example:

```
SELECT SUM(CURBAL) "Total Balance" FROM ACCT_MSTR;
```

Output:

```
Total Balance
-------------
        11000
```

Numeric Functions

ABS: Returns the absolute value of **'n'**.

Syntax:

```
ABS(n)
```

Example:

SELECT ABS(-15) "Absolute" **FROM DUAL;**

Output:

```
Absolute
---------
       15
```

POWER: Returns **m** raised to the **n**[th] power. **n** must be an integer, else an error is returned.

Syntax:

```
POWER(m,n)
```

Example:

SELECT POWER(3,2) "Raised" **FROM DUAL;**

Output:

```
Raised
---------
       9
```

ROUND: Returns **n**, rounded to **m** places to the right of a decimal point. If **m** is omitted, **n** is rounded to **0** places. **m** can be negative to round off digits to the left of the decimal point. **m** must be an integer.

Syntax:

```
ROUND(n[,m])
```

Example:

SELECT ROUND(15.19,1**)** "Round" **FROM DUAL;**

Output:

```
Round
---------
  15.2
```

SQRT: Returns square root of **n**. If **n**<0, NULL. SQRT returns a **real** result.

Syntax:

```
SQRT(n)
```

Example:

SELECT SQRT(25) "Square Root" **FROM DUAL;**

Output:

```
Square Root
-----------
          5
```

EXP: Returns **e** raised to the **nth** power, where **e = 2.71828183**.

Syntax:

EXP(n)

Example:

SELECT EXP(5) "Exponent" **FROM DUAL;**

Output:

```
  Exponent
----------
148.413159
```

EXTRACT: Returns a value extracted from a date or an interval value. A DATE can be used only to extract YEAR, MONTH, and DAY, while a timestamp with a time zone datatype can be used only to extract TIMEZONE_HOUR and TIMEZONE_MINUTE.

Syntax:

```
EXTRACT( {year | month | day | hour | minute | second | timezone_hour |
          timezone_minute | timezone_region | timezone_abbr}
   FROM { date_value | interval_value } )
```

Example:

SELECT EXTRACT(YEAR FROM DATE '2004-07-02'**)** "Year",
EXTRACT(MONTH FROM SYSDATE) "Month" **FROM DUAL;**

Output:

```
 Year  Month
------------
 2004      7
```

GREATEST: Returns the greatest value in a list of expressions.

Syntax:

GREATEST(expr1, expr2, ... expr_n)

where, **expr1**, **expr2**, ... **expr_n** are expressions that are evaluated by the greatest function.

Example:

SELECT GREATEST(4, 5, 17) "Num", **GREATEST(**'4', '5', '17') "Text" **FROM DUAL;**

Output:

```
 Num  Text
----------
  17     5
```

LEAST: Returns the least value in a list of expressions.

Syntax:

```
LEAST(expr1, expr2, ... expr_n)
```

where, **expr1**, **expr2**, ... **expr_n** are expressions that are evaluated by the least function.

Example:

SELECT LEAST(4, 5, 17**)** "Num", **LEAST(**'4', '5', '17'**)** "Text" **FROM DUAL;**

Output:

```
 Num  Text
-----------
   4    17
```

Note: *In the **GREATEST()** and **LEAST()** function if the datatypes of the expressions are different, all expressions will be converted to whatever is datatype of the first expression in the list. If the comparison is based on a character comparison, one character is considered greater than another if it has a higher character set value.*

MOD: Returns the remainder of a first number divided by second number passed a parameter. If the second number is zero, the result is the same as the first number.

Syntax:

```
MOD(m, n)
```

Example:

SELECT MOD(15, 7**)** "Mod1", **MOD(**15.7, 7**)** "Mod2" **FROM DUAL;**

Output:

```
 Mod1  Mod2
-----------
    1   1.7
```

TRUNC: Returns a number truncated to a certain number of decimal places. The decimal place value must be an integer. If this parameter is omitted, the TRUNC function will truncate the number to 0 decimal places.

Syntax:

```
TRUNC(number, [decimal_places])
```

Example:

SELECT TRUNC(125.815, 1**)** "Trunc1", **TRUNC(**125.815, -2**)** "Trunc2" **FROM DUAL;**

Output:

```
 Trunc1  Trunc2
---------------
  125.8     100
```

FLOOR: Returns the largest integer value that is equal to or less than a number.

Syntax:

FLOOR(n)

Example:

SELECT FLOOR(24.8) "Flr1", **FLOOR(**13.15) "Flr2" **FROM DUAL;**

Output:

```
 Flr1  Flr2
-----------
   24    13
```

CEIL: Returns the smallest integer value that is greater than or equal to a number.

Syntax:

CEIL(n)

Example:

SELECT CEIL(24.8) "Ceil1",**CEIL(**13.15) "Ceil2" **FROM DUAL;**

Output:

```
 Ceil  Ceil
    1     2
-----------
   25    14
```

Note: Several other Numeric functions are available in Oracle. These include the following:

- **ACOS()**, **ASIN()**, **ATAN()**, **ATAN2()**,
- **COS()**, **COSH()**, **SIN()**, **SINH()**, **TAN()**, **TANH()**,
- **COVAR_POP()**, **COVAR_SAMP()**, **VAR_POP()**, **VAR_SAMP()**,
- **CORR()**, **SIGN()**

String Functions

LOWER: Returns char, with all letters in lowercase.

Syntax:

LOWER(char)

Example:

SELECT LOWER('IVAN BAYROSS') "Lower" **FROM DUAL;**

Output:

```
Lower
-------------------
ivan bayross
```

INITCAP: Returns a string with the first letter of each word in **upper case**.

Syntax:

INITCAP(char)

Example:

SELECT INITCAP('IVAN BAYROSS'**)** "Title Case" **FROM DUAL;**

Output:

```
Title Case
----------------
Ivan Bayross
```

UPPER: Returns char, with all letters forced to uppercase.

Syntax:

```
UPPER (char)
```

Example:

SELECT UPPER('Ms. Carol'**)** "Capitalised" **FROM DUAL;**

Output:

```
Capitalised
----------------
MS. CAROL
```

SUBSTR: Returns a portion of characters, beginning at character **m**, and going upto character **n.** If **n** is omitted, the result returned is upto the last character in the string. The first position of char is **1**.

Syntax:

```
SUBSTR(<string>, <start_position>, [<length>])
```

where, **string** is the source string.

start_position is the position for extraction. The first position in the string is always 1.

length is the number of characters to extract.

Example:

SELECT SUBSTR('SECURE',3,4) "Substring" **FROM DUAL;**

Output:

```
Substring
----------------
CURE
```

ASCII: Returns the NUMBER code that represents the specified character. If more than one character is entered, the function will return the value for the first character and ignore all of the characters after the first.

Syntax:

```
ASCII(<single_character>)
```

where, **single_character** is the specified character to retrieve the NUMBER code for.

Example:

SELECT ASCII('a'**)** "ASCII1", **ASCII(**'A'**)** "ASCII2" **FROM DUAL;**

Output:

```
ASCII1 ASCII2
-------------
    97     65
```

COMPOSE: Returns a Unicode string. It can be a **char**, **varchar2**, **nchar**, **nvarchar2**, **clob**, or **nclob**.

Syntax:

COMPOSE(<single>)

Below is a listing of **unistring** values that can be combined with other characters in the compose function.

Unistring Value	Resulting character
UNISTR('\0300')	grave accent (`)
UNISTR('\0301')	acute accent (')
UNISTR('\0302')	circumflex (^)
UNISTR('\0303')	tilde (~)
UNISTR('\0308')	umlaut (¨)

Example:

SELECT COMPOSE('a' **|| UNISTR(**'\0301'**))** "Composed" **FROM DUAL;**

Output:

```
Composed
--------
á
```

DECOMPOSE: Accepts a string and returns a Unicode string.

Syntax:

DECOMPOSE(<single>)

Example:

SELECT DECOMPOSE(COMPOSE('a' **|| UNISTR(**'\0301'**)))** "Decomposed" **FROM DUAL;**

Output:

```
Decomposed
----------
a´
```

INSTR: Returns the location of a substring in a string.

Syntax:

INSTR(<string1>, <string2>, [<start_position>], [<nth_appearance>])

where, **string1** is the string to search.

string2 is the substring to search for in string1.

start_position is the position in **string1** where the search will start. If omitted, it defaults to 1. The first position in the string is 1. If the **start_position** is negative, the function counts back **start_position** number of characters from the end of **string1** and then searches towards the beginning of **string1**.

nth_appearance is the **nth** appearance of **string2**. If omitted, it defaults to 1.

Example:

SELECT INSTR('SCT on the net', 't'**)** "Instr1", **INSTR(**'SCT on the net', 't', 1, 2**)** "Instr2"
FROM DUAL;

Output:

```
 Instr1  Instr2
----------------
      8      14
```

TRANSLATE: Replaces a sequence of characters in a string with another set of characters. However, it replaces a single character at a time. For example, it will replace the 1st character in the string_to_replace with the 1st character in the replacement_string. Then it will replace the 2nd character in the string_to_replace with the 2nd character in the replacement_string, and so on.

Syntax:

TRANSLATE(<string1>, <string_to_replace>, <replacement_string>)

where, **string1** is the string to replace a sequence of characters with another set of characters.

string_to_replace is the string that will be searched for in string1.

All characters in the **string_to_replace** will be replaced with the corresponding character in the **replacement_string**.

Example:

SELECT TRANSLATE('1sct523', '123', '7a9'**)** "Change" **FROM DUAL;**

Output:

```
Change
-----------
7sct5a9
```

LENGTH: Returns the length of a word.

Syntax:

LENGTH(word)

Example:

SELECT LENGTH('RAJESH'**)** "Length" **FROM DUAL;**

Output:

```
Length
--------
       8
```

LTRIM: Removes characters from the left of char with initial characters removed upto the first character not in set.

Syntax:

LTRIM(char[,set])

Example:

SELECT LTRIM('NISHA','N') "LTRIM" **FROM DUAL;**

Output:

```
LTRIM
-----
ISHA
```

RTRIM: Returns char, with final characters removed after the last character not in the set. **'set'** is optional, it defaults to spaces.

Syntax:

RTRIM (char,[set])

Example:

SELECT RTRIM('SUNILA','A') "RTRIM" **FROM DUAL;**

Output:

```
RTRIM
-----
SUNIL
```

TRIM: Removes all specified characters either from the beginning or the ending of a string.

Syntax:

TRIM([leading | trailing | both [<trim_character> FROM]] <string1>)

where, **leading** - remove **trim_string** from the front of **string1**.

trailing - remove **trim_string** from the end of **string1**.

both - remove **trim_string** from the front and end of **string1**.

If none of the above option is chosen, the **TRIM** function will remove **trim_string** from both the front and end of **string1**.

trim_character is the character that will be removed from string1. If this parameter is omitted, the trim function will remove all leading and trailing spaces from string1.

string1 is the string to trim.

Example:

SELECT TRIM(' Hansel   '**)** "Trim both sides" **FROM DUAL;**

Output:

```
Trim both sides
---------------
Hansel
```

Example:

SELECT TRIM(LEADING 'x' **FROM** 'xxxHanselxxx'**)** "Remove prefixes" **FROM DUAL;**

Output:

```
Remove prefixes
---------------
Hanselxxx
```

Example:

SELECT TRIM(BOTH 'x' **FROM** 'xxxHanselxxx'**)** "Remove prefixes N suffixes" **FROM DUAL;**

Output:

```
Remove prefixes N suffixes
--------------------------
Hansel
```

Example:

SELECT TRIM(BOTH '1' **FROM** '123Hansel12111'**)** "Remove string" **FROM DUAL;**

Output:

```
Remove string
-------------
23Hansel12
```

LPAD: Returns **char1**, left-padded to length **n** with the sequence of characters specified in **char2**. If **char2** is not specified Oracle uses blanks by default.

Syntax:

```
LPAD(char1,n [,char2])
```

Example:

SELECT LPAD('Page 1',10,'*'**)** "LPAD" **FROM DUAL;**

Output:

```
LPAD
----------
****Page1
```

RPAD: Returns **char1**, right-padded to length **n** with the characters specified in **char2**. If **char2** is not specified, Oracle uses blanks by default.

Syntax:

```
RPAD(char1,n[,char2])
```

Example:

SELECT RPAD(FNAME,10,'x') "RPAD Example" **FROM** CUST_MSTR
WHERE FNAME = 'Ivan';

Output:

```
RPAD Example
------------
Ivanxxxxxx
```

VSIZE: Returns the number of bytes in the internal representation of an expression.

Syntax:

VSIZE(<expression>)

Example:

SELECT VSIZE('SCT on the net') "Size" **FROM DUAL;**

Output:

```
Size
-----
  14
```

Date Functions

To manipulate and extract values from the date column of a table Oracle provides some date functions. These are discussed below:

ADD_MONTHS: Returns date after adding the number of months specified in the function.

Syntax:

ADD_MONTHS(d,n)

Example:

SELECT ADD_MONTHS(SYSDATE, 4) "Add Months" **FROM DUAL;**

Output:

```
Add Months
-----------
01-NOV-04
```

LAST_DAY: Returns the last date of the month specified with the function.

Syntax:

LAST_DAY(d)

Example:

SELECT SYSDATE, LAST_DAY(SYSDATE) "LastDay" **FROM DUAL;**

Output:

```
SYSDATE    LastDay
--------------------
01-JUL-04  31-JUL-04
```

MONTHS_BETWEEN: Returns number of months between **d1** and **d2**.

Syntax:

MONTHS_BETWEEN(d1, d2)

Example:

SELECT MONTHS_BETWEEN('02-FEB-92', '02-JAN-92') "Months" **FROM DUAL;**

Output:

```
Months
-------
      1
```

NEXT_DAY: Returns the date of the first weekday named by **char** that is after the date named by **date**. **char** must be a day of the week.

Syntax:

NEXT_DAY(date, char)

Example:

SELECT NEXT_DAY('06-JULY-02', 'Saturday') "NEXT DAY" **FROM DUAL;**

Output:

```
NEXT_DAY
-----------
13-July-02
```

ROUND: Returns a date rounded to a specific unit of measure. If the second parameter is omitted, the **ROUND** function will round the date to the nearest day.

Syntax:

ROUND(date, [format])

Below are the valid format parameters:

Unit	Format parameters	Rounding Rule
Year	SYYYY, YYYY, YEAR, SYEAR, YYY, YY, Y	Rounds up on July 1st
ISO Year	IYYY, IY, I	
Quarter	Q	Rounds up on the 16th day of the second month of the quarter
Month	MONTH, MON, MM, RM	Rounds up on the 16th day of the month
Week	WW	Same day of the week as the first day of the year
IW	IW	Same day of the week as the first day of the ISO year

W	W	Same day of the week as the first day of the month
Day	DDD, DD, J	
Hour	HH, HH12, HH24	
Unit	**Format parameters**	**Rounding Rule**
Start day of the week	DAY, DY, D	
Minute	MI	

Example:

SELECT ROUND(TO_DATE('01-JUL-04'), 'YYYY'**)** "Year" **FROM DUAL;**

Output:

```
Year
-----------------
01-JAN-05
```

NEW_TIME: Returns the date after converting it from **time zone1** to a date in **time zone2**.

Syntax:

NEW_TIME(date, zone1, zone2)

Value	Description	Value	Description
AST	Atlantic Standard Time	ADT	Atlantic Daylight Time
BST	Bering Standard Time	BDT	Bering Daylight Time
CST	Central Standard Time	CDT	Central Daylight Time
EST	Eastern Standard Time	EDT	Eastern Daylight Time
GMT	Greenwich Mean Time	HST	Alaska-Hawaii Standard Time
HDT	Alaska-Hawaii Daylight Time	MST	Mountain Standard Time
MDT	Mountain Daylight Time	NST	Newfoundland Standard Time
PST	Pacific Standard Time	PDT	Pacific Daylight Time
YST	Yukon Standard Time	YDT	Yukon Daylight Time

Example:

The following example converts an Atlantic Standard Time into a Mountain Standard Time:

SELECT NEW_TIME(TO_DATE('2004/07/01 01:45', 'yyyy/mm/dd HH24:MI'), 'AST', 'MST') "MST"

FROM DUAL;

Output:

```
MST
------------------
30-JUN-04
```

Note:	*Several other Date function are available in Oracle. These include the following:* ***DbTimeZone(), SessionTimeZone(), SysTimestamp(), Tz_Offset()***

The above Oracle date functions are **just a few** selected from the many date functions that are built into Oracle. These Oracle functions are commonly used in commercial application development.

Subqueries

A **subquery** is a form of an SQL statement that appears inside another SQL statement. It is also termed as **nested query**. The statement containing a subquery is called a **parent** statement. The parent statement uses the rows (i.e. the result set) returned by the subquery.

It can be used for the following:

- To insert records in a target table
- To create tables and insert records in the table created
- To update records in a target table
- To create views
- To provide values for **conditions** in WHERE, HAVING, IN and so on used with SELECT, UPDATE, and DELETE statements

Example:

Retrieve the address of a customer named 'Ivan Bayross'.

Synopsis:

Tables:	CUST_MSTR, ADDR_DTLS
Columns:	CUST_MSTR: CUST_NO, FNAME, LNAME ADDR_DTLS: CODE_NO, ADDR1, ADDR2, CITY, STATE, PINCODE
Technique:	**Sub-Queries**, **Operators:** IN, **Clauses:** WHERE, **Other:** Concat (||)

Solution:

```
SELECT CODE_NO "Cust. No.", ADDR1 || ' ' || ADDR2 || ' ' || CITY || ', ' || STATE || ', ' ||
    PINCODE "Address"
  FROM ADDR_DTLS WHERE CODE_NO IN(SELECT CUST_NO FROM CUST_MSTR
    WHERE FNAME = 'Ivan' AND LNAME = 'Bayross');
```

Output:

```
Cust. No. Address
--------------------------------------------------------------------------------
C1        F-12, Diamond Palace, West Avenue, North Avenue,
          Santacruz (West), Mumbai, Maharashtra, 400056
```

Explanation:

In the above example, the data that has to be retrieved is available in the **ADDR_DTLS** table, which holds the address for customer named '**Ivan Bayross**'. This table holds all the address details identified by the customer number i.e. **CODE_NO**.

However, the **ADDR_DTLS** table does not contain the field, which holds the customer's name, which is required to make a comparison.The Customers Name is available in the **CUST_MSTR** table where each customer is identified by a unique number (i.e. **CUST_NO**). So it is required to access the table **CUST_MSTR** and retrieve the **CUST_NO** based on which a comparison can be made with the **CODE_NO** field held in the table **ADDR_DTLS**.

Using the **CUST_NO** retrieved from the **CUST_MSTR** table, it is now possible to retrieve the address(es) from the **ADDR_DTLS** table by finding a matching value in the **CODE_NO** field in that table.

This type of processing can be done elegantly using a subquery.

In the above solution the sub-query is as follows:

```
SELECT CUST_NO FROM CUST_MSTR
    WHERE FNAME = 'IVAN' AND LNAME = 'BAYROSS';
```

The target table will be as follows:

Output:

```
CUST_NO
-------
C1
```

The outer sub-query output will simplify the solution as shown below:

```
SELECT CODE_NO "Cust. No.", ADDR1 || ' ' || ADDR2 || ' ' || CITY || ', ' || STATE || ', ' ||
    PINCODE "Address" FROM ADDR_DTLS WHERE CODE_NO IN('C1');
```

When the above SQL query is executed the resulting output is equivalent to the desired output of the SQL query using two levels of Sub-queries.

Example:

Find the customers who do not have bank branches in their vicinity.

Synopsis:

Tables:	CUST_MSTR, ADDR_DTLS
Columns:	CUST_MSTR: CUST_NO, FNAME, LNAME ADDR_DTLS: CODE_NO, PINCODE
Technique:	**Sub-Queries**, **Operators:** IN, **Clauses:** WHERE, **Other:** Concat (||)

Solution:

```
SELECT (FNAME || ' ' || LNAME) "Customer" FROM CUST_MSTR
    WHERE CUST_NO IN(SELECT CODE_NO FROM ADDR_DTLS
        WHERE CODE_NO LIKE 'C%' AND PINCODE NOT IN(SELECT PINCODE
        FROM ADDR_DTLS WHERE CODE_NO LIKE 'B%'));
```

Output:

```
Customer
------------------------------------
Ivan Bayross
Namita Kanade
Chriselle Bayross
Mamta Muzumdar
Chhaya Bankar
Ashwini Joshi
Hansel Colaco
Anil Dhone
Alex Fernandes
Ashwini Apte
10 rows selected.
```

Explanation:

In the above example, the data that has to be retrieved is available in the **CUST_MSTR**, which holds the Customer details. The **CUST_MSTR** table will only provide all the customer names but to retrieve only those customers who do not have any bank branches in their vicinity, one more tables will be involved that is **ADDR_DTLS** table, which holds the branch as well as customer addresses. This table holds all the address details identified by the branch / customer number i.e. **CODE_NO**. This table will help comparing the value held in the **PINCODE** field belonging to the customer addresses with the ones of bank branch addresses.

To understand the solution the query mentioned above needs to be simplified. The inner most sub-queries should be handled first and then proceeded outwards.

The **first step** is to identify the vicinities in which the branches are located. This is done by extracting the **PINCODE** from the address details table (i.e. **ADDR_DTLS**) for all entries belonging to the branches. The SQL query for this will be as follows:

SELECT PINCODE **FROM** ADDR_DTLS **WHERE** CODE_NO **LIKE** 'B%'

The target table will be as follows:

Output:

```
PINCODE
---------------
400057
400058
400004
400045
400078
110004
6 rows selected.
```

The resulting output simplifies the solution as shown below:

```
SELECT (FNAME || ' ' || LNAME) "Customer" FROM CUST_MSTR
    WHERE CUST_NO IN(SELECT CODE_NO FROM ADDR_DTLS
        WHERE CODE_NO LIKE 'C%' AND PINCODE NOT IN('400057', '400058',
                    '400004', '400045', '400078', '110004'));
```

The **second step** is to identify the customers who are not resident near a branch. To do this the customer numbers (i.e. **CODE_NO**) have to be retrieved from the Address details table (i.e. **ADDR_DTLS**). The SQL query for this will be as follows:

```
SELECT CODE_NO FROM ADDR_DTLS WHERE CODE_NO LIKE 'C%'
    AND PINCODE NOT IN('400057', '400058', '400004', '400045', '400078', '110004')
```

The target table will be as follows:

Output:

```
CODE_NO
----------
C1
C2
C3
C4
C5
C6
C7
C8
C9
C10
10 rows selected.
```

The outer sub-query output will simplify the solution as shown below:

```
SELECT (FName || ' ' || LName) "Customer" FROM Cust_Mstr
    WHERE Cust_No IN('C1', 'C2', 'C3', 'C4', 'C5', 'C6', 'C7', 'C8', 'C9', 'C10');
```

When the above SQL query is executed the resulting output is equivalent to the desired output of the SQL query using two levels of Sub-queries.

Example:

List customers holding Fixed Deposits in the bank of amount more than 5,000.

Synopsis:

Tables:	CUST_MSTR, ACCT_FD_CUST_DTLS, FD_DTLS
Columns:	CUST_MSTR: CUST_NO, FNAME, LNAME ACCT_FD_CUST_DTLS: CUST_NO, ACCT_FD_NO FD_DTLS: FD_SER_NO, AMT
Technique:	**Sub-Queries**, **Operators:** IN() **Clauses:** WHERE, **Other:** Concat (||)

Solution:

```
SELECT (FNAME || ' ' || LNAME) "Customer" FROM CUST_MSTR WHERE CUST_NO
    IN(SELECT CUST_NO FROM ACCT_FD_CUST_DTLS WHERE ACCT_FD_NO
        IN(SELECT FD_SER_NO FROM FD_DTLS WHERE AMT > 5000));
```

Output:

```
Customer
------------------------------
Chriselle Bayross
Mamta Muzumdar
Chhaya Bankar
Ashwini Joshi
```

Explanation:

In the above example, the data that has to be retrieved is available in the **CUST_MSTR**, which holds the Customer details. The **CUST_MSTR** table will only provide all the customer names but to retrieve only those customers who hold fixed deposits of amount exceeding Rs.5000, two more tables will be involved that is **ACCT_FD_DTLS** and **FD_DTLS.** The **ACCT_FD_DTLS** acts as a link between the **CUST_MSTR** and **FD_DTLS** table and hold details identified by the **ACCT_FD_NO** field.

The **FD_DTLS** table actually holds all the details related to the fixed deposits held by the customers in a bank identified by the **FD_SER_NO** field.

To understand the solution the query mentioned above needs to be simplified. The inner most sub-queries should be handled first and then proceeded outwards.

The **first step** is to identify the fixed deposits of amount more than 5000. This is done by extracting the value held by the **FD_SER_NO** field from the fixed deposits details table (i.e. **FD_DTLS**). The SQL query for this will be as follows:

```
SELECT FD_SER_NO FROM FD_DTLS WHERE AMT > 5000
```

The target table will be as follows:

Output:

```
FD_SER_NO
---------
FS1
FS2
FS2
FS5
```

The data retrieved by the above **SELECT** statement will be passed to the outer sub-query as in:

SELECT (FNAME || ' ' || LNAME) "Customer" **FROM** CUST_MSTR **WHERE** CUST_NO
    IN(SELECT CUST_NO **FROM** ACCT_FD_CUST_DTLS **WHERE** ACCT_FD_NO
        IN('FS1', 'FS2', 'FS2', 'FS5'**));**

The **second step** is to identify the customer numbers who hold these FDs i.e. ('FS1', 'FS2', 'FS2', 'FS5'). To do this the customer numbers (i.e. **CUST_NO**) have to be retrieved from the Account FD details table (i.e. **ACCT_FD_DTLS**). The SQL query for this will be as follows:

SELECT CUST_NO **FROM** ACCT_FD_CUST_DTLS
    WHERE ACCT_FD_NO **IN(**'FS1', 'FS2', 'FS2', 'FS5'**)**

The target table will be as follows:

Output:

```
CUST_NO
----------
C2
C3
C4
C5
C5
C5
6 rows selected.
```

The outer sub-query output will simplify the solution as shown below:

SELECT (FNAME || ' ' || LNAME) "Customer" **FROM** CUST_MSTR
    WHERE CUST_NO **IN(**'C2', 'C3', 'C4', 'C5', 'C5', 'C5'**);**

When the above SQL query is executed the resulting output is equivalent to the desired output of the SQL query using two levels of Sub-queries.

Using Sub-query In The FROM Clause

A subquery can be used in the **FROM** clause of the **SELECT** statement. The concept of using a subquery in the **FROM** clause of the **SELECT** statement is called an **inline view**. A subquery in the **FROM** clause of the **SELECT** statement defines a **data source** from that particular **Select** statement.

Example:

List accounts along with the current balance, the branch to which it belongs and the average balance of that branch, having a balance more than the average balance of the branch, to which the account belongs.

Synopsis:

Tables:	ACCT_MSTR
Columns:	ACCT_NO, CURBAL, BRANCH_NO
Technique:	**Sub-Queries**, **Join**, **Functions:** AVG(), **Clauses:** WHERE, GROUP BY

Solution:

```
SELECT A.ACCT_NO, A.CURBAL, A.BRANCH_NO, B.AVGBAL
   FROM ACCT_MSTR A, (SELECT BRANCH_NO, AVG(CURBAL) AVGBAL FROM
ACCT_MSTR
      GROUP BY BRANCH_NO) B
   WHERE A.BRANCH_NO = B.BRANCH_NO AND A.CURBAL > B.AVGBAL;
```

Output:

```
ACCT_NO  CURBA BRANCH_NO   AVGBAL
         L
---------------------------------
CA7       22000 B1        7666.67
CA2        3000 B2        2833.33
CA12       5000 B2        2833.33
CA4       12000 B5          11000
CA10      32000 B6          11000
```

Explanation:

In the above example, the data that has to be retrieved is available in the **ACCT_MSTR**, which holds the accounts held by the bank. The output requirements are the **account number**, the **current balance** of that account, the **branch** to which that account belongs and the **average balance** of that branch. The first three requirements can be retrieved from the **ACCT_MSTR** table.

The average of the balance on a per branch basis requires use of another select query and a group by clause. This means a sub query can be used, but in this case, the sub query will return a value, which will be a part of the output. Since this query is going to act as a source of data it is placed in the **FROM** clause of the outer query and given an alias **B**. Finally to produce the output a join is used to get the data on the basis of the outer query i.e. (**A.**BRANCH_NO = **B.**BRANCH_NO) followed by a **WHERE** clause which actually filters the data before producing the output.

To understand the solution the query mentioned above needs to be simplified. The inner most sub-queries should be handled first and then continued outwards.

The **first step** is to identify the branch numbers and their average balance. This is done by, extracting the value held by the **BRANCH_NO** field from the **BRANCH_MSTR** table. The SQL query for this will be as follows:

```
SELECT BRANCH_NO, AVG(CURBAL) AVGBAL FROM ACCT_MSTR
   GROUP BY BRANCH_NO
```

The target table will be as follows:

Output:

```
BRANCH_NO  AVGBAL
-------------------
B1          7666.67
B2          2833.33
B3              500
B4              500
B5            11000
B6            11000
6 rows selected.
```

The **second step** is to associate the data returned by the inner query with the outer. This is done by binding the Sub-query with the **FROM** clause and using join. The output shown above is treated as an individual (temporary) table. This new table is referred as **B**, the alias name specified in the main **SELECT** statement.

The **third step** is to filter the data to output only those records where the current balance is more than the average balance of the branch to which they belong This is done using a **WHERE** clause i.e.(**A.**CURBAL **>** **B.**AVGBAL)

Finally, the **SELECT** statement is executed as a JOIN i.e. (**WHERE A.**BRANCH_NO = **B.**BRANCH_NO). This is explained in greater depth later in this chapter.

Using Correlated Sub-queries

A sub-query becomes correlated when the subquery references a column from a table in the parent query. A correlated subquery is evaluated once for each row processed by the parent statement, which can be any of SELECT, DELETE or UPDATE.

A correlated subquery is one way of reading every row in a table and comparing values in each row against related data. It is used whenever a subquery must return a different result for each candidate row considered by the parent query.

Example:

List accounts along with the current balance and the branch to which it belongs, having a balance more than the average balance of the branch, to which the account belongs.

Synopsis:

Tables:	ACCT_MSTR
Columns:	ACCT_NO, CURBAL, BRANCH_NO
Technique:	**Sub-Queries**, **Join**, **Functions:** AVG(), **Clauses:** WHERE

Solution:

```
SELECT ACCT_NO, CURBAL, BRANCH_NO FROM ACCT_MSTR A
   WHERE CURBAL > (SELECT AVG(CURBAL) FROM ACCT_MSTR
      WHERE BRANCH_NO = A.BRANCH_NO);
```

Output:

```
ACCT_NO  CURBAL    BRANCH_NO
-----------------------------
CA2          3000 B2
CA4         12000 B5
CA7         22000 B1
CA10        32000 B6
CA12         5000 B2
```

Explanation:

In the above example, the data that has to be retrieved is available in the **ACCT_MSTR**, which holds the accounts held by the bank. The output requirements are the **account number**, the **current balance** of that account, the **branch** to which that account belongs.

These requirements can be retrieved from the **ACCT_MSTR** table. However the average balance on a per branch basis requires use of another select query.

This means a correlated sub query can be used. The correlated sub-query specifically computes the average balance of each branch. Since both the queries (i.e. Outer and the Inner) use **ACCT_MSTR** table an alias is allotted to the table in the outer query. It is because of this **alias** the inner query is able to distinguish the inner column from the outer column.

Using Multi Column Subquery

Example:

Find out all the customers having same names as the employees.

Synopsis:

Tables:	CUST_MSTR, EMP_MSTR
Columns:	CUST_MSTR: FNAME, LNAME, EMP_MSTR: FNAME, LNAME
Technique:	**Sub_Queries, Operators:** IN, **Clauses:** WHERE

Solution:

```
SELECT FNAME, LNAME FROM CUST_MSTR
   WHERE (FNAME, LNAME) IN(SELECT FNAME, LNAME FROM EMP_MSTR);
```

Output:

```
FNAME    LNAME
---------------------
Ivan     Bayross
```

Explanation:

In the above example, each row of the outer query is compared to the values from the inner query (Multi Row and Multi Column). This means that the values of **FNAME** and **LNAME** from the outer query are compared with **FNAME** and **LNAME** values retrieved by the inner query.

Using Sub-query in CASE Expressions

Example:

List the account numbers along with the transaction date, transaction type **i.e.** whether it's a deposit or withdrawal, the mode of transaction **i.e.** Cash or Cheque and the amount of transaction.

Synopsis:

Tables:	TRANS_MSTR, TRANS_DTLS
Columns:	TRANS_MSTR: ACCT_NO, DT, DR_CR, TRANS_NO, AMT, TRANS_DTLS: TRANS_NO
Technique:	**Operators:** IN, **Clauses:** CASE WHEN ... THEN

Solution:

```
SELECT ACCT_NO, DT, DR_CR, (CASE WHEN TRANS_NO IN(SELECT TRANS_NO
   FROM TRANS_DTLS) THEN 'Cheque' ELSE 'Cash' END) "Mode", AMT FROM TRANS_MSTR;
```

Output:

ACCT_NO	DT	DR_CR	Mode	AMT
SB1	05-NOV-03	D	Cash	500
CA2	10-NOV-03	D	Cash	2000
CA2	13-NOV-03	D	Cash	3000
SB3	22-NOV-03	D	Cash	500
CA2	10-DEC-03	W	Cash	2000
CA4	05-DEC-03	D	Cheque	2000
SB5	15-DEC-03	D	Cheque	500
SB6	27-DEC-03	D	Cash	500
CA7	14-JAN-04	D	Cheque	2000
SB8	29-JAN-04	D	Cash	500
SB9	05-FEB-04	D	Cash	500
SB9	15-FEB-04	D	Cheque	3000
SB9	17-FEB-04	W	Cash	2500
CA10	19-FEB-04	D	Cheque	2000
SB9	05-APR-04	D	Cheque	3000
SB9	27-APR-04	W	Cash	2500
SB11	05-MAR-04	D	Cash	500

Output: (Continued)

```
CA12    10-MAR-04   D      Cash      2000
SB13    22-MAR-04   D      Cash       500
CA14    05-APR-04   D      Cheque    2000
20 rows selected.
```

Explanation:

In the above example, the inner query will return a value (i.e. if a record exists in the **TRANS_DTLS** table then the transaction is done via a Cheque). Based on the value returned the outer query will display the Transaction mode as either Cheque or Cash.

Using Subquery In An ORDER BY Clause

Example:

List the employees of the bank in the order of the branch names at which they are employed.

Synopsis:

Tables:	EMP_MSTR,
Columns:	EMP_MSTR: EMP_NO, FNAME, LNAME, DEPT
Technique:	**Clauses:** ORDER BY **Others:** Alias, Concat (||)

Solution:

```
SELECT EMP_NO, (FNAME || ' ' || LNAME) "Name", DEPT FROM EMP_MSTR E
    ORDER BY (SELECT NAME FROM BRANCH_MSTR B
        WHERE E.BRANCH_NO = B.BRANCH_NO);
```

Output:

```
EMP_NO  Name            DEPT
----------------------------------------------
E2      Amit Desai      Loans And Financing
E9      Vikram Randive  Marketing
E3      Maya Joshi      Client Servicing
E8      Seema Apte      Client Servicing
E6      Sonal Khan      Administration
E10     Anjali Pathak   Administration
E5      Mandhar Dalvi   Marketing
E7      Anil Kambli     Marketing
E1      Ivan Bayross    Administration
E4      Peter Joseph    Loans And Financing
10 rows selected.
```

Explanation:

In the above example, the output needs to be ordered on the basis of branch names in which they are employed. The Data required is available in the **EMP_MSTR** table.

Since the output needs to be ordered on the basis of branch names, which are available in the **BRANCH_MSTR** table, there is a need of a separate query, which can return the branch names from the **BRANCH_MSTR** table to which the employees belong. Based on the values returned from the inner query the output produced by the outer query will be ordered. This is done, by placing the inner query, in the **ORDER BY** clause and further correlated with the outer query on the basis of the **BRANCH_NO** being **the common field** in the tables **EMP_MSTR** and **BRANCH_MSTR**.

Using EXISTS / NOT EXISTS Operator

The **EXISTS** operator is usually used with correlated subqueries. This operator enables to test whether a value retrieved by the outer query exists in the results set of the values retrieved by the inner query. If the subquery returns at least one row, the operator returns **TRUE**. If the value does not exist, it returns **FALSE**.

The **EXISTS** operator ensures that the search in the inner query terminates when at least one match is found.

Similarly, the **NOT EXISTS** operator enables to test whether a value retrieved by the outer query is not a part of the result set of the values retrieved by the inner query.

Example:

List employees who have verified at least one account.

Synopsis:

Tables:	EMP_MSTR, ACCT_MSTR
Columns:	EMP_MSTR: EMP_NO, FNAME, LNAME, ACCT_MSTR: VERI_EMP_NO
Technique:	**Operators:** EXISTS(), **Clauses:** WHERE

Solution:

```
SELECT EMP_NO, FNAME, LNAME FROM EMP_MSTR E WHERE EXISTS(SELECT 'SCT'
    FROM ACCT_MSTR WHERE VERI_EMP_NO = E.EMP_NO);
```

Output:

```
EMP_NO  FNAME   LNAME
-----------------------------
E1      Ivan    Bayross
E4      Peter   Joseph
```

Explanation:

In the above example, the inner query is correlated with the outer query via the **EMP_NO** field As soon as the search in the inner query retrieves at least one match, i.e. **VERI_EMP_NO = E.EMP_NO**, the search is terminated. This means that the inner query stops it's processing and the outer query then produces the output. In the case of the inner query there is no need to return a specific value, hence a constant **'SCT'** is used instead. This is useful in terms of performance as it will be faster to select a constant than a column.

Example:

List those branches, which don't have employees yet.

Synopsis:

Tables:	BRANCH_MSTR, EMP_MSTR
Columns:	BRANCH_MSTR: BRANCH_NO, NAME, LNAME, EMP_MSTR: BRANCH_NO
Technique:	Operators: NOT, EXISTS(), Clauses: WHERE Others: Alias

Solution:

SELECT BRANCH_NO, NAME **FROM** BRANCH_MSTR **B WHERE NOT EXISTS(SELECT** 'SCT'
FROM EMP_MSTR **WHERE** BRANCH_NO = **B.**BRANCH_NO);

Output:

```
BRANCH_NO   NAME
---------------------------------
B5          Borivali
```

Explanation:

In the above example, the inner query is correlated with the outer query via the **BRANCH_NO** field. Since the **NOT EXISTS** operator is used, if the inner query retrieves no rows at all i.e. the condition **BRANCH_NO = B.BRANCH_NO** fails, the outer query produces the output. This means after the inner query stops it's processing, the outer query sends the output based on the operator used.

In the case of the inner query there is no need to return a specific value, hence a constant **'SCT'** is used instead. This is useful in terms of performance as it will be faster to select a constant than a column.

Joins

Joining Multiple Tables (Equi Joins)

Sometimes it is necessary to work with multiple tables as though they were a single entity. Then a single SQL sentence can manipulate data from all the tables. **Joins** are used to achieve this. Tables are joined on columns that have the same **data type** and **data width** in the tables.

Tables in a database can be related to each other with keys. A primary key is a column with a unique value for each row. The purpose is to bind data together, across tables, without repeating all of the data in every table.

The JOIN operator specifies how to relate tables in the query.

Types of JOIN:

- INNER
- OUTER (LEFT, RIGHT, FULL)
- CROSS

INNER JOIN: Inner joins are also known as **Equi Joins**. There are the most common joins used in SQL*Plus. They are known as equi joins because the where statement generally compares two columns from two tables with the equivalence operator **=**. This type of join is by far the most commonly used. In fact, many systems use this type as the default join. This type of join can be used in situations where selecting only those rows that have values in common in the columns specified in the ON clause, is required. In short, the INNER JOIN returns all rows from both tables where there is a match

OUTER JOIN: Outer joins are similar to inner joins, but give a bit more flexibility when selecting data from related tables. This type of join can be used in situations where it is desired, to select all rows from the table on the left (or right, or both) regardless of whether the other table has values in common and (usually) enter NULL where data is missing.

CROSS JOIN: A cross join returns what's known as a Cartesian product. This means that the join combines every row from the left table with every row in the right table. As can be imagined, sometimes this join produces a mess, but under the right circumstances, it can be very useful. This type of join can be used in situations where it is desired, to select all possible combinations of rows and columns from both tables. This kind of join is usually not preferred as it may run for a very long time and produce a huge result set that may not be useful.

Syntax:

ANSI-style

```
SELECT <ColumnName1>, <ColumnName2>, <ColumnName N> FROM <TableName1>
    INNER JOIN <TableName2>
        ON <TableName1>.<ColumnName1>=<TableName2>.<ColumnName2>
            WHERE <Condition>
        ORDER BY <ColumnName1>, <ColumnName2>, <ColumnNameN>
```

Theta-style

```
SELECT <ColumnName1>, <ColumnName2>, <ColumnNameN>
    FROM <TableName1>,<TableName2>
    WHERE <TableName1>.<ColumnName1> = <TableName2>.<ColumnName2>
        AND <Condition>
        ORDER BY <ColumnName1>, <ColumnName2>, <ColumnNameN>
```

In the above syntax:

- **ColumnName1** in **TableName1** is usually that table's **Primary Key**
- **ColumnName2** in **TableName2** is a **Foreign Key** in that table
- **ColumnName1** and **ColumnName2** must have the **same Data Type** and for certain data types, the same size

Inner Join

Example:

List the employee details along with branch names to which they belong.

Synopsis:

Tables:	EMP_MSTR, BRANCH_MSTR
Columns:	EMP_MSTR: EMP_NO, FNAME, MNAME, LNAME, DEPT, DESIG, BRANCH_NO BRANCH_MSTR: NAME, BRANCH_NO
Technique:	**Join:** INNER JOIN ... ON, SIMPLE, **Clauses:** WHERE, **Others:** Concat (||)

Solution 1 (Ansi-style):

```
SELECT E.EMP_NO, (E.FNAME || ' ' || E.MNAME || ' ' || E.LNAME) "Name", B.NAME "Branch",
        E.DEPT, E.DESIG
    FROM EMP_MSTR E INNER JOIN BRANCH_MSTR B
        ON B.BRANCH_NO = E.BRANCH_NO;
```

Solution 2 (Theta-style):

```
SELECT E.EMP_NO, (E.FNAME || ' ' || E.MNAME || ' ' || E.LNAME) "Name", B.NAME "Branch",
        E.DEPT, E.DESIG
    FROM EMP_MSTR E, BRANCH_MSTR B WHERE B.BRANCH_NO = E.BRANCH_NO;
```

Output:

```
EMP Name                  Branch           DEPT            DESIG
 NO
-------------------------------------------------------------------------------------
E1  Ivan Nelson Bayross   Vile Parle (HO) Administration  Managing Director
E4  Peter Iyer Joseph     Vile Parle (HO) Loans And       Clerk
                                          Financing
E2  Amit Desai            Andheri         Loans And       Finance Manager
                                          Financing
E9  Vikram Vilas Randive  Andheri         Marketing       Sales Asst.
E3  Maya Mahima Joshi     Churchgate      Client          Sales Manager
                                          Servicing
E8  Seema P. Apte         Churchgate      Client          Clerk
                                          Servicing
E5  Mandhar Dilip Dalvi   Mahim           Marketing       Marketing Manager
E7  Anil Ashutosh Kambli  Mahim           Marketing       Sales Asst.
E6  Sonal Abdul Khan      Darya Ganj      Administration  Admin. Executive
E10 Anjali Sameer Pathak  Darya Ganj      Administration  HR Manager
10 rows selected.
```

Explanation:

In the above example, in the **EMP_MSTR** table, the **EMP_NO** column is the **primary key**, meaning that no two rows can have the same **EMP_NO**. The **EMP_NO** distinguishes two persons even if they have the same name. The data required in this example is available in two tables i.e. **EMP_MSTR** and **BRANCH_MSTR**.

This is because branch names are going to be a part of the output but are not available in the **EMP_MSTR** table.

Notice that:

- The **EMP_NO** column is the primary key of the **EMP_MSTR** table
- The **BRANCH_NO** column is the primary key of the **BRANCH_MSTR** table
- The **BRANCH_NO** column in the **EMP_MSTR** table is used to refer to the branches in the **BRANCH_MSTR** table without using their names

On the basis of the reference available in the **EMP_MSTR** table i.e. the **BRANCH_NO** field it's possible to link to the **BRANCH_MSTR** table and fetch the Branch names for display. This is easily possible with the use of inner join based on the condition (**B.**BRANCH_NO = **E.**BRANCH_NO).

Note: *If the column names on which the join is to be specified are the same in each table reference the columns using TableName.ColumnName.*

Example:

List the customers along with their multiple address details.

Synopsis:

Tables:	CUST_MSTR, ADDR_DTLS
Columns:	CUST_MSTR: CUST_NO, FNAME, MNAME, LNAME ADDR_DTLS: CODE_NO, ADDR1, ADDR2, CITY, STATE, PINCODE
Technique:	**Join:** INNER JOIN ... ON, SIMPLE, **Clauses:** WHERE **Others:** Concat (||)

Solution 1 (Ansi-style):

```
SELECT C.CUST_NO, (C.FNAME || ' ' || C.MNAME || ' ' || C.LNAME) "Customer", (A.ADDR1 ||
    ' ' || A.ADDR2 || ' ' || A.CITY || ', ' || A.STATE || ', ' || A.PINCODE) "Address"
  FROM CUST_MSTR C INNER JOIN ADDR_DTLS A ON C.CUST_NO = A.CODE_NO
  WHERE C.CUST_NO LIKE 'C%' ORDER BY C.CUST_NO;
```

Solution 2 (Theta-style):

```
SELECT C.CUST_NO, (C.FNAME || ' ' || C.MNAME || ' ' || C.LNAME) "Customer", (A.ADDR1 ||
    ' ' || A.ADDR2 || ' ' || A.CITY || ', ' || A.STATE || ', ' || A.PINCODE) "Address"
  FROM CUST_MSTR C, ADDR_DTLS A WHERE C.CUST_NO = A.CODE_NO
     AND C.CUST_NO LIKE 'C%' ORDER BY C.CUST_NO;
```

Output:

```
CUST_NO Customer
-------------------------------------------
Address
------------------------------------------------------------------------------------------
C1      Ivan Nelson Bayross
F-12, Diamond Palace, West Avenue, North Avenue, Santacruz (West),
Mumbai, Maharashtra, 400056
```

Output: (Continued)

```
C10      Namita S. Kanade
B-10, Makarand Society, Cadal Road, Mahim, Mumbai, Maharashtra,
400016
C2       Chriselle Ivan Bayross
F-12, Silver Stream, Santacruz (East), Mumbai, Maharashtra, 400056
C3       Mamta Arvind Muzumdar
Magesh Prasad, Saraswati Baug, Jogeshwari(E), Mumbai, Maharashtra,
400060
C4       Chhaya Sudhakar Bankar
4, Sampada, Kataria Road, Mahim, Mumbai, Maharashtra, 400016
C5       Ashwini Dilip Joshi
104, Vikram Apts. Bhagat Lane, Shivaji Park, Mahim, Mumbai,
Maharashtra, 400016
C6       Hansel I. Colaco
12, Radha Kunj, N.C Kelkar Road, Dadar, Mumbai, Maharashtra, 400028
C6       Hansel I. Colaco
203/A, Prachi Apmt., Andheri (East), Mumbai, Maharashtra, 400058
C7       Anil Arun Dhone
A/14, Shanti Society, Mogal Lane, Mahim, Mumbai, Maharashtra,
400016
C8       Alex Austin Fernandes
5, Vagdevi, Senapati Bapat Rd., Dadar, Mumbai, Maharashtra, 400016
C9       Ashwini Shankar Apte
A-10 Nutan Savita, Shivaji Park, Mahim, Mumbai, Maharashtra, 400016
11 rows selected.
```

Explanation:

In the above example, the data required is available in two tables i.e. CUST_MSTR and ADDR_DTLS. Both the tables are linked via a common field. This is because the data is spread across the tables based on a normalization schema.

Notice that:

- The **CUST_NO** column is the primary key of the **CUST_MSTR** table
- The **ADDR_DTLS** is a table that holds the address details of customers.

  In **ADDR_DTLS** table:

  - **ADDR_NO** column is the primary key of that table.
  - **CODE_NO** column is used to refer to the customers in the **CUST_MSTR** table via the **CUST_NO** column

To retrieve the data required, both the tables have to linked on the basis of a common column using joins as follows:

- **C.**CUST_NO = **A.**CODE_NO

This means the CUST_NO field of CUST_MSTR table is joined with CODE_NO field of the ADDR_DTLS table

Now since both the tables are linked using a join, data can be retrieved as if they are all in one table using the alias as:

C.CUST_NO, (**C.**FNAME || ' ' || **C.**MNAME || ' ' || **C.**LNAME) "Customer", (**A.**ADDR1 || ' ' || **A.**ADDR2 || ' ' || **A.**CITY || ', ' || **A.**STATE || ', ' || **A.**PINCODE) "Address"

Finally the output is ordered on the basis of Customers.

Example:

List the Customers along with the account details associated with them.

Synopsis:

Tables:	CUST_MSTR, ACCT_MSTR, ACCT_FD_CUST_DTLS, BRANCH_MSTR
Columns:	ACCT_FD_CUST_DTLS: ACCT_FD_NO, CUST_NO CUST_MSTR: CUST_NO, FNAME, MNAME, LNAME ACCT_MSTR: ACCT_NO, BRANCH_NO, CURBAL BRANCH_MSTR: NAME, BRANCH_NO
Technique:	**Join:** INNER JOIN ... ON, **Operators:** || **Join:** SIMPLE, **Operators:** ||, **Clauses:** WHERE

Solution 1 (Ansi-style):

```
SELECT C.CUST_NO, (C.FNAME || ' ' || C.MNAME || ' ' || C.LNAME) "Customer", A.ACCT_NO,
        B.NAME "Branch", A.CURBAL
    FROM CUST_MSTR C INNER JOIN ACCT_FD_CUST_DTLS L
        ON C.CUST_NO = L.CUST_NO INNER JOIN ACCT_MSTR A
        ON L.ACCT_FD_NO = A.ACCT_NO INNER JOIN BRANCH_MSTR B
        ON A.BRANCH_NO = B.BRANCH_NO ORDER BY C.CUST_NO, A.ACCT_NO;
```

Solution 2 (Theta-style):

```
SELECT C.CUST_NO, (C.FNAME || ' ' || C.MNAME || ' ' || C.LNAME) "Customer", A.ACCT_NO,
        B.NAME "Branch", A.CURBAL
    FROM CUST_MSTR C, ACCT_FD_CUST_DTLS L, ACCT_MSTR A, BRANCH_MSTR B
        WHERE C.CUST_NO = L.CUST_NO AND L.ACCT_FD_NO = A.ACCT_NO
            AND A.BRANCH_NO = B.BRANCH_NO ORDER BY C.CUST_NO, A.ACCT_NO;
```

Output:

```
CUST_NO Customer                ACCT_NO  Branch              CURBAL
-------------------------------------------------------------------
C1      Ivan Nelson Bayross     SB1      Vile Parle (HO)        500
C1      Ivan Nelson Bayross     SB11     Vile Parle (HO)        500
C1      Ivan Nelson Bayross     SB15     Darya Ganj             500
C1      Ivan Nelson Bayross     SB5      Darya Ganj             500
C10     Namita S. Kanade        CA10     Darya Ganj           32000
C10     Namita S. Kanade        SB9      Mahim                  500
C2      Chriselle Ivan          CA12     Andheri               5000
        Bayross
C2      Chriselle Ivan          CA2      Andheri               3000
        Bayross
C3      Mamta Arvind Muzumdar   CA12     Andheri               5000
C3      Mamta Arvind Muzumdar   CA2      Andheri               3000
C3      Mamta Arvind Muzumdar   SB9      Mahim                  500
C4      Chhaya Sudhakar         CA14     Borivali             10000
        Bankar
C4      Chhaya Sudhakar         CA4      Borivali             12000
        Bankar
C4      Chhaya Sudhakar         SB13     Churchgate             500
        Bankar
C4      Chhaya Sudhakar         SB15     Darya Ganj             500
        Bankar
C4      Chhaya Sudhakar         SB3      Churchgate             500
        Bankar
C4      Chhaya Sudhakar         SB5      Darya Ganj             500
        Bankar
C5      Ashwini Dilip Joshi     CA14     Borivali             10000
C5      Ashwini Dilip Joshi     CA4      Borivali             12000
C5      Ashwini Dilip Joshi     SB6      Mahim                  500
C6      Hansel I. Colaco        CA7      Vile Parle (HO)      22000
C7      Anil Arun Dhone         SB6      Mahim                  500
C8      Alex Austin Fernandes   CA7      Vile Parle (HO)      22000
C9      Ashwini Shankar Apte    CA10     Darya Ganj           32000
C9      Ashwini Shankar Apte    SB8      Andheri                500
25 rows selected.
```

Explanation:

In the above example, the data required is available in four tables i.e. CUST_MSTR, ACCT_FD_CUST_DTLS, ACCT_MSTR and BRANCH_MSTR. All the four tables are linked via some field in the other table. This is because the data is spread across the tables based on a normalization scheme.

Notice that:

- The **CUST_NO** column is the primary key of the **CUST_MSTR** table
- The **ACCT_NO** column is the primary key of the **ACCT_MSTR** table
- The **ACCT_FD_CUST_DTLS** is a link table between the CUST_MSTR and the ACCT_MSTR table. This table holds information related to which accounts belong to which customers.

  In **ACCT_FD_CUST_DTLS** table:
  - The **ACCT_FD_NO** column is used to refer to the accounts in the **ACCT_MSTR** table via the **ACCT_NO** column
  - The **CUST_NO** column is used to refer to the customers in the **CUST_MSTR** table via the **CUST_NO** column
- The **BRANCH_NO** column is the primary key of the **BRANCH_MSTR** table

To retrieve the data required, all the four tables have to linked on the basis of common columns using joins as follows:

- **C.**CUST_NO **= L.**CUST_NO

This means the CUST_NO field of CUST_MSTR table is joined with CUST_NO field of the ACCT_FD_CUST_DTLS table

- **L.**ACCT_FD_NO = **A.**ACCT_NO

This means the ACCT_FD_NO field of ACCT_FD_CUST_DTLS table is joined with ACCT_NO field of the ACCT_MSTR table

- **A.**BRANCH_NO **= B.**BRANCH_NO

This means the BRANCH_NO field of ACCT_MSTR table is joined with BRANCH_NO field of the BRANCH_MSTR table

Now since the tables are linked using a join, data can be retrieved as if they are all in one table using the alias as:

C.CUST_NO, (**C.**FNAME **||** ' ' **||** **C.**MNAME **||** ' ' **||** **C.**LNAME) "Customer", **A.**ACCT_NO, **B.**NAME "Branch", **A.**CURBAL

Finally the output is ordered on the basis of Customers and within Customer, Account numbers.

<u>Adding An Additional WHERE Clause Condition</u>

Example:

List the employee details of only those employees who belong to the Administration department along with branch names to which they belong.

Synopsis:

Tables:	EMP_MSTR, BRANCH_MSTR
Columns:	EMP_MSTR: EMP_NO, FNAME, MNAME, LNAME, DEPT, DESIG, BRANCH_NO BRANCH_MSTR: NAME, BRANCH_NO
Technique:	**Join:** INNER JOIN ... ON, **Clauses:** WHERE, **Others:** Alias

Solution:

```
SELECT E.EMP_NO, (E.FNAME || ' ' || E.MNAME || ' ' || E.LNAME) "Name", B.NAME "Branch",
    E.DEPT, E.DESIG
  FROM EMP_MSTR E INNER JOIN BRANCH_MSTR B ON B.BRANCH_NO =
E.BRANCH_NO
    WHERE E.DEPT = 'Administration';
```

Output:

```
EMP  Name                  Branch       DEPT            DESIG
_NO
-------------------------------------------------------------------------------
E1   Ivan Nelson Bayross   Vile Parle   Administration  Managing Director
                           (HO)
E6   Sonal Abdul Khan      Darya Ganj   Administration  Admin. Executive
E10  Anjali Sameer Pathak  Darya Ganj   Administration  HR Manager
```

Explanation:

In the above example, the data required is available in two tables i.e. EMP_MSTR and BRANCH_MSTR. Both the tables are linked via a common field. This is because the data is spread across the tables based on a normalization schema.

Notice that:

- The **EMP_NO** column is the primary key of the **EMP_MSTR** table
- The **BRANCH_NO** column is used to refer to the branch names in the BRANCH_MSTR table via the BRANCH_NO column
- The **BRANCH_NO** column is the primary key of the **BRANCH_MSTR** table

To retrieve the data required, both the tables have to linked on the basis of a common column using joins as follows:

- **B.**BRANCH_NO = **E.**BRANCH_NO

This means the BRANCH_NO field of BRANCH_MSTR table is joined with BRANCH_NO field of the EMP_MSTR table

Now since both the tables are linked using a join, data can be retrieved as if they are all in one table using the alias as:

E.EMP_NO, (**E.**FNAME || ' ' || **E.**MNAME || ' ' || **E.**LNAME) "Name", **B.**NAME "Branch", **E.**DEPT, **E.**DESIG

Finally the output is filtered to display only those employees belonging to the administration department using WHERE clause as:

E.DEPT = 'Administration'

Outer Join

Example:

List the employee details along with the contact details (if any) Using Left Outer Join.

Synopsis:

Tables:	EMP_MSTR, CNTC_DTLS
Columns:	EMP_MSTR: EMP_NO, FNAME, LNAME, DEPT CNTC_DTLS: CODE_NO, CNTC_TYPE, CNTC_DATA
Technique:	**Join:** LEFT JOIN ... ON, **Clauses:** WHERE **Others:** Alias, Concat (||)

Solution 1 (Ansi-style):

```
SELECT (E.FNAME || ' ' || E.LNAME) "Name", E.DEPT, C.CNTC_TYPE, C.CNTC_DATA
   FROM EMP_MSTR E LEFT JOIN CNTC_DTLS C ON E.EMP_NO = C.CODE_NO;
```

Solution 2 (Theta-style):

```
SELECT (E.FNAME || ' ' || E.LNAME) "Name", E.DEPT, C.CNTC_TYPE, C.CNTC_DATA
   FROM EMP_MSTR E, CNTC_DTLS C WHERE E.EMP_NO = C.CODE_NO(+);
```

Output:

```
Name            DEPT                 CNTC_TYPE    CNTC_DATA
Amit Desai      Loans And Financing  R            28883779
Maya Joshi      Client Servicing     R            28377634
Peter Joseph    Loans And Financing  R            26323560
Mandhar Dalvi   Marketing            R            26793231
Sonal Khan      Administration       R            28085654
Anil Kambli     Marketing            R            24442342
Seema Apte      Client Servicing     R            24365672
Vikram          Marketing            R            24327349
Randive
Anjali Pathak   Administration       R            24302579
Ivan Bayross    Administration
10 rows selected.
```

Explanation:

In the above example, the data required is all the employee details along with their contact details **if any**. This means all the employee details have to be listed even though their corresponding contact information is not present.

The data is available in two tables i.e. EMP_MSTR and CNTC_DTLS

In such a situation, the **LEFT JOIN** can be used which returns all the rows from the first table (i.e. EMP_MSTR), even if there are no matches in the second table (CNTC_DTLS). This means, if there are employees in **EMP_MSTR** that do not have any contacts in **CNTC_DTLS**, those rows will also be listed. Notice the keyword **LEFT JOIN** in the first solution (Ansi-style) and the **(+)** in the second solution (Theta-style). This indicates that all rows from the first table i.e. EMP_MSTR will be displayed even though there exists no matching rows in the second table i.e. CNTC_DTLS.

Notice that:

- The **EMP_NO** column is the primary key of the **EMP_MSTR** table
- The **CNTC_DTLS** is a table that holds the contact details of employees.

  In **CNTC_DTLS** table:
  - **ADDR_NO** column is used to refer to the addresses in the ADDR_DTLS table via the ADDR_NO column.
  - **CODE_NO** column is used to refer to the employees in the **EMP_MSTR** table via the **EMP_NO** column

To retrieve the data required, both the tables have to linked on the basis of common columns using joins as follows:

- **E.**EMP_NO = **C.**CODE_NO

This means the EMP_NO field of EMP_MSTR table is joined with CODE_NO field of the CNTC_DTLS table

Example:

List the employee details along with the contact details (if any) Using Right Outer Join.

Synopsis:

Tables:	EMP_MSTR, CNTC_DTLS
Columns:	EMP_MSTR**:** EMP_NO, FNAME, LNAME, DEPT CNTC_DTLS**:** CODE_NO, CNTC_TYPE, CNTC_DATA
Technique:	**Join:** RIGHT JOIN ... ON, **Clauses:** WHERE

Solution 1 (Ansi-style):

```
SELECT E.FNAME, E.LNAME, E.DEPT, C.CNTC_TYPE, C.CNTC_DATA FROM CNTC_DTLS C
    RIGHT JOIN EMP_MSTR E ON C.CODE_NO = E.EMP_NO;
```

Solution 2 (Theta-style):

```
SELECT E.FNAME, E.LNAME, E.DEPT, C.CNTC_TYPE, C.CNTC_DATA
    FROM CNTC_DTLS C, EMP_MSTR E WHERE C.CODE_NO(+) = E.EMP_NO;
```

Output:

```
FNAME   LNAME   DEPT                 CNTC_TYPE CNTC_DATA
---------------------------------------------------------
Ivan    Bayross Administration       R         26045953
Anjali  Pathak  Administration       R         24302579
Amit    Desai   Loans And Financing  R         28883779
Maya    Joshi   Client Servicing     R         28377634
Peter   Joseph  Loans And Financing  R         26323560
Mandhar Dalvi   Marketing            R         26793231
Sonal   Khan    Administration       R         28085654
Anil    Kambli  Marketing            R         24442342
Seema   Apte    Client Servicing     R         24365672
Vikram  Randive Marketing            R         24327349
10 rows selected.
```

Explanation:

In the above example, the data required is all the employee details along with their contact details **if any**. But in this case **RIGHT JOIN** is being used. This means all the employee details have to be listed even though their corresponding contact information is not present. The data is available in two tables i.e. EMP_MSTR and CNTC_DTLS

Since the **RIGHT JOIN** returns all the rows from the second table even if there are no matches in the first table. The first table in the FROM clause will have to be **CNTC_DTLS** and the second table **EMP_MSTR**. This means, if there are employees in **EMP_MSTR** that do not have any contacts in **CNTC_DTLS**, those rows will also be listed. Notice the keyword **RIGHT JOIN** in the first solution (Ansi-style) and the **(+)** in the second solution (Theta-style).

This indicates that all rows from the second table i.e. EMP_MSTR will be displayed even though there exists no matching rows in the first table i.e. CNTC_DTLS.

Notice that:

- The **EMP_NO** column is the primary key of the **EMP_MSTR** table
- The **CNTC_DTLS** is a table that holds the contact details of employees.

  In **CNTC_DTLS** table:
  - **ADDR_NO** column is used to refer to the addresses in the ADDR_DTLS table via the ADDR_NO column.
  - **CODE_NO** column is used to refer to the employees in the **EMP_MSTR** table via the **EMP_NO** column

To retrieve the data required, both the tables have to linked on the basis of common columns using joins as follows:

- **C.**CODE_NO = **E.**EMP_NO

This means the CODE_NO field of CNTC_DTLS table is joined with EMP_NO field of the EMP_MSTR table

Cross Join

Suppose it is desired to combine each deposit amount with a Fixed Deposits Interest Slab table so as to analyze each deposit amount at each interest rate and their minimum and maximum periods. This is elegantly done using a cross join.

Example:

Create a report using **cross join** that will display the maturity amounts for pre-defined deposits, based on the Minimum and Maximum periods fixed / time deposits. Ensure that a temporary table called TMP_FD_AMT stores the amounts for pre-defined deposits in the FD_AMT column.

Synopsis:

Tables:	TMP_FD_AMT, FDSLAB_MSTR
Columns:	TMP_FD_AMT: FD_AMT, FDSLAB_MSTR: MINPERIOD, MAXPERIOD, INTRATE
Technique:	**Join:** CROSS JOIN, **Operators:** (*), (/)

Prior executing the SQL statement a table called TMP_FD_AMT has to be created and filled in with some sample data.

```
CREATE TABLE "DBA_BANKSYS"."TMP_FD_AMT"("FD_AMT" NUMBER(6));
```

Insert Statements for the table TMP_FD_AMT:

```
INSERT INTO TMP_FD_AMT (FD_AMT) VALUES(5000);
INSERT INTO TMP_FD_AMT (FD_AMT) VALUES(10000);
INSERT INTO TMP_FD_AMT (FD_AMT) VALUES(15000);
INSERT INTO TMP_FD_AMT (FD_AMT) VALUES(20000);
INSERT INTO TMP_FD_AMT (FD_AMT) VALUES(25000);
INSERT INTO TMP_FD_AMT (FD_AMT) VALUES(30000);
INSERT INTO TMP_FD_AMT (FD_AMT) VALUES(40000);
INSERT INTO TMP_FD_AMT (FD_AMT) VALUES(50000);
```

Solution:

```
SELECT T.FD_AMT, S.MINPERIOD, S.MAXPERIOD, S.INTRATE,
    ROUND(T.FD_AMT + (T.FD_AMT * (S.INTRATE/100) * (S.MINPERIOD/365)))
        "Amt. Min. Period",
    ROUND(T.FD_AMT + (T.FD_AMT * (S.INTRATE/100) * (S.MAXPERIOD/365)))
        "Amt. Max. Period"
    FROM FDSLAB_MSTR S CROSS JOIN TMP_FD_AMT T;
```

Output:

```
 FD_AM MINPERIO MAXPERIO INTRATE         Amt. Min.          Amt. Max.
     T        D        D                    Period             Period
-------------------------------------------------------------------------
  5000        1       30       5              5001               5021
  5000       31       92     5.5              5023               5069
  5000       93      183       6              5076               5050
. . .
 20000       31       92     5.5             20093              20277
 20000       93      183       6             20306              20602
 20000      184      365     6.5             20655              21300
 20000      366      731     7.5             21504              23004
. . .
 50000      184      365     6.5             51638              53250
 50000      366      731     7.5             53760              57510
 50000      732     1097     8.5             58523              62773
 50000     1098     1829      10             65041              75055
56 rows selected.
```

Explanation:

In the above example, the data required is available in two tables i.e. TMP_FD_AMT and FDSLAB_MSTR. In the table TMP_FD_AMT, there exists, the deposit amounts. In the second table FDSLAB_MSTR, there exists a list of fixed deposits slabs comprising of minimum and maximum periods and the interest rates applicable for those periods.

The output is required in the form of a report, which will display calculation based on the FDSLAB_MSTR table for each row held in the TMP_FD_AMT. In such a situation, a CROSS JOIN can be used which will combine each record from the left table with that of the right table. In this example a cross join will combine each deposit amount (i.e. FD_AMT) from the TMP_FD_AMT table with each slab i.e. each record in the FDSLAB_MSTR table after applying some calculations. Using Cross Join, a matrix between the temporary table named TMP_FD_AMT table and the FDSLAB_MSTR table can be created.

The above SELECT statement creates a record for each deposit amount with the calculated maturity amount based on the interest rates and the minimum and maximum periods. The results are known as a Cartesian product, which combines every record in the left table i.e. FDSLAB_MSTR with every record in the right table i.e. TMP_FD_AMT.

Oracle versions **prior to 9i** don't support an explicit cross join, but the same results can be obtained by using the following statement:

SELECT T.FD_AMT, **S.**MINPERIOD, **S.**MAXPERIOD, **S.**INTRATE,
 ROUND(T.FD_AMT + **(T.**FD_AMT * **(S.**INTRATE/100) * **(S.**MINPERIOD/365**)))**
 "Amt. Min. Period",

```
ROUND(T.FD_AMT + (T.FD_AMT * (S.INTRATE/100) * (S.MAXPERIOD/365)))
    "Amt. Max. Period"
FROM FDSLAB_MSTR S, TMP_FD_AMT T;
```

Guidelines for Creating Joins

- When writing a select statement that joins tables, precede the column name with the table name for clarity
- If the same column name appears in more than one table, the column name must be prefixed with the table name
- The WHERE clause, is the most critical clause in a join select statement. Always make sure to include the WHERE clause

Joining A Table To Itself (Self Joins)

In some situations, it is necessary to join a table to itself, as though joining two separate tables. This is referred to as a **self-join**. In a self-join, two rows from the same table combine to form a result row.

To join a table to itself, **two** copies of the very same table have to be opened in memory. Hence in the **FROM** clause, the table name needs to be mentioned twice. Since the table names are the same, the second table will overwrite the first table and in effect, result in only one table being in memory. This is because a table name is translated into a specific memory location. To avoid this, each table is opened using an alias. Now these table aliases will cause two identical tables to be opened in different memory locations. This will result in two identical tables to be physically present in the computer's memory.

Using the table alias names these two identical tables can be joined.

```
FROM <TableName> [<Alias1>], <TableName> [<Alias2>] ....
```

Example:

Retrieve the names of the employees and the names of their respective managers from the employee table.

Synopsis:

Tables:	EMP_MNGR
Columns:	FNAME
Technique:	**Joins:** SELF, **Clauses**: WHERE **Others:** Alias

Solution:

```
SELECT EMP.FNAME "Employee", MNGR.FNAME "Manager"
  FROM EMP_MSTR EMP, EMP_MSTR MNGR
     WHERE EMP.MNGR_NO = MNGR.EMP_NO;
```

Note: *In this query, the EMP_MSTR table is treated as two separate tables named EMP and MNGR, using the table alias feature of SQL.*

Output:

Employee	Manager
Peter	Amit
Sonal	Ivan
Anil	Mandhar
Seema	Maya
Vikram	Anil
Anjali	Ivan

6 rows selected.

Explanation:

In the above example, the data required are all the employees and the names of their respective managers to whom they report. This data is available in the table **EMP_MSTR**. The EMP_MSTR table holds the employee number, their names and the manager numbers who in turn are employees in the same table.

The table EMP_MSTR holds the following data:

Emp_No	Fname	Lname	Mngr_No
E1	Ivan	Bayross	
E2	Amit	Desai	
E3	Maya	Joshi	
E4	Peter	Joseph	E2
E5	Mandhar	Dalvi	
E6	Sonal	Khan	E1
E7	Anil	Kambli	E5
E8	Seema	Apte	E3
E9	Vikram	Randive	E7
E10	Anjali	Pathak	E1

As can be seen from the data above employees named **Peter** having employee number **E4** reports to a manager (employee) named **Amit** having employee number **E2**.

Similarly, employees numbered **E6, E7, E8, E9, E10** report to managers (employees) numbered **E1, E5, E3, E7, E1** respectively.

This means:

- The **EMP_NO** column is the primary key of the **EMP_MSTR** table
- The **MNGR_NO** column is used to refer to the Employee details in the same table i.e. **EMP_MSTR** via the **EMP_NO** column

This simply means that MNGR_NO is a foreign key mapping to the EMP_NO which is the primary key of the table.

From the data available in the EMP_MSTR table seen above, it is possible to extract the manager number to which the employee reports, but in order to extract the manager name i.e. the employee's name (since the manager is also an employee) a reference to the same table EMP_MSTR has to be made. This can be done using a SELF JOIN i.e. making a copy of the same table EMP_MSTR and then referring to the columns to get the employee name against the manager number.

To form a copy of the same table alias have to be used in the FROM clause as:

FROM EMP_MSTR **EMP**, EMP_MSTR **MNGR**

Here the **EMP** is the **first copy** of the table **EMP_MSTR** and **MNGR** is the **second copy** of the table **EMP_MSTR**.

To retrieve the data required, both the copies of the same tables have to linked on the basis of common columns using joins as follows:

- **EMP.**MNGR_NO = **MNGR.**EMP_NO

  This means the MNGR_NO field of EMP_MSTR table (First Copy: EMP) is joined with EMP_NO field of the EMP_MSTR (Second Copy: MNGR) table

Views

After a table is created and populated with data, it may become necessary to prevent all users from accessing all columns of a table, for data security reasons. This would mean creating several tables having the appropriate number of columns and assigning specific users to each table, as required. This will answer data security requirements very well but will give rise to a great deal of redundant data being resident in tables, in the database.

To reduce redundant data to the minimum possible, Oracle allows the creation of an object called a **View**. A View is mapped, to a SELECT sentence. The table on which the view is based is described in the FROM clause of the SELECT statement. The SELECT clause consists of a sub-set of the columns of the table. Thus a View, which is mapped to a table, will in effect have a sub-set of the actual columns of the table from which it is built. This technique offers a simple, effective way of hiding columns of a table.

An interesting fact about a View is that it is stored only as a definition in Oracle's system catalogue. When a reference is made to a View, its definition is scanned, the base table is opened and the View created on top of the base table. Hence, a view holds no data at all, until a specific call to the view is made. This reduces redundant data on the HDD to a very large extent. When a View is used to manipulate table data, the underlying base table will be completely invisible. This will give the level of data security required.

The Oracle engine treats a View just as though it was a base table. Hence a View can be queried exactly as though it was a base table. However, a query fired on a view will run slower that a query fired on a base table.

This is because the View definition has to be retrieved from Oracle's system catalogue, the base table has to be identified and opened in memory and then the View has to be constructed on top of the base table, suitably masking table columns. Only then will the query actually execute and return the active data set.

Some View's are used only for looking at table data. Other View's can be used to Insert, Update and Delete table data as well as View data. If a View is used to only look at table data and nothing else the View is called a **Read-Only** View. A View that is used to Look at table data as well as Insert, Update and Delete table data is called an **Updateable** View.

The reasons why views are created are

- When Data security is required
- When Data redundancy is to be kept to the minimum while maintaining data security

Let's spend some time in learning how a View is

- Created

Used for only viewing and / or manipulating table data

- i.e. a read-only or updateable view

- Destroyed

Creation of views

Syntax:

```
CREATE VIEW viewname AS
        SELECT columnname, columnname
FROM tablename
WHERE columnname = expression list;
GROUP BY grouping criteria
HAVING operator
```

Note: *The ORDER BY clause cannot be used while creating a view.*

Example:

Create a view on the salesman_master table for the Sales Department.

CREATE VIEW **vw_sales** AS

SELECT * FROM **salesman_master**;

Note: *The columns of the table are related to the view on a **one-to-one** relationship.*

Example:

Create a view on the client_master table for the Administration Department.

CREATE VIEW **vw_clientadmin** AS

SELECT **name, address1, address2, city, pincode, state**

FROM **client_master**;

This creates a view by the name of **vw_clientadmin** based on the table **client_master**.

Renaming The Columns Of A View

The columns of the view can take on different names from the table columns, if required.

Example:

CREATE VIEW **vw_clientadmin** AS

SELECT **name, address1 add1, address2 add2, city, pincode, state**

FROM **client_master**;

Selecting A Data Set From A View

Once a view has been created, it can be queried exactly like a base table.

Syntax:

SELECT *columnname,columnname*

FROM *viewname;*

Note: *Instead of the table name in the FROM clause, a view name is used. The SELECT statement can have all the clauses like WHERE, ORDER BY etc.*

Example:

SELECT name, address1, address2, city, pincode, state

FROM vw_clientadmin

WHERE city IN ('BOMBAY', 'DELHI');

Updateable Views

Views can also be used for data manipulation (i.e. the user can perform the Insert, Update and Delete operations). Views on which data manipulation can be done are called Updateable Views. When you give an updateable view name in the Update, Insert or Delete SQL statement, modifications to data will be passed to the underlying table.

For a view to be updateable, it should meet the following criteria

Views defined from Single table

- If the user wants to **INSERT** records with the help of a view, then the PRIMARY KEY column/s and **all** the NOT NULL columns must be included in the view.
- The user can **UPDATE, DELETE** records with the help of a view even if the PRIMARY KEY column and NOT NULL column/s **are excluded** from the view definition.

Example:

Table Name: Client_master

Column Name	Data type	Size	Attributes
Client_no	Varchar2	6	Primary key
Name	Varchar2	15	Not Null
Address1	Varchar2	15	Not Null
Address2	Varchar2	15	
City	Varchar2	10	
Pincode	Number	8	
Bal_due	Number	8,2	

CREATE VIEW **vw_client** AS

SELECT **client_no, name, address1, bal_due**

FROM **client_master**;

When an INSERT operation is performed using the view

SQL> insert into vw_client values ('C0011', 'Robert', '1/101, Kurla', 1000);

Oracle returns the following message:

1 row created

When an MODIFY operation is performed using the view

SQL> update vw_client set bal_due=10000 where client_no='C0011';

Oracle returns the following message:

1 row updated.

When an DELETE operation is performed using the view

SQL> delete from vw_client where client_no='C0011';

Oracle returns the following message:

1 rows deleted.

A view can be created from more than one table. For the purpose of creating the View these tables will be linked by a join condition specified in the where clause of the View's definition.

The behavior of the View will vary for Insert, Update, Delete and Select table operations depending upon the following

- Whether the tables were created using a Referencing clause
- Whether the tables were created without any Referencing clause and are actually standalone tables not related in any way.

Views defined from Multiple tables (Which have no Referencing clause):

If a view is created from multiple tables, which were not created using a 'Referencing clause' (i.e. No logical linkage exists between the tables), then though the PRIMARY Key Column/ s as well as the NOT NULL columns are included in the View definition the view's behavior will be as follows:

The INSERT, UPDATE or DELETE operation is not allowed. If attempted Oracle displays the following error message:

For insert/modify:

ORA –01779: cannot modify a column, which maps to a non key-preserved table.

For delete:

ORA –01752: cannot delete from view without exactly one key-preserved table.

Views defined from Multiple tables (Which have been created with a Referencing clause):

If a view is created from multiple tables, which were created using a 'Referencing clause' (i.e. a logical linkage exists between the tables), then though the **PRIMARY Key** Column/ s as well as the **NOT NULL** columns are included in the View definition the view's behavior will be as follows:

- An **INSERT** operation is not allowed.
- The **DELETE** or **MODIFY** operations **do not** affect the Master table.
- The view can be used to **MODIFY** the columns of the **detail table** included in the view.
- If a **DELETE** operation is executed on the view, the corresponding records from the **detail table** will be deleted.

Example:

Table Name : sales_order

Column Name	Data Type	Size	Attributes
order_no	varchar2	6	Primary Key / first letter must start with 'O'
order_date	date		
client_no	varchar2	6	Foreign Key references client_no of client_master table
dely_Addr	varchar2	25	
salesman_no	Varchar2	6	Foreign Key references salesman_no of salesman_master table
dely_type	char	1	Delivery : part(P) / full (F), Default 'F'

billed_yn	char	1	
dely_date	date		cannot be less than order_date
order_status	varchar2	10	Values ('In Process', 'Fulfilled', 'BackOrder', 'Cancelled')

Table Name : sales_order_details

Column Name	Data Type	Size	Attributes
detorder_no	varchar2	6	Primary Key / Foreign Key references order_no of the sales_order table
product_no	Varchar2	6	Primary Key / Foreign Key references product_no of the product_master table.
qty_ordered	Number	8	
qty_disp	Number	8	
product_rate	Number	10,2	

Syntax for creating a Master/Detail View

```
CREATE VIEW vw_sales AS
SELECT order_no,order_date, dely_addr, product_no, qty_ordered ,qty_disp
FROM sales_order, sales_order_details
WHERE sales_order.order_no =sales_order_details.detorder_no;
```

- When an INSERT operation is performed using the view

```
SQL> insert into vw_sales values ('O00011','12-Jan-98','Malad','P00001',100,
              50);
```

Oracle returns the following error message:

ORA-01776: cannot modify more than one base table through a join view

- When an MODIFY operation is performed using the view

```
SQL> update vw_sales set qty_disp =100 where detorder_no='O0007';
```

Oracle returns the following message:

1 row updated.

- When an DELETE operation is performed using the view

```
SQL> delete from vw_sales where product_no ='P0001' and
          detorder_no='O0001';
```

Oracle returns the following message:

1 rows deleted.

Common restrictions on updateable views

The following condition holds true irrespective of the view being created from a single table or multiple tables.

- For the view to be updateable the view definition must not include:
  - Aggregate functions.
  - DISTINCT, GROUP BY or HAVING clause
  - Sub-queries.
  - Constants, Strings or Value Expressions like sell_price * 1.05.
  - UNION, INTERSECT or MINUS clause.
  - If a view is defined from another view, the second view should be updateable.

If the user tries to perform any of INSERT, UPDATE, DELETE operation, on a view, which is created from a non-updateable view Oracle returns the following error message:

```
ORA-01732: data manipulation operation not legal on this view
```

Destroying a view

The **DROP VIEW** command is used to remove a view from the database.

Syntax:

DROP VIEW ***viewname;***

Example:

Remove the view vw_clientadmin from the database.

DROP VIEW **VW_CLIENTADMIN**;

Self Review Questions

Fill In The Blanks

1. The SQL sentences that are used to create database objects are called ______________________.
2. The SQL sentences used to manipulate data within database objects are called ______________________.
3. The SQL sentences, which are used to control the behavior of database objects, are called ______________________.

4. In a DBMS a group of similar information or data, is called an ____________.
5. A table is a two dimensional matrix that consists of ______________________.
6. The characteristics of an entity are called __________________.
7. Business rules, which are enforced on data being stored in a table, are called __________.
8. If the column was created as __________ Oracle will place a NULL value in the column in the absence of a user-defined value.
9. When a column is defined as not null, then that column becomes a ___________ column.
10. The ______________ constraint can only be applied at column level.
11. A __________ value can be inserted into the columns of any data type.
12. A single column primary key is called a __________ key.
13. The data held across the primary key column must be __________.
14. ___________ keys represent relationships between tables.
15. The table in which the foreign key is defined is called a Foreign table or _________ table.
16. The default behavior of the foreign key can be changed by using the _____________________ option.
17. __________ constraints must be specified as a logical expression that evaluates either to TRUE or FALSE.
18. In a CHECK constraint the condition must be a __________ expression that can be evaluated using the values in the row being inserted or updated.

True Or False

19. The SQL sentences used to manipulate data within database objects are called Data Definition Language.
20. Entity information is stored in an object called Table.
21. A table is an single dimensional matrix.
22. Business rules that have to be applied to data are completely System dependent.
23. Constraints super control the data being entered into a table for temporary storage.
24. A NULL value is equivalent to a value of zero.
25. Setting a NULL value is appropriate when the actual value is unknown.
26. A table cannot contain multiple unique keys.
27. Oracle ignores any UNIQUE, FOREIGN KEY, CHECK constraints on a NULL value.
28. A primary key column in a table is an optional column.

29. Standard business rules do not allow multiple entries for the same product.
30. The master table can be referenced in the foreign key definition by using the clause REFERENCES tablename.columnname when defining the foreign key.
31. A CHECK constraint consists of subqueries and sequences.
32. The USER_CONSTRAINTS command displays only the column names, data type, size and the NOT NULL constraint.
33. Drop the constraint using the DROP TABLE command with the DELETE clause.
34. At the time of table creation a default value can be assigned to a column.
35. If a column level constraint is defined on the column with a default value, the default value clause must precede the constraint definition.

Objectives

1. Describe some of the main features of SQL?
2. What are DDL, DML and DCL statements?
3. What are Constraints? Describe some of the different types of Constraints available.
4. What are the differences (if any) between the UNIQUE and PRIMARY key Constraint?
5. What are the different Aggregate functions? Explain any three any three with simple examples?
6. What are the different String functions? Explain any three any three with simple examples?
7. What are the different Date functions? Explain with simple examples?
8. What is a subquery? What is a correlated subquery?
9. What are Joins? State the different types of Joins.
10. Define what a View, Read-only View and Updateable View are.
11. How is a View created? Describe using a simple example.

9. PL/SQL CONCEPTS

What is a cursor?

The Oracle Engine uses a work area for its internal processing in order to execute an SQL statement. This work area is private to SQL's operations and is called a **Cursor**.

The data that is stored in the cursor is called the **Active Data Set**. Conceptually, the size of the cursor in memory is the size required to hold the number of rows in the **Active Data Set**. The actual size, however, is determined by the Oracle engine's built in memory management capabilities and the amount of RAM available. Oracle has a pre-defined area in main memory set aside, within which cursors are opened. Hence the cursor's size will be limited by the size of this pre-defined area.

The values retrieved from a table are held in a cursor opened in memory by the Oracle Engine. This data is then transferred to the client machine via the network. In order to hold this data, a cursor is opened at the client end. If the number of rows returned by the Oracle engine is more than the area available in the cursor opened on the client, the cursor data and the retrieved data is swapped between the operating system's swap area and RAM.

Example:

When a user fires a select statement as:

SELECT EMP_NO, FNAME, DEPT **FROM** EMP_MSTR **WHERE** BRANCH_NO = 'B1';

The resultant data set in the cursor opened at the Server end is displayed as under:

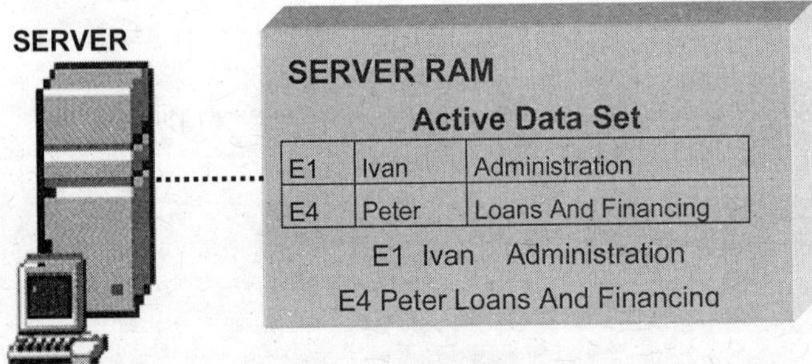

Diagram 9.1: Contents of a cursor.

When a cursor is loaded with multiple rows via a query the Oracle engine opens and maintains a row pointer. Depending on user's requests to view data the row pointer will be relocated within the cursor's Active Data Set. Additionally Oracle also maintains multiple cursor variables. The values held in these variables indicate the status of the processing being done by the cursor.

Types Of Cursors

Cursors are classified depending on the circumstances under which they are opened. If the Oracle engine opened a cursor for its internal processing it is known as an **Implicit Cursor**. A cursor can also be opened for processing data through a PL/SQL block, on demand. Such a user-defined cursor is known as an **Explicit Cursor**.

General Cursor Attributes:

When the Oracle engine creates an Implicit **or** Explicit cursor, cursor control variables are also created to control the execution of the cursor. These are a set of four system variables, which keep track of the **Current** status of a cursor. These cursor variables can be accessed and used in a PL/SQL code block.

Both **Implicit** and **Explicit** cursors have four attributes. They are described below:

Attribute Name	Description
%ISOPEN	Returns **TRUE** if **cursor** is **open**, **FALSE** otherwise.
%FOUND	Returns **TRUE** if **record** was **fetched** successfully, **FALSE** otherwise.
%NOTFOUND	Returns **TRUE** if **record** was **not fetched** successfully, **FALSE** otherwise.
%ROWCOUNT	Returns **number of records processed** from the cursor.

Implicit Cursor

The Oracle engine implicitly opens a cursor on the Server to process each SQL statement. Since the implicit cursor is opened and managed by the Oracle engine internally, the function of reserving an area in memory, populating this area with appropriate data, processing the data in the memory area, releasing the memory area when the processing is complete is taken care of by the Oracle engine. The resultant data is then passed to the client machine via the network. A cursor is then opened in memory on the client machine to hold the rows returned by the Oracle engine. The number of rows held in the cursor on the client is managed by the client's operating system and it's swap area.

Implicit cursor attributes can be used to access information about the status of the last insert, update, delete or single-row select statements. This can be done by preceding the implicit cursor attribute with the cursor name (i.e. SQL). The values of the cursor attributes always refer to the most recently executed SQL statement, wherever the statement appears. If an attribute value is to be saved for later use, it must be assigned to a (**boolean***)* memory variable.

Implicit Cursor Processing in Client Server Environment

Diagram 9.2: Client Server and Cursor processing.

Implicit Cursor Attributes

Attribute Name	Description
%ISOPEN	The Oracle engine automatically opens and closes the SQL cursor after executing its associated select, insert, update or delete SQL statement has been processed in case of implicit cursors. Thus the **SQL%ISOPEN** attribute of an implicit cursor cannot be referenced outside of its SQL statement. As a result, **SQL%ISOPEN** always evaluates to **FALSE**.
%FOUND	Evaluates to **TRUE**, if an insert, update or delete affected one or more rows, or a single-row select returned one or more rows. Otherwise, it evaluates to **FALSE**. The syntax for accessing this attribute is **SQL%FOUND**
%NOTFOUND	Is the logical opposite of **%FOUND**. It evaluates to **TRUE**, if an insert, update or delete affected no rows, or a single-row select returns no rows. Otherwise, it evaluates to **FALSE**. The syntax for accessing this attribute is **SQL%NOTFOUND**
%ROWCOUNT	Returns the number of rows affected by an insert, update or delete, or select into statement. The syntax for accessing this attribute is **SQL%ROWCOUNT**

Example:

The bank manager has decided to transfer employees across branches. Write a PL/SQL block to accept an employee number and the branch number followed by updating the branch number of that employee to which he belongs appropriately. Display an appropriate message using **SQL%FOUND** based on the existence of the record in the **EMP_MSTR** table. Display an appropriate message using **SQL%NOTFOUND** based on the non-existence of the record in the **EMP_MSTR** table.

```
BEGIN
   UPDATE EMP_MSTR SET BRANCH_NO = &BRANCH_NO WHERE EMP_NO =
&EMP_NO;
   IF SQL%FOUND THEN
      dbms_output.put_line('Employee Successfully Transferred');
   END IF;
   IF SQL%NOTFOUND THEN
      dbms_output.put_line('Employee Number does not Exist');
   END IF;
END;
```

Output:

```
Enter value for branch_no: 'B4'
old   2:  UPDATE EMP_MSTR SET BRANCH_NO = &BRANCH_NO
new   2:  UPDATE EMP_MSTR SET BRANCH_NO = 'B4'
Enter value for emp_no: 'E1'
old   3:   WHERE EMP_NO = &EMP_NO;
new   3:   WHERE EMP_NO = 'E1';
Employee Successfully Transferred
PL/SQL procedure successfully completed.
```

Note:	*Both SQL%FOUND and SQL%NOTFOUND attributes evaluate to NULL until they are set by an implicit or explicit cursor operation.*

Example:

For SQL%ROWCOUNT

The bank manager of **Darya Ganj** branch decides to activate all those accounts, which were previously marked as inactive for performing no transactions in last 365 days. Write a PL/SQL block to update the status of accounts. Display an appropriate message based on the number of rows affected by the update fired.

```
DECLARE
   Rows_Affected char(4);
BEGIN
   UPDATE ACCT_MSTR SET STATUS = 'A' WHERE STATUS = 'S' AND
      BRANCH_NO IN(SELECT BRANCH_NO FROM BRANCH_MSTR
         WHERE NAME = 'Darya Ganj');
   Rows_Affected := TO_CHAR(SQL%ROWCOUNT);
```

```
    IF SQL%ROWCOUNT > 0 THEN
        dbms_output.put_line(Rows_Affected || ' Account(s) Activated Successfully');
    ELSE
        dbms_output.put_line('Currently there exist no Inactive Accounts in the Darya Ganj Branch');
    END IF;
END;
```

Output:

```
2  Account(s) Activated Successfully
PL/SQL procedure successfully completed.
```

Explicit Cursor

When individual records in a table have to be processed inside a PL/SQL code block a cursor is used. This cursor will be declared and mapped to an SQL query in the Declare Section of the PL/SQL block and used within its Executable Section. A cursor thus created and used is known as an **Explicit Cursor**.

Explicit Cursor Management

The steps involved in using an explicit cursor and manipulating data in its active set are:

- Declare a cursor mapped to a SQL select statement that retrieves data for processing
- Open the cursor
- Fetch data from the cursor one row at a time into memory variables
- Process the data held in the memory variables as required using a loop
- Exit from the loop after processing is complete
- Close the cursor

Cursor Declaration

A cursor is defined in the declarative part of a PL/SQL block. This is done by naming the cursor and mapping it to a query. When a cursor is declared, the Oracle engine is informed that a cursor of the said name needs to be opened. The declaration is only an intimation. There is no memory allocation at this point in time. The three commands used to control the cursor subsequently are **open, fetch** and **close**.

The Functionality Of Open, Fetch And Close Commands

Initialization of a cursor takes place via the **open** statement, this:

- Defines a private SQL area named after the cursor name
- Executes a query associated with the cursor
- Retrieves table data and populates the named private SQL area in memory i.e. creates the **Active Data Set**
- Sets the cursor row pointer in the **Active Data Set** to the **first** record

A **fetch** statement then moves the data held in the **Active Data Set** into memory variables. Data held in the memory variables can be processed as desired.

The **fetch** statement is placed inside a **Loop ... End Loop** construct, which causes the data to be fetched into the memory variables and processed until all the rows in the **Active Data Set** are processed. The **fetch** loop then exits. The exiting of the **fetch** loop is user controlled.

After the **fetch** loop exits, the cursor must be closed with the **close** statement. This will release the memory occupied by the cursor and its **Active Data Set**. A PL/SQL block is necessary to declare a cursor and create an **Active Data Set**. The cursor name is used to reference the **Active Data Set** held within the cursor.

Syntax:

```
CURSOR CursorName IS SELECT statement;
```

Opening A Cursor

Opening a cursor executes the query and creates the active set that contains all rows, which meet the query search criteria. An open statement retrieves records from a database table and places the records in the cursor (i.e. named private SQL area in memory). A cursor is opened in the Server's memory.

Syntax:

```
OPEN CursorName;
```

The working of the Client Tool and Oracle Engine when an explicit cursor is opened using the OPEN command is represented diagrammatically below:

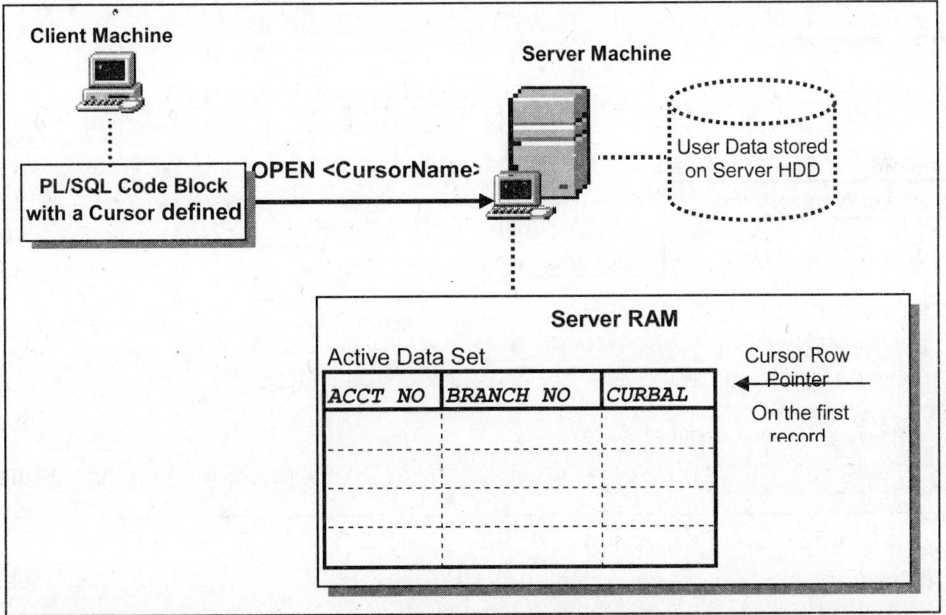

Diagram 9.3: Processing of OPEN CURSOR command in the Oracle Engine

Fetching A Record From The Cursor

The **fetch** statement retrieves the rows from the active set opened in the Server into memory variables declared in the PL/SQL code block on the client one row at a time. The memory variables are opened on the client machine. Each time a **fetch** is executed, the cursor pointer is advanced to the next row in the **Active Data Set**.

A standard loop structure (Loop-End Loop) is used to fetch records from the cursor into memory variables one row at a time.

Syntax:

```
FETCH CursorName INTO Variable1, Variable2, ...;
```

Note: *There must be a memory variable for each column value of the Active Data Set. Data types must match. These variables will be declared in the DECLARE section of the PL/SQL block.*

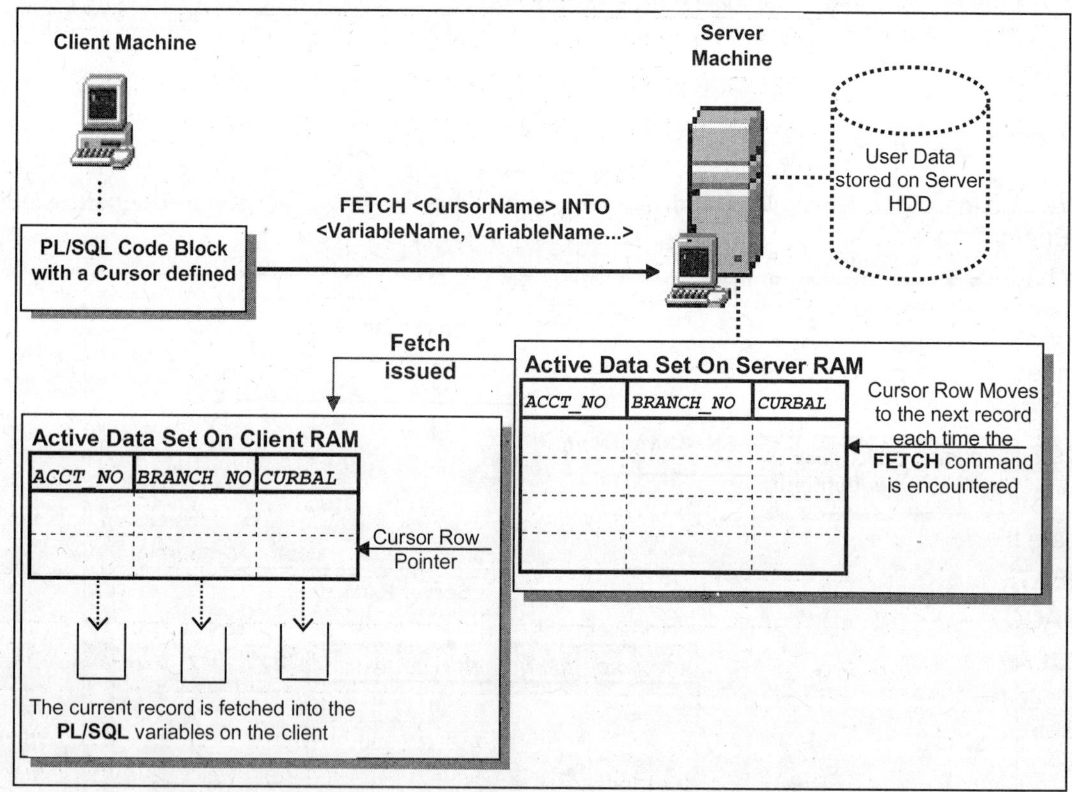

Diagram 9.4: Processing of FETCH command in the Oracle Engine

Closing A Cursor

The close statement disables the cursor and the active set becomes undefined. This will release the memory occupied by the cursor and its Data Set both on the Client and on the Server.

Syntax:

```
CLOSE CursorName;
```

Note: *Once a cursor is closed, the reopen statement causes the cursor to be reopened.*

Explicit Cursor Attributes

Similar to the cursor attributes in case of implicit cursors, four attributes are associated with explicit cursors. The attributes can be used in a PL/SQL code block for processing of data or exiting. The cursor name is appended to the attribute name when referencing the attribute.

Attribute Name	Description
%FOUND	Evaluates to TRUE, if the last fetch succeeded because a row was available; or to FALSE, if the last fetch failed because no more rows were available. The syntax for accessing this attribute is CursorName**%FOUND.**
%NOTFOUND	Is the logical opposite of %FOUND. It evaluates to TRUE, if the last fetch has failed because no more rows were available; or to FALSE, if the last fetch returned a row. The syntax for accessing this attribute is CursorName%NOTFOUND.
%ISOPEN	Evaluates to TRUE, if an explicit cursor is open; or to FALSE, if it is closed. The syntax for accessing this attribute is CursorName**%ISOPEN.**
%ROWCOUNT	Returns the number of rows fetched from the active set. It is set to zero when the cursor is opened. The syntax for accessing this attribute is CursorName**%ROWCOUNT.**

Example:

The bank manager has decided to mark all those accounts as inactive (I) on which there are no transactions performed in the last 365 days. Whenever any such update takes place, a record for the same is maintained in the **INACTV_ACCT_MSTR** table comprising of the account number, the opening date and the type of account. Write a PL/SQL block to do the same.

Table Name: INACTV_ACCT_MSTR

ACCT_NO	OPNDT	TYPE

Create the table INACTV_ACCT_MSTR as:

```
CREATE TABLE INACTV_ACCT_MSTR (
    ACCT_NO VARCHAR2(10), OPNDT DATE, TYPE VARCHAR2(2));
DECLARE
/* Declaration of the cursor named Crsr_NoTrans. The active data set will
include the account numbers and status of all the accounts held in the
ACCT_MSTR table. */
    CURSOR Crsr_NoTrans IS
        SELECT ACCT_NO, STATUS, OPNDT, TYPE FROM ACCT_MSTR
            WHERE ACCT_NO IN (SELECT ACCT_NO FROM TRANS_MSTR
```

```
            GROUP BY ACCT_NO HAVING MAX(SYSDATE - DT) >365);
/* Declaration of memory variable that holds data fetched from the cursor.
*/
    str_ACCT_NO ACCT_MSTR.ACCT_NO%type;
    str_STATUS ACCT_MSTR.STATUS%type;
    dt_OPNDT ACCT_MSTR.OPNDT%type;
    str_TYPE ACCT_MSTR.TYPE%type;
BEGIN
    OPEN Crsr_NoTrans;
/* If the cursor is open continue with the data processing else display an
appropriate error message. */
    IF Crsr_NoTrans%ISOPEN THEN
        LOOP
            FETCH Crsr_NoTrans INTO str_ACCT_NO, str_STATUS, dt_OPNDT, str_TYPE;
            EXIT WHEN Crsr_NoTrans%NOTFOUND;
            IF Crsr_NoTrans%FOUND THEN
            /* Updating status to 'S' and inserting each record into the
            INACTV_ACCT_MSTR table to keep track of the accounts marked as
            inactive. */
                UPDATE ACCT_MSTR SET STATUS = 'S' WHERE ACCT_NO =
str_ACCT_NO;
            /* Inserting a record in the INACTV_ACCT_MSTR table. */
                INSERT INTO INACTV_ACCT_MSTR
                    VALUES(str_ACCT_NO, dt_OPNDT, str_TYPE);
            END IF;
        END LOOP;
    /* Make the changes permanent. */
        COMMIT;
    ELSE
        dbms_output.put_line ('Unable to open Cursor');
    END IF;
/* Close cursor Crsr_NoTrans. */
    CLOSE Crsr_NoTrans;
END;
```

The above PL/SQL code marks all those accounts as inactive (S) on which there are no transactions performed in the last 365 days. To do this an Explicit cursor named **Crsr_NoTrans** is declared using the following query:

```
SELECT ACCT_NO, STATUS, OPNDT, TYPE FROM ACCT_MSTR
    WHERE ACCT_NO IN (SELECT ACCT_NO FROM TRANS_MSTR
        GROUP BY ACCT_NO HAVING MAX(SYSDATE - DT) >365);
```

The above query will retrieve account numbers, their status; the date on which the account was opened and the type of account. This information will be retrieved based on the following query:

```
SELECT ACCT_NO FROM TRANS_MSTR GROUP BY ACCT_NO
    HAVING MAX(SYSDATE - DT) >365
```

This query is responsible to retrieve only those account numbers from the **TRANS_MSTR** table where the difference between the current date and the date on which the last transaction was performed is more than 365 days i.e. one year. This means a concept of **Subquery** is applied here.

Since the above query will retrieve more than one value the following variables are declared to hold them.

```
str_ACCT_NO ACCT_MSTR.ACCT_NO%type;
str_STATUS ACCT_MSTR.STATUS%type;
dt_OPNDT ACCT_MSTR.OPNDT%type;
str_TYPE ACCT_MSTR.TYPE%type;
```

> **Note:** *The %type here means that the data type of these variables will be as that from the table.*

Since the above query may return more than one row a loop is created which is responsible to:

- Fetch the data retrieved by the cursor into the variable
- Check if any data is retrieved
  - Update the STATUS field of the ACCT_MSTR table to reflect the inactivity
  - Insert a record in the INACTV_ACCT_MSTR table to reflect the updation
- Repeat the above steps until the data retrieval process is complete.

Finally a COMMIT is fired to make the changes permanent

Example:

Write a PL/SQL block that will display the customer name, the fixed deposit number and the fixed deposit amount of the first 5 customers holding the highest amount in fixed deposits.

```
DECLARE
    CURSOR Crsr_HiFD IS SELECT FNAME || ' ' || LNAME, FD_NO, AMT
        FROM CUST_MSTR C, ACCT_FD_CUST_DTLS A, FD_DTLS F
            WHERE C.CUST_NO = A.CUST_NO AND A.ACCT_FD_NO = F.FD_SER_NO
                ORDER BY AMT Desc;
    str_NAME VARCHAR2(50);
    str_FD_NO FD_DTLS.FD_NO%type;
    num_AMT FD_DTLS.AMT%type;
```

```
BEGIN
    OPEN Crsr_HiFD;
    dbms_output.Put_line (' Name                    FD No.  Amount');
    dbms_output.Put_line (' ------------------------ ---------- ----------');
    LOOP
        FETCH Crsr_HiFD INTO str_NAME, str_FD_NO, num_AMT;
        EXIT WHEN (Crsr_HiFD%ROWCOUNT - 1) = 5 or Crsr_HiFD%NOTFOUND;
        dbms_output.Put_line(str_NAME || '  ' || str_FD_NO || '  ' || num_AMT);
    END LOOP;
END;
```

Output:

```
Name                FD No. Amount
------------------------------------------
Chriselle Bayross F1     15000
Mamta Muzumdar    F1     15000
Ashwini Joshi     F7     15000
Chhaya Bankar     F3     10000
Chhaya Bankar     F4     10000
PL/SQL procedure successfully completed.
```

The above PL/SQL code displays the customer name, the fixed deposit number and the fixed deposit amount of the first 5 customers holding the highest amount in a fixed deposit. To do this an Explicit cursor named **Crsr_HiFD** is declared using the following query:

```
SELECT FNAME || ' ' || LNAME, FD_NO, AMT
    FROM CUST_MSTR C, ACCT_FD_CUST_DTLS A, FD_DTLS F
        WHERE C.CUST_NO = A.CUST_NO AND A.ACCT_FD_NO = F.FD_SER_NO
        ORDER BY AMT Desc;
```

The above query will retrieve the customer name (Concatenating the first name and the last name), fixed deposit numbers and the amount of the fixed deposit. This information is available in CUST_MSTR, ACCT_FD_CUST_DTLS, FD_DTLS tables.

To retrieve the data required, both the tables have to linked on the basis of common columns using joins as follows:

- **C**.CUST_NO = **A**.CUST_NO: This means the CUST_NO field of CUST_MSTR table is joined with CUST_NO field of the ACCT_FD_CUST_DTLS table
- **A**.ACCT_FD_NO = **F**.FD_SER_NO: This means the ACCT_FD_NO field of ACCT_FD_CUST_DTLS table is joined with FD_SER_NO field of the FD_DTLS table

Since this query is responsible to retrieve only the first 5 customers holding the highest amount of fixed deposit, the ORDER BY clause is used to switch the order of display to DESCENDING.

Since the above query will retrieve more than one value the following variables are declared to hold them.

str_NAME VARCHAR2(50);

str_FD_NO FD_DTLS.FD_NO**%type;**

num_AMT FD_DTLS.AMT**%type;**

> **Note:** *The %type here means that the **data type** of these variables will be as that from the table.*

Since the above query may return more than one row a loop is created which is responsible to:

- Fetch the data retrieved by the cursor into the variable
- Repeat the above steps until the number of records retrieved becomes 5 (i.e. **Crsr_HiFD%ROWCOUNT - 1)** or the data retrieval process completes (i.e. **Crsr_HiFD%NOTFOUND)** whichever earlier.

Cursor For Loops

Another technique commonly used to control the Loop...End Loop within a PL/SQL block is the **FOR** variable **IN** value construct. This is an example of a machine defined loop exit i.e. when all the values in the **FOR** construct are exhausted looping stops.

Syntax:

FOR memory variable IN CursorName

Here, the verb **FOR** automatically creates the memory variable of the **%rowtype**. Each record in the opened cursor becomes a value for the memory variable of the **%rowtype**.

The **FOR** verb ensures that a row from the cursor is loaded in the declared **memory variable** and the loop executes once. This goes on until all the rows of the cursor have been loaded into the **memory variable**. After this the loop stops.

A cursor for loop automatically does the following:

- Implicitly declares its loop index as a **%rowtype** record
- Opens a cursor
- Fetches a row from the cursor for each loop iteration
- Closes the cursor when all rows have been processed

A cursor can be closed even when an **exit** or a **goto** statement is used to leave the loop prematurely, or if an **exception** is raised inside the loop.

Example:

The bank manager has decided to mark all those accounts as inactive (I) on which there are no transactions performed in the last 365 days. Whenever any such update takes place, a record for the same is maintained in the **INACTV_ACCT_MSTR** table comprising of the account number, the opening date and the type of account. Write a PL/SQL block to do the same.

Table Name: INACTV_ACCT_MSTR

ACCT_NO	OPNDT	TYPE

Create the table INACTV_ACCT_MSTR as:

```
CREATE TABLE INACTV_ACCT_MSTR(
    ACCT_NO VARCHAR2(10), OPNDT DATE, TYPE VARCHAR2(2));
DECLARE
/* Declaration of the cursor named Crsr_NoTrans. The active data set will include the account numbers and status of all the accounts held in the ACCT_MSTR table. */
    CURSOR Crsr_NoTrans IS
    SELECT ACCT_NO, STATUS, OPNDT, TYPE FROM ACCT_MSTR
        WHERE ACCT_NO IN (SELECT ACCT_NO FROM TRANS_MSTR
            GROUP BY ACCT_NO HAVING MAX(SYSDATE - DT) >365);
BEGIN
/* Use of a cursor FOR LOOP. */
    FOR NoTrans_Rec IN Crsr_NoTrans
    LOOP
    /* Updating status to 'S' and inserting each record into the INACTV_ACCT_MSTR table to keep track of the accounts marked as inactive. */
        UPDATE ACCT_MSTR SET STATUS = 'S' WHERE ACCT_NO = NoTrans_Rec.ACCT_NO;
    /* Inserting a record in the INACTV_ACCT_MSTR table. */
        INSERT INTO INACTV_ACCT_MSTR
            VALUES (NoTrans_Rec.ACCT_NO, NoTrans_Rec.OPNDT, NoTrans_Rec.TYPE);
    END LOOP;
    COMMIT ;
END;
```

Output:

PL/SQL procedure successfully completed.

The above PL/SQL code marks all those accounts as inactive (I) on which there are no transactions performed in the last 365 days. To do this an Explicit cursor named **Crsr_NoTrans** is declared using the following query:

```
SELECT ACCT_NO, STATUS, OPNDT, TYPE FROM ACCT_MSTR
    WHERE ACCT_NO IN (SELECT ACCT_NO FROM TRANS_MSTR
        GROUP BY ACCT_NO HAVING MAX(SYSDATE - DT) >365);
```

The above query will retrieve account numbers, their status, the date on which the account was opened and the type of account. This information will be retrieved based on the following query:

```
SELECT ACCT_NO FROM TRANS_MSTR GROUP BY ACCT_NO
    HAVING MAX(SYSDATE - DT) >365
```

This query is responsible to retrieve only those account numbers from the **TRANS_MSTR** table where the difference between the current date and the date on which the last transaction was performed is more than 365 days i.e. one year. This means a concept of **Subquery** is applied here.

Since a FOR LOOP is used in the process there is no need to declare any variable.

The **FOR NoTrans_Rec IN Crsr_NoTrans** here means an implicit declaration of memory variables, as a **%rowtype** record, required for the data retrieval process is undertaken.

The FOR LOOP is responsible to:

- Automatically fetch the data retrieved by the cursor into the **NoTrans_Rec** record set
- The sequence of statements inside the loop is executed once for every row that is fetched, i.e. check if any data is retrieved
  - Update the STATUS field of the ACCT_MSTR table to reflect the inactivity
  - Insert a record in the INACTV_ACCT_MSTR table to reflect the updation
- Automatically repeat the above steps until the data retrieval process is complete.
- The cursor closes automatically when all the records in the cursor have been processed. This is because there are no more rows left to load into **NoTrans_Rec**. This situation is sensed by the **FOR** verb which, causes the loop to exit.

Finally a COMMIT is fired to make the changes permanent

What Are Procedures / Functions?

A **Procedure** or **Function** is a logically grouped set of SQL and PL/SQL statements that perform a specific task. A **stored procedure** or function is a named PL/SQL code block that has been compiled and stored in one of the Oracle engine's system tables.

To make a **Procedure** or **Function dynamic** either of them can be passed parameters **before** execution. A **Procedure** or **Function** can then change the way it works depending upon the parameters passed prior to its execution.

Procedures and Functions are made up of:

- A declarative part
- An executable part
- An optional exception-handling part

Declarative Part

The declarative part may contain the declarations of cursors, constants, variables, exceptions and subprograms. These objects are local to the procedure or function. The objects become invalid once the procedure or function exits.

Executable Part

The executable part is a PL/SQL block consisting of SQL and PL/SQL statements that assign values, control execution and manipulate data. The action that the procedure or function is expected to perform is coded here.

The data that is to be returned back to the calling environment is also returned from here. The variables declared are put to use within this block.

Exception Handling Part

This part contains code that deals with exceptions that may be raised during the execution of code in the **executable** part. An Oracle exception handler can be redirected to the exception handling section of the procedure or function where the procedure or function determines the actual action that must be carried out by Oracle's exception handler.

The flow of code execution from the Exception Handling part **cannot** be transferred to the Executable part.

Where Do Stored Procedures And Functions Reside?

Procedures and **Functions** are stored in the Oracle database. They can be invoked or called by any PL/SQL block that appears within an application. Before a procedure or function is stored, the Oracle engine **parses** and **compiles** the procedure or function.

How Does The Oracle Engine Create A Stored Procedure / Function?

The following steps are performed automatically by the Oracle engine while creating a procedure:

- Compiles the procedure or function
- Stores the procedure or function in the database

The Oracle engine compiles the PL/SQL code block. If an error occurs during the compilation of the procedure or function, **an invalid** procedure or function gets created. The Oracle engine displays a message after creation that the procedure or function was created with **compilation errors**.

The compilation process does not display the errors. These errors can be viewed using the **SELECT** statement:

```
SELECT * FROM USER_ERRORS;
```

When a procedure or function is invoked, the Oracle engine loads the compiled procedure or function in a memory area called the **System Global Area** (**SGA**). This allows the code to be executed quickly. Once loaded in the SGA other users also access the same procedure or function if they have been granted permission to do so.

How Does The Oracle Engine Execute Procedures / Functions?

The Oracle engine performs the following steps to execute a procedure or function:

- Verifies user access
- Verifies procedure or function validity
- Executes the procedure or function

The Oracle engine checks if the user who called the procedure or function has the **execute privilege** for the procedure or function. If the user is invalid, then access is denied otherwise the Oracle engine proceeds to check whether the called procedure or function is valid or not. The status of a procedure or function is shown by the use of a **select** statement as follows:

```
SELECT <ObjectName>, <ObjectType>, <Status> FROM <UserObjects>
    WHERE <ObjectType> = <'PROCEDURE'>;
```

Or

```
SELECT <Object_Name>, <Object_Type>, <Status> FROM <User_Objects>
    WHERE <Object_Type> = <'FUNCTION'>;
```

Only if the status is **valid**, will a procedure or function be executed. Once found valid, the Oracle engine then loads a procedure or function into memory (**i.e.** if it is not currently present in memory) and executes it.

Advantages Of Using A Procedure Or Function

Security

Stored procedures and functions can help enforce data security. For **e.g.** by giving permission to a procedure or function that can query a table and granting the procedure or function to users, permissions to manipulate the table itself need not be granted to users.

Performance

It improves database performance in the following ways:

- Amount of information sent over a network is less
- No compilation step is required to execute the code
- Once the procedure or function is present in the shared pool of the SGA retrieval from disk is not required every time different users call the procedure or function **i.e.** reduction in disk I/O

Memory Allocation

The amount of memory used reduces as stored procedures or functions have shared memory capabilities. Only one copy of procedure needs to be loaded for execution by multiple users. Once a copy of a procedure or function is opened in the Oracle engine's memory, other users who have appropriate permission may access it when required.

Productivity

By writing procedures and functions redundant coding can be avoided, increasing productivity.

Integrity

A procedure or function needs to be tested only once to guarantee that it returns an accurate result. Since procedures and functions are stored in the Oracle engine they become a part of the engine's resource. Hence the responsibility of maintaining their integrity rests with the Oracle engine. The Oracle engine has high level of in-built security and hence integrity of procedures or functions can be safely left to the Oracle engine.

Procedures Versus Functions

The differences between Procedures and Functions can be listed as below:

- A function must return a value back to the caller. A function can return only one value to the calling PL/SQL code block
- By defining multiple OUT parameters in a procedure, multiple values can be passed to the caller. The OUT variable being global by nature, its value is accessible by any PL/SQL code block **including** the PL/SQL block via which it was called

Creating Stored Procedure

Syntax:

```
CREATE OR REPLACE PROCEDURE [Schema.] <ProcedureName>
    (<Argument> {IN, OUT, IN OUT} <Data type>, ...) {IS, AS}
    <Variable> declarations;
    <Constant> declarations;
BEGIN
    <PL/SQL subprogram body>;
EXCEPTION
    <Exception PL/SQL block>;
END;
```

Keywords And Parameters

The keywords and the parameters used for creating database procedures are explained below:

REPLACE	Recreates the procedure if it already exists. This option is used to change the definition of an existing procedure without dropping, recreating and re-granting object privileges previously granted on it. If a procedure is redefined the Oracle engine recompiles it.
Schema	Is the schema to contain the procedure. The Oracle engine takes the default schema to be the current schema, if it is omitted.
Procedure	Is the name of the procedure to be created.
Argument	Is the name of an argument to the procedure. Parentheses can be omitted if no arguments are present.
IN	Indicates that the parameter will accept a value from the user.
OUT	Indicates that the parameter will return a value to the user.
IN OUT	Indicates that the parameter will either accept a value from the user or return a value to the user.

Data type	Is the data type of an argument. It supports any data type supported by PL/SQL.
PL/SQL subprogram body	Is the definition of procedure consisting of PL/SQL statements.

Creating A Functions

Syntax:

```
CREATE OR REPLACE FUNCTION [Schema.] <FunctionName>
    (<Argument> IN <Data type>, ...)
    RETURN <Data type> {IS, AS}
    <Variable> declarations;
    <Constant> declarations;
BEGIN
    <PL/SQL subprogram body>;
EXCEPTION
    <Exception PL/SQL block>;
END;
```

Keywords and Parameters

The keywords and the parameters used for creating database functions are explained below:

REPLACE	Recreates the function if it already exists. This option is used to change the definition of an existing function without dropping, recreating and re-granting object privileges previously granted on it. If a function is redefined, Oracle recompiles it.
Schema	Is the schema to contain the function. Oracle takes the default schema to be the current schema, if it is omitted.
Function	Is the name of the function to be created.
Argument	Is the name of an argument to the function. Parentheses can be omitted if no arguments are present.
IN	Indicates that the parameter will accept a value from the user.
RETURN data type	Is the data type of the function's return value. Because every function must return a value, **this clause is required**. It supports any data type supported by PL/SQL.
PL/SQL subprogram body	Is the definition of function consisting of PL/SQL statements.

Diagrammatic representation of the working of a Procedure in Server RAM

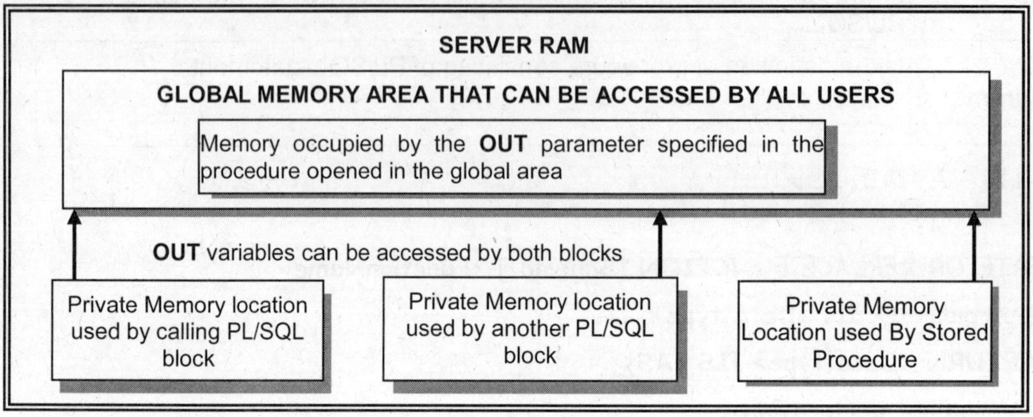

Diagram 9.5: Working of a Procedure within the Oracle Engine

Using A Function

Example:

Consider the tables **TRANS_MSTR** and **ACCT_MSTR**. Both the tables belong to the banking system. The TRANS_MSTR table is used to register the deposits or withdrawals, as performed. As a batch process, the initial opening balance value must be written to the TRANS_MSTR table whenever an account is opened with the bank.

Write a PL/SQL block of code that would insert a record representing the opening balance entry in the TRANS_MSTR table each time an account is opened. The insert in the TRANS_MSTR table depends on **ACCT_NO**. In case the ACCT_NO is not present in the TRANS_MSTR table i.e. there is no entry made for the initial deposit, then a record is inserted in the TRANS_MSTR table representing the initial payment made while opening an account. If there is already an entry made for the initial payment i.e. ACCT_NO is present in the TRANS_MSTR table then the insertion is skipped.

To help simplify this process (of batch insertion) a function called f_ChkAcctNo has been created. The function checks for the existence of ACCT_NO in the table TRANS_MSTR. The function has one argument, which receives a value. The function will search for a matching value in the TRANS_MSTR table when a value is passed to it when being invoked.

The function will return **1** indicating that a match is found or **0** indicating that no match is found.

This value returned by the function is used to make a decision to insert a record or skip the insertion in the TRANS_MSTR table.

Creating Function For Use

A stored function is created to perform the ACCT_NO check operation. f_ChkAcctNo() is the name of the function which accepts a variable ACCT_NO and returns a value to the host environment. The value changes from 0 (i.e. if ACCT_NO does not exist) to 1 (i.e. if ACCT_NO exists) depending on the records retrieved.

```
CREATE OR REPLACE FUNCTION F_CHKACCTNO(vACCT_NO IN VARCHAR2)
   RETURN NUMBER IS
/* Variable that hold data from the TRANS_MSTR table */
   dummyAcctNo VARCHAR2(10);
BEGIN
   SELECT DISTINCT ACCT_NO INTO dummyAcctNo FROM TRANS_MSTR
      WHERE ACCT_NO = vACCT_NO;

/* If the SELECT statement retrieves data, return value is set to 1. */
   RETURN 1;
EXCEPTION
/* If the SELECT statement does not retrieve data, return value is set to 0 */
   WHEN NO_DATA_FOUND THEN RETURN 0;
END;
```

Output:

```
Function created.
```

This function is then called in the PL/SQL block as follows. The return value is then checked and appropriate action is taken.

Calling The Function F_CHKACCTNO In A PL/SQL Code Block

```
DECLARE
/* Cursor SCANTABLE retrieves the required data from the table ACCT_MSTR */
   CURSOR SCANTABLE IS SELECT ACCT_NO, TYPE FROM ACCT_MSTR;
/* Variables that hold data from the cursor scantable */
   mACCT_NO ACCT_MSTR.ACCT_NO%type;
   mTYPE ACCT_MSTR.TYPE%type;
/* Variable that stores the value returned by the f_ChkAccctNo function i.e. 1 or 0 */
   valexists NUMBER(1);
BEGIN
   OPEN SCANTABLE;
   LOOP
      FETCH SCANTABLE INTO MACCT_NO, MTYPE;
      EXIT WHEN SCANTABLE%NOTFOUND;
   /* Call function F_CHKACCTNO to check if ACCT_NO is present in TRANS_MSTR table */
```

```
        valexists := F_CHKACCTNO(MACCT_NO);
    /* If ACCT_NO does not exist insert a record in the TRANS_MSTR table */
        IF valexists = 0 THEN
            IF mTYPE = 'SB' THEN
                INSERT INTO TRANS_MSTR (TRANS_NO, ACCT_NO, DT, TYPE, PARTICULAR,
                                        DR_CR, AMT, BALANCE)
                    VALUES((SELECT 'T' || TO_CHAR(MAX(TO_NUMBER(SUBSTR( TRANS_NO, 2)))
                            + 1) FROM TRANS_MSTR), mACCT_NO, SYSDATE, 'C', 'Initial
                            Payment', 'D', 500, 500);
            ELSE
                INSERT INTO TRANS_MSTR (TRANS_NO, ACCT_NO, DT, TYPE, PARTICULAR,
                                        DR_CR, AMT, BALANCE)
                    VALUES((SELECT 'T' || TO_CHAR(MAX(TO_NUMBER(SUBSTR( TRANS_NO, 2)))
                            + 1) FROM TRANS_MSTR), mACCT_NO, SYSDATE, 'C', 'Initial
                            Payment', 'D', 2000, 2000);
            END IF;
        END IF;
    END LOOP;
    CLOSE SCANTABLE;
    COMMIT;
END;
```

Output:

```
PL/SQL procedure successfully completed.
```

The Functionality Of The PL/SQL Block Of Code Will Be As Follows:

A cursor named **SCANTABLE** is created which is responsible to hold the ACCT_NO and TYPE from the ACCT_MSTR table. A call is made to the function and the value held in mACCT_NO is then passed as a parameter. The WHERE condition of the select statement within the function gets its value from the variable mACCT_NO and depending on whether the value exists in the TRANS_MTR table or not, a value of 0 or 1 is returned to the calling PL/SQL block.

If the select statement retrieves a record from the TRANS_MSTR table (**i.e.** the corresponding ACCT_NO is present in the TRANS_MSTR table) the insertion of a new records is skipped.

If the select retrieves no record (**i.e.** the ACCT_NO is not present in the TRANS_MSTR table), a new record is inserted into the TRANS_MSTR table.

The above process continues till all the records in the cursor, **SCANTABLE** are processed. When all the records have been processed the PL/SQL block exits the loop and the all the transactions are completed with the COMMIT statement.

Using A Procedure

Example:

The current example deals with the Fixed Deposit Maturity system. The tables involved with this processing are FD_DTLS, TRANS_MSTR and ACCT_MSTR.

Whenever a fixed deposit is due for payment and if there are instructions given to the bank for crediting the fixed deposit amount on maturity to their account held in the bank, an entry is passed in the TRANS_MSTR table for deposit of the fixed deposit amount as well as the ACCT_MSTR table is updated to reflect the increase of the current balance. Finally the status of that fixed deposits is updated as **M** i.e. Matured in the FD_DTLS table.

In order to simplify the job of insertion and updating, of three tables (TRANS_MSTR, FD_DTLS and ACCT_MSTR) each time a fixed deposit is due for payment, a procedure is created. This procedure is then called in the PL/SQL block while checking for those fixed deposits due for payment.

Creating Procedure For Use

A procedure called **PROC_INSUPD** is created and stored in the database. This procedure when called in a PL/SQL block updates the current balance in the ACCT_MSTR table and the status in the FD_DTLS table. It also inserts an entry to register the credit of the fixed deposit amount in the TRANS_MSTR table.

```
CREATE OR REPLACE PROCEDURE PROC_INSUPD(VFD_NO IN VARCHAR2, VACCT_NO
IN VARCHAR2, vAMT IN NUMBER) IS
/* Variable declarations */
    mCurBal number;
BEGIN
/* Retrieving the current balance */
    SELECT CURBAL INTO mCurBal FROM ACCT_MSTR WHERE ACCT_NO = vACCT_NO;
/* Inserting a record in the TRANS_MSTR table */
    INSERT INTO TRANS_MSTR (TRANS_NO, ACCT_NO, DT, TYPE, PARTICULAR, DR_CR,
                            AMT, BALANCE)
      VALUES((SELECT 'T' || TO_CHAR(MAX(TO_NUMBER(SUBSTR(TRANS_NO, 2))) + 1)
                            FROM TRANS_MSTR), vACCT_NO, SYSDATE, 'C', 'Fixed
                            Deposit Payment', 'D', vAMT, (mCurBal + vAMT));

/* Updating the CURBAL in the ACCT_MSTR table */
    UPDATE ACCT_MSTR SET CURBAL = CURBAL + vAMT WHERE ACCT_NO =
vACCT_NO;
/* Updating the STATUS in the FD_DTLS table */
    UPDATE FD_DTLS SET STATUS = 'M' WHERE FD_NO = vFD_NO;
END;
```

Output:

```
Procedure created.
```

Calling The Procedure In A PL/SQL Code Block:

```
DECLARE
/* Cursor CRSR_FDCHK retrieves all the records of table FD_DTLS which are active and due for payment */
   CURSOR CRSR_FDCHK IS
      SELECT FD_NO, PAYTO_ACCTNO, DUEAMT FROM FD_DTLS
         WHERE TO_CHAR(DUEDT,'DD-MM-YY') = TO_CHAR(SYSDATE,'DD-MM-YY')
            AND STATUS = 'A' AND PAYTO_ACCTNO IS NOT NULL;
/* Declaration of memory variables that will hold values */
   mFD_NO VARCHAR2(10);
   mPAYTO_ACCTNO VARCHAR2(10);
   mAMT NUMBER(8,2);
   mState NUMBER := 0;
BEGIN
/* Opening the cursor */
   OPEN CRSR_FDCHK;
   LOOP
      FETCH CRSR_FDCHK INTO mFD_NO, mPAYTO_ACCTNO, mAMT;
      EXIT WHEN CRSR_FDCHK%NOTFOUND;
      /* Call procedure proc_insupd to perform insert/update operations on tables. */
         proc_insupd(mFD_NO, mPAYTO_ACCTNO, mAMT);
      /* Updating the state to 1 i.e. there are fds due for payment */
         mState := 1;
   END LOOP;
/* Display a message if no FDs are due for payment based on the mState variable */
   IF mState = 0 THEN
      DBMS_OUTPUT.PUT_LINE('Currently there are no fixed deposits due for payment.');
   END IF;
      CLOSE CRSR_FDCHK;
   COMMIT;
END;
```

Output:

```
Currently there are no fixed deposits due for payment.
PL/SQL procedure successfully completed.
```

The Functionality Of The PL/SQL Block Of Code Will Be As Follows:

The above PL/SQL when fired will open a cursor called **CRSR_FDCHK** that will fetch the fixed deposit number, account number to which the fixed deposit amount will be credited and the fixed deposit due amount from the FD_DTLS table. The cursor will fetch only those records where the fixed deposits are active, due for payment and the account number to which the amount has to be credited is available.

Only when such records are fetched an insert/update operation on tables ACCT_MSTR, TRANS_MSTR AND FD_DTLS is performed via a procedure named **PROC_INSUPD**. This procedure takes three arguments i.e. fixed deposit number, account number that will be credited and the due amount.

On the basis of these three arguments:

- An insert is fired on the TRANS_MSTR table to register the maturity of the fixed deposit
- The current balance of the specified account number is increased in the ACCT_MSTR table
- The status of the fixed deposit is set to **M** i.e. the fixed deposit is now matured

In case no records are fetched by the cursor **CRSR_FDCHK** a message stating "Currently there are no fixed deposits due for payment"

Finally a COMMIT is fired to register the changes.

Deleting a Stored Procedure or Function

A procedure or function can be deleted by using the following syntax

Syntax:

```
DROP PROCEDURE <ProcedureName>;
```

Example:

DROP PROCEDURE PROC_INSUPD;

Output:

```
Procedure dropped.
```

Syntax:

```
DROP FUNCTION <FunctionName>;
```

Example:

DROP FUNCTION F_CHKACCTNO;

Output:

```
Function dropped.
```

Overloading Procedures And Functions

A package is an Oracle object that can hold a number of other objects like procedures and functions. More than one procedure or function with the **same name** but with **different parameters** can be defined within a package or within a PL/SQL declaration block.

Multiple procedures that are declared with the same name are called **Overloaded Procedures**. Similarly, multiple Functions that are declared with the same name are called **Overloaded Functions**.

The code in the overloaded functions or overloaded procedures can be same or completely different.

Example:

Create a package to check that a numeric value is greater than zero, and a date is less than or equal to sysdate.

```
CREATE OR REPLACE PACKAGE CHECK_FUNC IS
    FUNCTION VALUE_OK(DATE_IN IN DATE) RETURN VARCHAR2;
    FUNCTION VALUE_OK(NUMBER_IN IN NUMBER) RETURN VARCHAR2;
END;
```

Output:

```
Package created.
```

```
CREATE OR REPLACE PACKAGE BODY CHECK_FUNC IS
    FUNCTION VALUE_OK (DATE_IN IN DATE) RETURN VARCHAR2 IS
    BEGIN
        IF DATE_IN <= SYSDATE THEN
            RETURN 'Output From the First Over loaded Function: TRUE';
        ELSE
            RETURN 'Output From the First Over loaded Function: FALSE';
        END IF;
    END;
    FUNCTION VALUE_OK (NUMBER_IN IN NUMBER) RETURN VARCHAR2 IS
    BEGIN
        IF NUMBER_IN > 0 THEN
            RETURN 'Output From the Second Over loaded Function: TRUE';
        ELSE
            RETURN 'Output From the Second Over loaded Function: FALSE';
```

```
        END IF;
    END;
END;
```

Output:

```
Package body created.
```

Overloading can greatly simplify procedures and functions. The Overloading technique consolidates the call interface for many similar programs into a single procedure or function. When executing the procedure or function the Oracle engines **chooses** the **procedure** or **function** whose number of parameters and data type **match the values** passed by the caller.

As seen in the example, a function with the name **VALUE_OK** is created in the package **CHECK_FUNC**. The first function accepts a single parameter of type **date**. The second function also accepts a single parameter of type **number**.

Thus when the **VALUE_OK** function is called and passed a date value, as in

```
    IF CHECK_FUNC.VALUE_OK(TO_DATE('03-JAN-81')) THEN
        ....
    END IF;
```

The Oracle engine compares the data type of the values passed by the caller against the different parameter lists in the package **CHECK_DATA**. The Oracle engine then executes the code for first function that accepts date as in:

```
CREATE FUNCTION VALUE_OK (DATE_IN IN DATE) RETURN VARCHAR2 IS
BEGIN
    IF DATE_IN <= SYSDATE THEN
        RETURN 'Output From the First Over loaded Function: TRUE';
    ELSE
        RETURN 'Output From the First Over loaded Function: FALSE';
    END IF;
END;
```

Similarly, when the **'VALUE_OK'** function is called and a numeric value is passed by the caller, as in:

```
    IF CHECK_DATA.VALUE_OK (23) THEN
        ....
    END IF;
```

The Oracle engine executes the second function that accepts numeric value as in:

```
CREATE FUNCTION VALUE_OK (NUMBER_IN IN NUMBER) RETURN VARCHAR2 IS
BEGIN
    IF NUMBER_IN > 0 THEN
```

```
        RETURN 'Output From the Second Over loaded Function: TRUE';
    ELSE
        RETURN ' Output From the Second Over loaded Function: FALSE';
    END IF;
END;
```

Overloading Built-In PL/SQL Functions And Procedures

PL/ SQL itself makes extensive use of overloading. An Example of an overloaded function in PL/ SQL is the TO_CHAR function. Function overloading allows developers to use a single function to convert both numbers and dates to character format.

Example:

```
DATE_STRING := TO_CHAR(SYSDATE, 'DD/MM/YY');
NUMBER_STRING := TO_CHAR(10000, '$099,999');
```

In this example, the PL/SQL interpreter examines the value passed to the TO_CHAR function. Based on the data type of this value, it executes the appropriate TO_CHAR function.

Benefits Of Overloading

The benefits of overloading are:

1. Overloading can greatly simplify the processing logic of a program by eliminating multiple **IF** constructs or **CASE** constructs that would check the parameters passed and perform appropriate operations.
2. The overloading technique transfers the burden of knowledge from the developer to the software. For example if multiple procedures with different names are written, the programmer will have to remember the names of each of the procedures along with the parameters of each function.
3. If procedures or functions are overloaded, the programmer needs to remember a single procedure or function name and pass values as required.

Where To Overload Functions And Procedures

There are only two places in PL/SQL programs where the procedures and functions can be overloaded:

- Inside the declaration section of a PL/SQL block
- Inside a package

Tip:	*Standalone programs cannot be overloaded nor can two independent modules be created with the same name but different parameter lists.*

Example:

If an attempt is made to create or replace the following procedures of **revise estimates**, the second attempt will fail.

```
CREATE PROCEDURE REVISE_ESTIMATES (DATE_IN IN DATE) IS
BEGIN
  ...
END;
```

Output:

```
Procedure created.
```

```
CREATE PROCEDURE REVISE_ESTIMATES (DOLLARS_IN IN NUMBER) IS
BEGIN
  ...
END;
```

Output:

```
ORA-0955: name is already used by an existing object.
```

Because a procedure with the name used is present, PL/SQL rejected the attempt to replace it with the procedure created in the second attempt.

Restrictions On Overloading

There are several restrictions on how the procedures and functions can be overloaded. The following restrictions apply since the PL/SQL engine compares overloaded modules (functions or procedure) before executing the appropriate module.

1. The data subtype of at least one of the parameters of the overloaded function or procedure must differ

For example an overloaded procedure distinguished by parameters of different types of numeric data types is not allowed. Similarly, an overloaded procedure distinguished by parameters with varchar2 and char data types is not allowed.

Example:

```
CREATE OR REPLACE PACKAGE BODY STRING_FNS IS
   PROCEDURE TRIM_AND_CENTER (STRING_IN IN CHAR, STRING_OUT OUT CHAR)
   BEGIN
      ...
   END;
   PROCEDURE TRIM_AND_CENTER (STRING_IN IN VARCHAR2, STRING_OUT OUT
                                           VARCHAR2)
   BEGIN
      ...
   END;
END;
```

Caution:	*Such procedure overloading is not allowed.*

2. The parameter list of overloaded functions must differ by more than name or parameter mode

The parameter name is replaced by the values sent to the objects when the package is called, so differences in name do not offer a guide to the overloaded objects that must be used.

Example:

A procedure definition will be as:

```
CREATE OR REPLACE PACKAGE BODY CHECK_DATE IS
    FUNCTION VALUE_OK(DATE_IN IN DATE) RETURN BOOLEAN IS
    BEGIN
        RETURN DATE_IN <= SYSDATE;
    END;
    FUNCTION VALUE_OK(DATE_OUT IN DATE)RETURN BOOLEAN IS
    BEGIN
        RETURN DATE_OUT >= SYSDATE;
    END;
END;
```

The call to the function will be:

```
    IS_DATE_OK := CHECK_DATA.VALUE_OK(TO_DATE('03-JAN-81'))
```

The name of the parameter is not available in the module call and thus PL/SQL interpreter **cannot** distinguish objects by name.

Similarly, even if a parameter in the first module is IN and the same parameter is IN OUT in another module, PL/SQL interpreter **cannot** distinguish using the package call.

The overloading attempts will result in the following error messages:

```
PLS-00307: too many declarations of 'value_check' match this call.
```

3. Overloaded functions must differ by more than their return data type.

At the time that the overloaded function is called, the PL/SQL interpreter does not know what type of data that function will return. The interpreter therefore cannot distinguish between different overloaded functions based on the return data type.

Example:

```
CREATE OR REPLACE PACKAGE BODY CHECK_RETURN IS
    FUNCTION VALUE_OK(DATE_IN IN DATE) RETURN BOOLEAN IS
    BEGIN
        RETURN DATE_IN <= SYSDATE ;
    END;
    FUNCTION VALUE_OK(DATE_OUT IN DATE ) RETURN NUMBER IS
```

```
    BEGIN
        IF DATE_OUT >= SYSDATE THEN
            RETURN 1;
        ELSE
            RETURN 0;
        END IF;
    END;
END;
```

4. All the overloaded modules must be defined within the same PL/SQL scope or block (PL/SQL block or package).

Two modules cannot be overloaded across two PL/SQL blocks or across two packages.

Example:

```
PROCEDURE DEVELOP_ANALYSIS (QUARTER_END_IN IN DATE, SALES_IN IN NUMBER) IS
    PROCEDURE REVISE_ESTIMATE (DATE_IN IN DATE) IS
    BEGIN
        PROCEDURE REVISE_ESTIMATE (DOLLAR_IN IN NUMBER) IS
        BEGIN
            ...
        END;
        BEGIN
            REVISE_ESTIMATE(QUARTER_END_IN);
            REVISE_ESTIMATE(DOLLARS_IN);
        END;
    END;
```

When the above code is interpreted, the PL/SQL interpreter displays the following error message.

```
Error in Line 12 / Column 3:
PLS-00306: wrong number or type of arguments in call to
'REVISE_ESTIMATE'
```

PL/ SQL displays the error message because the scope and visibility of both the procedures is different. The scope of the date **REVISE_ESTIMATES** is the entire scope of the body **DEVELOP_ANALYSIS**. The scope of the **numeric REVISE_ESTIMATES** is the inner block only and it takes precedence over the date **REVISE_ESTIMATES**.

Function Or Procedure Overloading

Example:

The bank manager decides to activate all those accounts, which were previously marked as inactive for performing no transactions in last 365 days.

Create a package spec and package body named **ACCT_MNTC** that includes two procedures of the same name. The procedure name is **ACT_ACCTS**. The first procedure accepts BRANCH_NO and the second procedure accepts branch name.

Package Specification:

```
CREATE OR REPLACE PACKAGE ACCT_MNTC IS
    PROCEDURE ACT_ACCTS(vBRANCH_NO IN NUMBER);
    PROCEDURE ACT_ACCTS (vNAME IN VARCHAR2);
END;
```

Output:

```
Package created.
```

Package Body:

```
CREATE OR REPLACE PACKAGE BODY ACCT_MNTC IS
    PROCEDURE ACT_ACCTS(vBRANCH_NO IN NUMBER) IS
    BEGIN
        UPDATE ACCT_MSTR SET STATUS = 'A'
            WHERE BRANCH_NO = 'B' || vBRANCH_NO AND STATUS = 'S';
        IF SQL%ROWCOUNT > 0 THEN
            DBMS_OUTPUT.PUT_LINE(TO_CHAR(SQL%ROWCOUNT) || ' Account(s) Activated
                                        Successfully');
        ELSE
            DBMS_OUTPUT.PUT_LINE('Currently there exist no Inactive Accounts in the
                                        branch no ' || vBRANCH_NO);
        END IF;
    END;
    PROCEDURE ACT_ACCTS(vNAME IN VARCHAR2) IS
    BEGIN
        UPDATE ACCT_MSTR SET STATUS = 'A' WHERE STATUS = 'S'
            AND BRANCH_NO IN(SELECT BRANCH_NO FROM BRANCH_MSTR
                WHERE NAME = vNAME);
        IF SQL%ROWCOUNT > 0 THEN
            DBMS_OUTPUT.PUT_LINE(TO_CHAR(SQL%ROWCOUNT) || ' Account(s) Activated
                                        Successfully');
```

```
        ELSE
            DBMS_OUTPUT.PUT_LINE('Currently there exist no Inactive Accounts in the branch ' ||
                                  vNAME);
        END IF;
    END;
END ACCT_MNTC;
```

Output:

```
Package body created.
```

Execution of the above PL/SQL block will be as follows:

Calling the Procedure by passing the branch number

```
SQL> EXECUTE ACCT_MNTC.ACT_ACCTS(1);
3 Account(s) Activated Successfully
PL/SQL procedure successfully completed.
```

Calling the Procedure by passing the branch name

```
SQL> EXECUTE ACCT_MNTC.ACT_ACCTS('Vile Parle (HO)');
3 Account(s) Activated Successfully
PL/SQL procedure successfully completed.
```

Database Triggers

Database triggers are database objects created via the SQL* Plus tool on the client and stored on the Server in the Oracle engine's system table. These database objects consist of the following distinct sections:

- A named database event
- A PL/SQL block that will execute when the event occurs

The occurrence of the database event is strongly bound to table data being changed.

The Oracle engine allows the definition of procedures that are implicitly executed (i.e. executed by the Oracle engine itself), when an insert, update or delete is issued against a table from SQL* Plus or through an application. These procedures are called **database triggers**.

The major issues that make these triggers stand-alone are that, they are fired implicitly (**i.e.** internally) by the Oracle engine itself and not explicitly **i.e.** called by the user.

Use Of Database Triggers

Since the Oracle engine supports database triggers it provides a highly customizable database management system. Some of the uses to which the database triggers can be put, to customize management information by the Oracle engine are as follows:

- A trigger can permit DML statements against a table only if they are issued, during regular business hours or on predetermined weekdays
- A trigger can also be used to keep an audit trail of a table (i.e. to store the modified and deleted records of the table) along with the operation performed and the time on which the operation was performed
- It can be used to prevent invalid transactions
- Enforce complex security authorizations

Note: *When a trigger is fired, an SQL statement inside the trigger's PL/SQL code block can also fire the same or some other trigger. This is called cascading triggers.*

Excessive use of triggers for customizing the database can result in complex interdependencies between the triggers, which may be difficult to maintain in a large application.

Database Triggers V/S Procedures

There are very few differences between database triggers and procedures. Triggers do not accept parameters whereas procedures can. A trigger is executed implicitly by the Oracle engine itself upon modification of an associated table or its data. To execute a procedure, it has to be explicitly called by a user.

Database Triggers V/S Declarative Integrity Constraints

Triggers as well as declarative integrity constraints can be used to constrain data input. However both have significant differences as mentioned below:

- A declarative integrity constraint is a statement about a database that is always true. A constraint applies to existing data in the table and any statement that manipulates the table
- Triggers constrain what a transaction can do. A trigger does not apply to data loaded before the trigger was created, so it does not guarantee all data in table conforms to the rules established by an associated trigger
- A trigger enforces a transitional constraint, which cannot be enforced by a declarative integrity constraint

How To Apply Database Triggers

A trigger has three basic parts:

- A triggering event or statement
- A trigger restriction
- A trigger action

Each part of the trigger is explained below

Triggering Event or Statement

It is a SQL statement that causes a trigger to be fired. It can be INSERT, UPDATE or DELETE statement for a specific table. (**i.e.** Table write operations)

Trigger Restriction

A trigger restriction specifies a Boolean (logical) expression that must be **TRUE** for the trigger to fire. It is an option available for triggers that are fired for each row. Its function is to conditionally control the execution of a trigger. A trigger restriction is specified using a **WHEN** clause.

Trigger Action

A trigger action is the PL/SQL code to be executed when a triggering statement is encountered and any trigger restriction evaluates to TRUE. The PL/SQL block can contain SQL and PL/SQL statements, can define PL/SQL language constructs and can call stored procedures. Additionally, for row triggers, the statements the PL/SQL block have access to column values (**:new** and **:old**) of the current row being processed.

Types Of Triggers

While defining a trigger, the number of times the trigger action is to be executed can be specified. This can be once for every row affected by the triggering statement (such as might be fired by an UPDATE statement that updates many rows), or once for the triggering statement, no matter how many rows it affects.

Row Triggers

A row trigger is fired each time a row in the table is affected by the triggering statement. For example, if an UPDATE statement updates multiple rows of a table, a row trigger is fired once for each row affected by the UPDATE statement. If the triggering statement affects no rows, the trigger is not executed at all. Row triggers should be used when some processing is required whenever a triggering statement affects a single row in a table.

Statement Triggers

A **statement trigger** is fired once on behalf of the triggering statement, independent of the number of rows the triggering statement affects (even if no rows are affected). Statement triggers should be used when a triggering statement affects rows in a table but the processing required is completely independent of the number of rows affected.

Before V/S After Triggers

When defining a trigger it is necessary to specify the trigger timing, i.e. specifying when the triggering action is to be executed in relation to the triggering statement. **BEFORE** and **AFTER** apply to both row and the statement triggers.

Before Triggers

BEFORE triggers execute the trigger action before the triggering statement. These types of triggers are commonly used in the following situations:

- BEFORE triggers are used when the trigger action should determine whether or not the triggering statement should be allowed to complete. By using a BEFORE trigger, user can eliminate unnecessary processing of the triggering statement
- BEFORE triggers are used to derive specific column values before completing a triggering INSERT or UPDATE statement

After Triggers

AFTER trigger executes the trigger action after the triggering statement is executed. These types of triggers are commonly used in the following situations:

- AFTER triggers are used when the triggering statement should complete before executing the trigger action
- If a BEFORE trigger is already present, an AFTER trigger can perform different actions on the same triggering statement

Combinations Triggers

Using the options explained above, four types of triggers could be created

BEFORE statement trigger

Before executing the triggering statement, the trigger action is executed.

BEFORE row trigger

Before modifying each row affected by the triggering statement and **before** applying appropriate integrity constraints, the trigger is executed.

AFTER Statement Trigger

After executing the triggering statement and applying any deferred integrity constraints, the trigger action is executed.

AFTER Row Trigger

After modifying each row affected by the triggering statement and applying appropriate integrity constraints, the trigger action is executed for the current row. Unlike BEFORE row triggers, AFTER row triggers have **rows locked**.

Syntax For Creating A Trigger:

```
CREATE OR REPLACE TRIGGER [Schema.] <TriggerName>
    {BEFORE, AFTER}
    {DELETE, INSERT, UPDATE [OF Column, ...]}
ON [Schema.] <TableName>
    [ REFERENCING { OLD AS old, NEW AS new }]
    [ FOR EACH ROW [ WHEN Condition ] ]
DECLARE
    <Variable declarations>;
```

```
    <Constant declarations>;
BEGIN
    <PL/SQL subprogram body>;
EXCEPTION
    <Exception PL/SQL block>;
END;
```

Keywords And Parameters

The keywords and the parameters used for creating database triggers are explained below:

OR REPLACE	Recreates the trigger if it already exists. This option can be used to change the definition of an existing trigger without requiring the user to drop the trigger first.
Schema	Is the schema, which contains the trigger. If the schema is omitted, the Oracle engine creates the trigger in the users own schema.
TriggerName	Is the name of the trigger to be created.
BEFORE	Indicates that the Oracle engine fires the trigger before executing the triggering statement.
AFTER	Indicates that the Oracle engine fires the trigger after executing the triggering statement.
DELETE	Indicates that the Oracle engine fires the trigger whenever a DELETE statement removes a row from the table.
INSERT	Indicates that the Oracle engine fires the trigger whenever an INSERT statement adds a row to table.
UPDATE	Indicates that the Oracle engine fires the trigger whenever an UPDATE statement changes a value in one of the columns specified in the OF clause. If the OF clause is omitted, the Oracle engine fires the trigger whenever an UPDATE statement changes a value in any column of the table.
ON	Specifies the schema and name of the table, which the trigger is to be created. If schema is omitted, the Oracle engine assumes the table is in the users own schema. A trigger cannot be created on a table in the schema SYS.
REFERENCING	Specifies correlation names. Correlation names can be used in the PL/SQL block and WHEN clause of a row trigger to refer specifically to old and new values of the current row. The default correlation names are **OLD** and **NEW**. If the row trigger is associated with a table named OLD or NEW, this clause can be used to specify different correlation names to avoid confusion between table name and the correlation name.

FOR EACH ROW	Designates the trigger to be a row trigger. The Oracle engine fires a row trigger once for each row that is affected by the triggering statement and meets the optional trigger constraint defined in the WHEN clause. If this clause is omitted the trigger is a statement trigger.
WHEN	Specifies the trigger restriction. The trigger restriction contains a SQL condition that must be satisfied for the Oracle engine to fire the trigger. This condition must contain correlation names and cannot contain a query. Trigger restriction can be specified only for the row triggers. The Oracle engine evaluates this condition for each row affected by the triggering statement.
PL/SQL block	Is the PL/SQL block that the Oracle engine executes when the trigger is fired.

Note: *The PL/SQL block cannot contain transaction control SQL statements (COMMIT, ROLLBACK, and SAVEPOINT)*

Deleting a Trigger

Syntax:

```
DROP TRIGGER <TriggerName>;
```

where, **TriggerName** is the name of the trigger to be dropped.

Applications Using Database Triggers

Example:

Create a transparent audit system for a table **CUST_MSTR**. The system must keep track of the records that are being deleted or updated. The functionality being when a record is deleted or modified the original record details and the date of operation are stored in the audit table, **then** the delete or update operation is allowed to go through.

The table definition for audit system is given below:

Table Name:	AUDIT_CUST
Description:	This is the table, which keeps track of the records deleted or updated when such operations are carried out. Records in this table will be inserted when the database trigger fires due to an update or delete statement fired on the table **CUST_MSTR**.

Column Definition:

Column Name	Data Type	Size	Attributes
CUST_NO	VarChar2	10	
FNAME	VarChar2	25	
MNAME	VarChar2	25	
LNAME	VarChar2	25	
DOB_INC	Date/Time		
OCCUP	VarChar2	25	
PHOTOGRAPH	VarChar2	25	
SIGNATURE	VarChar2	25	
PANCOPY	VarChar2	1	
FORM60	VarChar2	1	
Operation	VarChar2	10	
Userid	VarChar2	10	
Odate	Date		

Table Description:

Column Name	Description
CUST_NO	A system generated number auto posted to this table column
FNAME	Customer's first name
MNAME	Customer's middle name
LNAME	Customer's last name
DOB_INC	Customer's date of birth (for individuals) or data of incorporation (for organizations)
OCCUP	Customer's occupation or line of business
PHOTOGRAPH	Location to customer's scanned photograph (for individuals only)
SIGNATURE	Location to customer's scanned signature (for individuals only)
PANCOPY	Holds **Y** if a copy of PAN card has been submitted
FORM60	Holds **Y** if the Form 60 has been submitted
Operation	The operation performed on the CUST_MSTR table
Userid	The date when the operation was performed
Odate	The name of the user performing the operation

Solution

Create table statement for the AUDIT_CUST table:

```
CREATE TABLE "DBA_BANKSYS"."AUDIT_CUST"(
    "CUST_NO" VARCHAR2(10), "FNAME" VARCHAR2(25), "MNAME" VARCHAR2(25),
    "LNAME" VARCHAR2(25), "DOB_INC" DATE NOT NULL, "OCCUP" VARCHAR2(25),
    "PHOTOGRAPH" VARCHAR2(25), "SIGNATURE" VARCHAR2(25), "PANCOPY"
VARCHAR2(1),
    "FORM60" VARCHAR2(1), "OPERATION" VARCHAR2(20), "USERID" VARCHAR2(20),
    "ODATE" DATE);
```

Output:

```
Table created.
```

This trigger is fired when an update or delete operation is performed on the table **CUST_MSTR**. The trigger first checks for the operation being performed on the table. Then depending on the operation being performed, a variable is assigned the value **update** or **delete**. Previous values of the modified record of the table **CUST_MSTR** are inserted into the AUDIT_CUST table.

```
CREATE TRIGGER AUDIT_TRAIL
    AFTER UPDATE OR DELETE ON CUST_MSTR
        FOR EACH ROW
DECLARE
/* The value in the OPER variable will be inserted into the operation
field in the AUDIT_CUST table */
    OPER VARCHAR2(8);
BEGIN
/* If the records are updated in the CUST_MSTR table then OPER is set to
'UPDATE'. */
    IF updating THEN
        OPER := 'UPDATE';
    END IF;
/* If the records are deleted from the CUST_MSTR table then OPER is set to
'DELETE'. */
    IF deleting THEN
        OPER := 'DELETE';
    END IF;
/* Insert the old values in the AUDIT_CUST table. */
```

```
INSERT INTO AUDIT_CUST VALUES (:OLD.CUST_NO, :OLD.FNAME, :OLD.MNAME,
        :OLD.LNAME, :OLD.DOB_INC, :OLD.OCCUP, :OLD.PHOTOGRAPH,
        :OLD.SIGNATURE, :OLD.PANCOPY, :OLD.FORM60, OPER, USER, SYSDATE);
END;
```

Output:

```
Trigger created.
```

The creation of the database trigger AUDIT_TRAIL results in an auditing system for the table **CUST_MSTR**. The owner of the table can keep track of time of modification or deletion of a record in **CUST_MSTR** by querying the table **AUDIT_CUST**.

Observations:

The actual working of the auditing system can be confirmed as follows:

This is the data in the table **CUST_MSTR** before the Database Trigger had been fired.

SELECT CUST_NO, FNAME, MNAME, LNAME, DOB_INC **FROM** CUST_MSTR;

Output:

CUST_NO	FNAME	MNAME	LNAME	DOB_INC
C1	Ivan	Nelson	Bayross	25-JUN-52
C2	Chriselle	Ivan	Bayross	29-OCT-82
C3	Mamta	Arvind	Muzumdar	28-AUG-75
C4	Chhaya	Sudhakar	Bankar	06-OCT-76
C5	Ashwini	Dilip	Joshi	20-NOV-78
C6	Hansel	I.	Colaco	01-JAN-82
C7	Anil	Arun	Dhone	12-OCT-83
C8	Alex	Austin	Fernandes	30-SEP-62
C9	Ashwini	Shankar	Apte	19-APR-79
C10	Namita	S.	Kanade	10-JUN-78
O11				14-NOV-97
O12				23-OCT-92
O13				05-FEB-89
O14				24-MAY-80
O15				02-APR-00
O16				13-JAN-02

16 rows selected.

Following is the data in the table **AUDIT_CUST** before the Database Trigger has been fired.

SELECT CUST_NO, FNAME, MNAME, LNAME, DOB_INC, OPERATION, ODATE, USER
    FROM AUDIT_CUST;

Output:

```
No Rows Selected
```

Case 1:

When an update statement modifies a record in the table **CUST_MSTR**.

The following update statement modifies the CUST_MSTR.

UPDATE CUST_MSTR **SET** DOB_INC = '1-FEB-1981' **WHERE** FNAME = 'Hansel';

Once the update is complete the contents of the table **Client_Master** have been modified as shown below. The content of the column Bal_due in the table **Client_Master** where the value was 2000 is updated to 2200.

SELECT CUST_NO, FNAME, MNAME, LNAME, DOB_INC **FROM** CUST_MSTR;

Output:

CUST_NO	FNAME	MNAME	LNAME	DOB_INC
C1	Ivan	Nelson	Bayross	25-JUN-52
C2	Chriselle	Ivan	Bayross	29-OCT-82
C3	Mamta	Arvind	Muzumdar	28-AUG-75
C4	Chhaya	Sudhakar	Bankar	06-OCT-76
C5	Ashwini	Dilip	Joshi	20-NOV-78
C6	***Hansel***	***I.***	***Colaco***	***01-FEB-81***
C7	Anil	Arun	Dhone	12-OCT-83
C8	Alex	Austin	Fernandes	30-SEP-62
C9	Ashwini	Shankar	Apte	19-APR-79
C10	Namita	S.	Kanade	10-JUN-78
O11				14-NOV-97
O12				23-OCT-92
O13				05-FEB-89
O14				24-MAY-80
O15				02-APR-00
O16				13-JAN-02

```
16 rows selected.
```

The changes made to the table CUST_MSTR must be reflected in the table AUDIT_CUST. AUDIT_CUST keeps track of the previous contents of CUST_MSTR whose records were modified as well as the operation and the date when the operation was performed.

SELECT CUST_NO, FNAME, MNAME, LNAME, DOB_INC, OPERATION, ODATE, USER
FROM AUDIT_CUST;

Output:

```
CUST_NO  FNAME   MNAME LNAME   DOB_INC   OPERATION ODATE
-------------------------------------------------------------
USER
---------------
C6       Hansel  I.    Colaco  01-JAN-82 UPDATE    13-JUL-04
DBA_BANKSYS
```

Case 2:

When a record is deleted from the table **CUST_MSTR**.

The following delete statement deletes all those customers from the **CUST_MSTR** table whose names start with 'A'.

DELETE FROM CUST_MSTR WHERE FNAME LIKE 'A%';

The following SELECT statement confirms that four record have been deleted.

SELECT CUST_NO, FNAME, MNAME, LNAME, DOB_INC **FROM** CUST_MSTR;

Output:

```
CUST_NO FNAME      MNAME    LNAME    DOB_INC
--------------------------------------------
C1      Ivan       Nelson   Bayross  25-JUN-52
C2      Chriselle  Ivan     Bayross  29-OCT-82
C3      Mamta      Arvind   Muzumdar 28-AUG-75
C4      Chhaya     Sudhakar Bankar   06-OCT-76
C6      Hansel     I.       Colaco   01-FEB-81
C10     Namita     S.       Kanade   10-JUN-78
O11                                  14-NOV-97
O12                                  23-OCT-92
O13                                  05-FEB-89
O14                                  24-MAY-80
O15                                  02-APR-00
O16                                  13-JAN-02
12 rows selected.
```

The records deleted from the table CUST_MSTR must be reflected in the table AUDIT_CUST. Records are inserted into this table when an update or delete operation is performed on the table. It can be observed that four more records have been inserted into the table AUDIT_CUST.

SELECT CUST_NO, FNAME, MNAME, LNAME, DOB_INC, OPERATION, ODATE, USER
FROM AUDIT_CUST;

Output:

CUST_NO	FNAME	MNAME	LNAME	DOB_INC	OPERATION	ODATE	USER
C6	Hansel	I.	Colaco	01-JAN-82	UPDATE	13-JUL-04	DBA_BANKSYS
C5	Ashwini	Dilip	Joshi	20-NOV-78	DELETE	13-JUL-04	DBA_BANKSYS
C7	Anil	Arun	Dhone	12-OCT-83	DELETE	13-JUL-04	DBA_BANKSYS
C8	Alex	Austin	Fernandes	30-SEP-62	DELETE	13-JUL-04	DBA_BANKSYS
C9	Ashwini	Shankar	Apte	19-APR-79	DELETE	13-JUL-04	DBA_BANKSYS

Note: *If the user performs a ROLLBACK after this, then the records, which were modified and deleted from the table **CUST_MSTR** are restored to their original status. Since all these changes are being done via the SQL* Plus tool at the SQL> prompt, a single ROLLBACK will also cause the records inserted into AUDIT_CUST to be rolled back as well.*

If a PL/ SQL code block is performing this type of table operations, the same table behavior will result.

Raise_Application_Error Procedure

The Oracle engine provides a procedure named **RAISE_APPLICATION_ERROR** that allows programmers to issue user-defined error messages.

Syntax:

RAISE_APPLICATION_ERROR (<ErrorNumber>, <Message>);

where, **ErrorNumber** is a negative integer in the range **-20000 to -20999** while,

Message is a character string up to 2048 bytes in length.

An application can call **RAISE_APPLICATION_ERROR** only while executing a stored subprogram like stored procedures, functions and database triggers. Typically, **RAISE_APPLICATION_ERROR** is used in database **Triggers**.

RAISE_APPLICATION_ERROR ends the subprogram, rolls back any database changes it made and returns a user-defined error number and message to the application.

Example:

Write a database trigger on the TRANS_MSTR that checks the following:

- The account number for which the transaction is being performed is a valid account number
- The Transaction Amount is not zero and is positive and
- In case of a withdrawal the amount does not exceed the current balance for that account number

```
CREATE OR REPLACE TRIGGER TRANS_CHECK
    BEFORE INSERT ON TRANS_MSTR FOR EACH ROW
DECLARE
    v_CNT_ACCT_NO VARCHAR2(10);
```

```
    v_CURBAL NUMBER(10);
BEGIN
/* Checking if the account number is a valid account number. */
    SELECT COUNT(ACCT_NO) INTO v_CNT_ACCT_NO
        FROM ACCT_MSTR WHERE ACCT_NO = :new.ACCT_NO;
    IF v_CNT_ACCT_NO = 0 THEN
        RAISE_APPLICATION_ERROR(-20000,'The Account number is invalid.');
    END IF;
/* Checking if the transaction amount is a positive number. */
    IF :new.AMT <= 0 THEN
        RAISE_APPLICATION_ERROR(-20001,'The Transaction amount cannot be negative or
                                zero.');
    END IF;
/* Checking if the transaction amount exceeds the current balance in case
of withdrawals. */
    SELECT CURBAL INTO v_CURBAL
        FROM ACCT_MSTR WHERE ACCT_NO = :new.ACCT_NO;
    IF v_CURBAL < :new.AMT AND :new.DR_CR = 'W' THEN
        RAISE_APPLICATION_ERROR(-20002,'The amount of withdrawal cannot exceed the
                                balance held in the account.');
    END IF;
END;
```

Output:

```
Trigger created.
```

Case 1:

```
INSERT INTO TRANS_MSTR (TRANS_NO, ACCT_NO, DT, TYPE, PARTICULAR, DR_CR,
                        AMT, BALANCE)
    VALUES('T32', 'SB3', '15-DEC-2003', 'B', 'Initial Payment', 'D', -2, 500);
```

```
INSERT INTO TRANS_MSTR (TRANS_NO, ACCT_NO, DT, TYPE, PARTICULAR, DR_CR,
AMT, BALANCE)
*
ERROR at line 1:
ORA-20001: The Transaction amount cannot
be negative or zero.
ORA-06512: at "DBA_BANKSYS.TRANS_CHECK", line 16
ORA-04088: error during execution of trigger 'DBA_BANKSYS.TRANS_CHECK'
```

Case 2:

INSERT INTO TRANS_MSTR (TRANS_NO, ACCT_NO, DT, TYPE, PARTICULAR, DR_CR, AMT, BALANCE)
VALUES('T32', 'SB33', '15-DEC-2003', 'B', 'Initial Payment', 'W', -2, 500**);**

```
INSERT INTO TRANS_MSTR (TRANS_NO, ACCT_NO, DT, TYPE, PARTICULAR, DR_CR,
AMT, BALANCE)
*
ERROR at line 1:
ORA-20000: The Account number is invalid.
ORA-06512: at "DBA_BANKSYS.TRANS_CHECK", line 11
ORA-04088: error during execution of trigger 'DBA_BANKSYS.TRANS_CHECK'
```

Case 3:

INSERT INTO TRANS_MSTR (TRANS_NO, ACCT_NO, DT, TYPE, PARTICULAR, DR_CR, AMT, BALANCE)
VALUES('T32', 'SB3', '15-DEC-2003', 'B', 'Initial Payment', 'W', 99999, 500);

```
INSERT INTO TRANS_MSTR (TRANS_NO, ACCT_NO, DT, TYPE, PARTICULAR, DR_CR,
AMT, BALANCE)
*
ERROR at line 1:
ORA-20002: The amount of withdrawal cannot
exceed the balance held in the account.
ORA-06512: at "DBA_BANKSYS.TRANS_CHECK", line 25
ORA-04088: error during execution of trigger 'DBA_BANKSYS.TRANS_CHECK'
```

Self Review Questions

Fill In The Blanks

1. The data that is stored in the cursor is called the ___________________.
2. When a cursor is loaded with multiple rows via a query the Oracle engine opens and maintains a _____________.
3. If the Oracle Engine for its internal processing has opened a cursor they are known as _________ Cursors.
4. Cursors defined by the users are called ______________.
5. ____________ is always evaluated to false in case of implicit cursors.
6. All LOOP statements must end with an ______________ statement.
7. The __________ statement retrieves the rows from the active set opened in the Server.

8. In case of Explicit cursors the ____________ attribute returns the number of rows fetched from the active set.
9. _________________ allows passing values dynamically to a cursor while opening a cursor.
10. A ____________ or __________ is a logically grouped set of SQL and PL/SQL statements that perform a specific task.
11. Procedures and Functions are stored in the ____________ ___________.
12. When the procedure or function is invoked, the Oracle engine loads the compiled procedure or function in the memory area called the ______________________.
13. Only ________ copy of procedure needs to be loaded for execution by multiple users.
14. Multiple procedures that are declared with the same name are called __________________.
15. A ________ trigger is fired each time a row in the table is affected by the triggering statement.
16. ___________ ____________ should be used when a triggering statement affects rows in a table but the processing required is completely independent of the number of rows affected.
17. __________ trigger executes the trigger action after the triggering statement is executed.
18. The Oracle engine provides a procedure named ____________________ that allows programmers to issue user-defined error messages.
19. The process of breaking the SQL sentence into words and then checking them for syntax and object privileges is called __________.
20. The process of dividing the cursor into appropriate columns as per the SELECT list is called as _______________.
21. A ________________ procedure is called after a row has been fetched to transfer the value from the SELECT list of the cursor into a local variable.

True Or False

22. A ROLLBACK statement at the SQL prompt is used to make permanent changes.
23. A Rollback statement cannot be used to close a transaction.
24. ROLLBACK cannot be fired from the SQL prompt without the SAVEPOINT clause.
25. The use of cursors provides manipulation of table data in batch processing mode.
26. The cursor defined system variables that are associated with a user defined cursor are SQL%IsOpen, SQL%Found, SQL%NotFound, SQL%RowCount.
27. COMMIT can be fired upto a savepoint.
28. The close statement disables the cursor and the active set becomes undefined.
29. Only constant values can be passed as parameters to parameterized cursors.
30. Fetch statement is used to get the data from the table into the cursor.

31. An Oracle exception handler can be redirected to the executable section of the procedure or function.
32. One cannot transfer the flow of execution from the Exception Handling part to the Executable part.
33. The Oracle engine checks if the user who called the procedure or function has the write privilege for the procedure or function.
34. A function or a procedure can return only one value to the calling PL/SQL code block.
35. Triggers are fired implicitly.
36. A trigger is executed implicitly by the Oracle engine itself upon modification of an associated table or its data.
37. A trigger restriction specifies a Boolean (logical) expression that must be False for the trigger to fire.
38. BEFORE and AFTER apply to only the statement triggers.
39. The PL/SQL block in the trigger cannot contain transaction control SQL statements i.e. COMMIT, ROLLBACK, and SAVEPOINT.
40. An application can call 'raise_application_error' only while executing a stored subprogram like stored procedures, functions and database triggers.

Objective Questions

1. What is a cursor?
2. How does a cursor work?
3. What are the different types of cursors? Briefly explain each of them.
4. What are the different attributes of Implicit and Explicit Cursors?
5. What are the steps involved in using an explicit cursor and manipulating data in its active set?
6. What are the three commands used to control a cursor? Briefly explain each of the commands.
7. What are procedures? State the advantages of using procedures.
8. State the differences between a procedure and a function?
9. Define: Overloaded Procedures and Overloaded Functions
10. What are the benefits and drawbacks of Overloading?
11. Explain the different types of Triggers
12. What are the advantages of using Triggers?

Answers To Self Review Questions

1. Introductory Concepts Of DBMS

Fill In The Blanks

1 database
2 Database Management System (DBMS)
3 ANSI-SQL
4 American National Standards Institute (ANSI)
5 cell
6 record
7 read
8 read
9 model
10 Return On Investment
11 Report extraction
12 transaction
13 coherent
14 two
15 any
16 table
17 returns
18 collated
19 audit
20 Database Administrator (DBA)

True Or False

21 False
22 True
23 False
24 True
25 True
26 False
27 True
28 False
29 True
30 True
31 False
32 True
33 False
34 True
35 False
36 True
37 False
38 True
39 False
40 True
41 False
42 True

2. Relational Model

Fill In The Blanks

1 Hierarchical
2 Relational
3 DataBase Management Systems

True Or False

22 True
23 False
24 True

4 Systems and Application
5 child
6 keyboard
7 tables
8 Structured Query Language (SQL)
9 American National Standards Institute (ANSI)
10 Named
11 Tuples
12 Attributes
13 controller
14 period
15 operations
16 procedural language
17 Intersection
18 concatenation
19 syntactically
20 Create Table
21 UPDATE

25 False
26 True
27 False
28 True
29 True
30 False
31 True
32 False
33 True
34 True

4. Transaction Management

Fill In The Blanks

1 column, table
2 relationships
3 Premium
4 NOT NULL
5 decomposed
6 Normalization
7 two
8 First Normal
9 Third Normal
10 Join dependencies
11 table data
12 Repeating Group

True Or False

13 False
14 True
15 False
16 True
17 True
18 False
19 True
20 True
21 True
22 False
23 False
24 True

5. Query Processing And Query Optimization

Fill In The Blanks

1 query
2 query optimizer
3 Optimization
4 SQL *Net
5 Public Global Area
6 efficiently
7 execution plan
8 row source
9 Sorts, sort-merge joins
10 EXPLAIN PLAN
11 Access
12 PLAN_TABLE
13 utlxplan.sql
14 rule-based
15 cost-based
16 lower
17 full table
18 multi-block
19 data file, data block
20 ROWID
21 index scan
22 range
23 expected elapsed time
24 cost-based
25 cost-based
26 OPTIMIZER_MODE
27 COST
28 RULE
29 OPTIMIZER_GOAL
30 FIRST_ROWS
31 one

True Or False

32 False
33 True
34 True
35 False
36 False
37 True
38 False
39 True
40 False
41 True
42 False
43 True
44 False
45 True
46 False
47 False
48 True
49 False
50 True
51 True
52 True
53 False
54 False
55 True
56 False
57 True
58 True
59 True
60 False
61 True

6. Transaction Management

Fill In The Blanks

1 Transaction
2 COMMIT
3 COMMIT
4 SAVEPOINT
5 Concurrency Control
6 Locking
7 Read, Write
8 Exclusive
9 exclusive
10 page level
11 Explicit Locking
12 NOWAIT
13 commit, unqualified Rollback
14 Row
15 deadlock
16 lock
17 Exclusive (X) mode
18 transaction
19 matrix
20 protocol
21 serializability
22 deadlocks
23 rollbacks
24 Intention
25 lock
26 low concurrency
27 Locks
28 Implicit Locking
29 fields
30 Commit or rollback

True Or False

34 False
35 True
36 False
37 False
38 False
39 True
40 True
41 True
42 False
43 False
44 True
45 False
46 True
47 False
48 True
49 True
50 False
51 False
52 False
53 True
54 False
55 False
56 False
57 True
58 False
59 True
60 True
61 False
62 False
63 False

31 Active
32 Without
33 With

64 True
65 True
66 True
67 False

7. Security

Fill In The Blanks

1 Data management
2 security policy
3 data audit policy
4 CREATE ANY USER
5 System privileges
6 Roles

True Or False

7 False
8 True
9 True
10 True
11 False

8. SQL Concepts

Fill In The Blanks

1 Data Definition Language
2 Data Manipulation Language
3 Data Control Language
4 Entity
5 rows and columns
6 Attributes
7 Constraints
8 NULLABLE
9 mandatory
10 NOT NULL
11 NULL
12 Simple
13 UNIQUE
14 Foreign
15 Detail
16 ON DELETE CASCADE
17 CHECK
18 Boolean

True Or False

19 False
20 True
21 False
22 True
23 False
24 False
25 True
26 False
27 True
28 False
29 True
30 True
31 False
32 True
33 False
34 True
35 True

9. PL / SQL Concepts

Fill In The Blanks

1 Active Data Set
2 row pointer
3 Implicit
4 Explicit cursors
5 SQL%ISOPEN
6 End Loop
7 fetch
8 %ROWCOUNT
9 Parameterized Cursor
10 procedure, function
11 Oracle database
12 System Global Area
13 one
14 Overloaded Procedures
15 row
16 Statement triggers
17 AFTER
18 raise_application_error
19 Parsing
20 Binding
21 COLUMN_VALUE

True Or False

22 False
23 False
24 False
25 True
26 False
27 True
28 True
29 False
30 False
31 False
32 True
33 False
34 False
35 True
36 True
37 False
38 False
39 True
40 True

Index

P

R

S

T

U

V

W